NOT A PROPER
JOURNALIST

NOT A PROPER JOURNALIST

Bob Humphrys

YELLOW JERSEY PRESS

LONDON

Published by Yellow Jersey Press 2008

2 4 6 8 10 9 7 5 3 1

First published in Great Britain in 2008 by
Yellow Jersey Press
Random House, 20 Vauxhall Bridge Road,
London SW1V 2SA

www.rbooks.co.uk

Addresses for companies within The Random House Group Limited can be found at:
www.randomhouse.co.uk/offices.htm

The Random House Group Limited Reg. No. 954009

A CIP catalogue record for this book
is available from the British Library

ISBN 9780224082754

The Random House Group Limited makes every effort to ensure that the papers used in its books
are made from trees that have been legally sourced from well-managed and credibly certified forests.
Our paper procurement policy can be found at: www.rbooks.co.uk/environment

Mixed Sources
Product group from well-managed
forests and other controlled sources
www.fsc.org Cert no. TT-COC-2139
© 1996 Forest Stewardship Council
FSC

Typeset by SX Composing DTP, Rayleigh, Essex
Printed and bound in the UK by
CPI Mackays, Chatham ME5 8TD

In memory of Bob Humphrys

1952–2008

Contents

Preface

When you're appointed as the coach of the Welsh national rugby team you need to work out very quickly who the people are that you can trust and who are those that you can't.

Wales can be a lonely place for a Kiwi a long way from home (especially when your team is on a losing run), and it helps to know who your friends are – the sort that stick by you through thick and thin.

It was obvious from the moment I landed that Bob Humphrys was one of those people for me. That's not to question his integrity as a journalist. Bob's style was firm but fair and, most importantly, admirably consistent.

He had a genuine enthusiasm for rugby, which put him in that relatively small category of journalists who make you care about the game. He brought it to life. He dealt with the people involved as real human beings. Not just professionals doing a job.

His passion for Wales, for sport and rugby in particular, dedication to journalism and professionalism as a broadcaster shone through in everything he did, but he had a refreshingly adult perspective on it all – rugby was rugby, television was television and neither were the 'be all and end all'.

And that is why he had no problem in regarding me as a friend. We both did our jobs, which sometimes involved uncomfortable interviews, but at the end of the day he was happy to put down his microphone, loosen his tie and buy me a pint. And I was very happy with that too – my time in Wales was a rollercoaster ride but Bob was a reliable constant among all the silliness.

His passion for Wales was obvious and infectious. On a television assignment to New Zealand in 1999, my wife Raewyn and I took Bob to Akaroa, a mountainous coastal region where they bottle the best wine and catch the finest seafood in the world, all framed by scenery that makes the Brecon Beacons look like a municipal park.

The highlight of our visit should have been cod and chips for lunch from what every New Zealander knows is the best fish and chip shop in the world. Bob of course begged to differ and was adamant that his fish, pulled out of the Pacific that very morning, was not a patch on that served by the Top Gun fish bar in Whitchurch High Street back in Cardiff.

It was on that visit that I got a sense of Bob's integrity. Halfway through the trip he asked his bewildered producer if he could go home. The by-now angry producer refused, pointing out how much money the trip had cost and what was at stake if he went back with a half-finished programme. So, reluctantly, Bob agreed to see the trip out. It was only afterwards he revealed that he'd asked to go home upon receiving a call saying that his young son had been taken to hospital after an accident.

He knew where he should have been and only assurances from his wife back in Wales that his son was fine, along with his own high professional standards, kept him going. But from that moment on his only thoughts were for home.

Speaking to his former colleagues, they all agree that among the many professional qualities that Bob possessed, it was his writing that shone through. Those of us who only knew him as a television sports presenter were surprised to learn that Bob was actually first and foremost a writer, having cut his teeth on newspapers, and he spent much of his early broadcasting career breaking exclusives in hard news.

But this pedigree is obvious really when you consider how his prose stood out from the other cliché-ridden sports hacks' copy, and how he seemed to know what was actually a story that could justify its place in a bulletin alongside the train wrecks and gloomy economic forecasts, as opposed to the inconsequential tittle-tattle talked up and packaged as vital news by many of his colleagues.

And a mark of his true passion for sport was his encyclopedic knowledge, which went far beyond the big teams and the famous stars. He spent as much time rooting out stories from Wales's sporting hinterland, among the unknowns and up-and-coming athletes, as he did seeking out the company of Welsh superheroes.

So much so that, when it came to choosing the candidates for the Young Sports Personality of the Year, the entire sports department of BBC Wales more often than not scratched their collective heads and turned to Bob for a few suggestions.

As well as interviewing me on countless occasions, Bob also wrote a television series that I was presenting, the excuse being that I was too busy to sit down in front of a word processor. But in reality I could have never matched his knowledge, wit, insight and speed.

He researched and wrote six half-hour shows on the culture and history of the Six Nations on my behalf, while still working full time as a television sports reporter in his own right. Bob had stamina.

And if that wasn't impressive enough, he adeptly altered his writing style to suit 'my voice', which, as well as being hugely difficult, was remarkably skilful, and was obviously a good thing. I've been told that the copy he wrote for himself, which was so poetic to listen to in his broadcasts, was almost impossible for anyone else to read – such was its unique style.

Bob wasn't the only writer in his family of course and his brother John led the way and took a lot of the glory as a London-based broadcaster. But Bob never once felt in his older sibling's shadow. In fact, it was quite the opposite. He was hugely proud of his brother's achievements. On a filming assignment in London some years ago, there was only one person that he wanted me to meet, and I spent a fascinating and memorable evening in the company of the Humphrys brothers. Bob enjoyed listening to John's anecdotes as much if not more than I did.

Talking to his friends and former colleagues, I get a sense that Bob could be quite difficult to work with at times. But no one has suggested that awkwardness and confrontation came because an ego was at work. It was his determination to be as professional as possible. He had very high standards and fully expected everyone around him to match them, and this could lead to frustration.

At the same time they tell me he was patient, gentle and kind to the new boys and girls in the BBC newsroom. And there are now generations of hacks who have passed through that place, on to bigger and better things, who would admit to having learned a lot from Bob, especially about writing to pictures. Many great scribes whose background is in newspapers fail to adapt their technique to the extra dimension that television brings – Bob not only made the switch, he became a master of the medium.

And yet despite his obvious talents as a writer and broadcaster, he could be, at times, hugely underconfident. I remember myself doing live shots from the Millennium Stadium with him and, once we were off air, him asking if I thought it had gone OK a split second before I could ask him the very same question.

He left the BBC at a time of their choosing, and his departure left him feeling not so well disposed to the organisation that he had loved and served for a great part of his career. It seems to me that, although he may have served his purpose as a TV front man, he had plenty more to give as an elder statesman of Welsh journalism.

Thank goodness for us that he decided to approach his premature retirement with the same drive and vigour that he had applied to his working life. Once free of his broadcasting commitments, he sat down at his kitchen table and wrote this book. He had some great tales to tell and the odd score to settle. For most, this book will be a delightful treasure trove of memories and anecdotes, full of larger-than-life characters, as told by a master storyteller. For a small number of others, its searing honesty could make uncomfortable reading.

Life, just like sport, is full of cruel twists and turns. Bob had played a blinder in the first half, and after a rocky spell at the beginning of the second, was beginning to get back into his stride.

Then disaster struck. It became obvious that Bob wasn't going to be allowed to play the full eighty minutes, much to his own distress, as well his family's, friends' and fans'.

He decided to attack the news of his career-ending 'injury' in typical fashion. He wrote about it for a national newspaper, and the raw emotion shone through in a stunningly honest article, winning him a whole new legion of fans and admirers.

This book is sure to do the same, and we have to be grateful that he managed to file this 'report' on his remarkable life and career before the end of transmission.

Graham Henry

Chapter 1

Beginnings

The boy and the young man were talking. It was the sixties. The house where they sat was the young man's, an off-the-shelf semi in a village just outside Cardiff before what was left of its rural identity was swallowed by its neighbour. Three bedrooms, two downstairs rooms, a couple of toilets, the perfect, unpretentious package for the up-and-coming professional, first step on the path to the bigger and the better.

The two didn't often talk, not beyond the mundane. The young man was older than the boy, nine years older. They'd missed out on the comfortable, shared conversations of childhood, separated by short trousers and cigarettes. The young man spoke with the wisdom of one whom life had yet to prove wrong and the boy listened, not intently but politely enough, sufficiently impressed by the seniority that girlfriends and a 1963 white Mini could bring.

Tonight though was different. The subject under discussion was the future, more precisely the boy's future. It was a land he'd thought about but travelled to only fitfully in an imagination fuelled by the romantic not the real. Farmer, fireman? Get a grip. The young man's made-to-measure house in Llandeilo Close would not have the suave salesman salivating on today's *Location, Location, Location*, but it was a far cry from the working-class sprawl of Splott and the little terraced house with the outside loo – not that they'd ever heard of the word – where they had both been born.

Splott was a Cardiff suburb described by the man from the *Telegraph* as 'a place as ugly as it sounds'. The boy thought that was unfair. It made him think of a dollop of wet mud dropped on the pavement . . . S-p-l-o-t-t! But something about the place confused him.

Step out of the house on Pearl Street, walk to the corner of the road, turn right down Blanche Street and you came to the New Dock Tavern. The New Dock was a down-at-heel boozer, unexceptional by Cardiff standards, where a woman walking in had male heads turning and conversations stopping. It wasn't the type of rundown dive, of which there were some not too far away, where the locals could scupper a petrol bomb by drinking it before it went off. No, what made the New Dock notable was where it was, on a street of scruffy second-hand car dealers, pawnshops and houses unloved and uncared for by a population passing through not staying. This was Broadway . . . and that was what puzzled the boy.

They say the neon lights are bright on Broadway
They say there's always magic in the air
But when you're walking down the street
And you ain't had enough to eat
The glitter rubs right off and you're nowhere.

'Neon lights', 'magic in the air': that wasn't the boy's Broadway, not the one sung about by the Drifters and Ol' Blue Eyes. 'You ain't had enough to eat' was closer to the mark. The boy's father told him of the soup kitchen that had been there during the Depression, and how he'd been beaten by his own father for taking a bowl. 'No one in our family has ever gone hungry, lad . . . and we don't want any bloody do-gooders thinking we're going hungry now,' he'd said. The boy still failed to understand why *his* Broadway had such worldwide celebrity.

His world was defined by a few mean streets. When he threw off their shackles and travelled himself, would the Taj Mahal pale into insignificance alongside Ebenezer Chapel just over the road from his house? Were the Hanging Gardens of Babylon but a cheap imitation of Splott Park and Jessie the Steam Engine (later removed to the relative safety of North Wales as local vandals found their form)? Was Harry's Bar in Venice really the equal of the Roath Cons? But even if they were all better, it wouldn't matter, because this was his world, such as it was. Splott was in his blood, not farming. Neither was being a vet – he had an aversion to pets dying (his guinea pig had shown him that). Or a fireman. The boy didn't like heights. Or fires.

But there was the young man's work. The young man had left the school he hated for a job on a local newspaper in the small seaside town of Penarth. Their father's attempts to lure him to a bank in Cardiff Docks and the security of the nine-to-five existence he'd never known had failed. The boy had looked on with interest, not much more, as he began to move up the career ladder. He was curious - and thankful for a bedroom of his own - when the young man moved out of the family house for a job on the Merthyr *Express*.

The boy had visited the young man's house in the town at the top of the valleys. At one time Merthyr's ironworks had been the largest in the world; now the town had all the traits of the Wild West before the Wild West knew it existed. Ernest Street, where the young man rented a tumbledown part of Merthyr's industrial legacy, made Splott look like Mayfair. Cats went AWOL at the threat of rats the size of small deer. If this was life in the fast lane, the boy wasn't sure he wanted to get on.

But the young man didn't slow down. A job as the *Western Mail*'s crime correspondent had a certain cachet to it, even if it meant the family bedroom had to be shared again. By now the boy was old enough to be forming his own opinions; he wondered whether the young man was right to quit print journalism for Television Wales and the West and the more constrained world of TV news. He was soon convinced. Interviews with an up-and-coming Morecambe and Wise – a clowning Eric turned an old-fashioned microphone into a pipe – and an impossibly youthful Clint Eastwood told of a life more interesting than the shellac polish and strippers of their father's french-polishing business.

The conversion was complete one Friday lunchtime in 1966. The boy was home for a lunch that went largely untasted as the voice of William Hardcastle on the BBC's *World at One* told of a catastrophic pit slide onto a school in Aberfan. He went back to afternoon lessons; the young man stayed in the devastated village and 'watched through the hours and days that followed as the tiny coffins mounted up in the little chapel'. 'There is nothing so poignant as a child's coffin,' the young man wrote later. 'By the end of it there were 116 of them. One hundred and sixteen dead children and twenty-eight adults.'

A little while later, as their conversation ended in the comfort of the house on Dinas Powys, the boy's future was formed. No more fanciful notions, no more farming or firefighting. The path first forged by the young man would be followed by the boy. But before the journey of a thousand miles started with the first step there was a word of caution.

'There is, though, one thing you want to avoid,' the young man warned. 'Sports journalism.' The boy could sense the shudder of distaste that went through him. 'Sports journalism is not PROPER journalism.'

Thirty years and more later, the now not-so-young man brought out his first book, John Humphrys' *Devil's Advocate*. Page 129 was testament to how his advice had been taken to heart. 'Whenever I think of football I recall the old man who was asked why he never read books. "Because I read one once and I didn't like it," he said. That's me and football. I went with my younger brother, Rob, to see Cardiff City play when I was a boy. He was hooked and eventually turned hobby into career and became the finest sports journalist in Wales. I never went again.'

'The finest sports journalist in Wales'? That smacks of a soft side unknown to the sacrificial lambs sent shaking into the studios of the *Today* programme for a breakfast-time intellectual disembowelling. Then again, he could be damning with faint praise. My brother has been known to do that!

Chapter 2

Bob's Your Name!

I was no longer Rob. A sub-editor on the *Western Mail* – I never found out which one – made sure of that. The abbreviation that had been good enough for friends and family for twenty-two years disappeared overnight when I was visiting my fiancée at the university she was still at, and I'd just graduated from, in Exeter. I'd left behind my first bylined piece commissioned by the deputy editor who'd shared my brother's name, though not its spelling, during his time at the newspaper . . . John Humphrys was never to be seen in Wales's national newspaper . . . instead John Desmond ruled the crime correspondent columns while John Humphries gave the orders.

One of those orders was to his new news trainee, fresh out of the Thomson group's training school in 1974 but not quite wet enough behind the ears to expect to write a hard-hitting leader on American involvement in Vietnam on day one. Instead, Humphries briefed me on . . . glamour models. 'Apparently the industry's suffering, not enough girls want to get into it. Find out who they are, find out where they are, find out . . . find out what makes them tick,' he instructed in his curiously manic way. 'And get the pictures . . .'

This was obviously the PROPER journalism the other Humphrys had talked about in his fraternal advice of a few years before. He knew his stuff. It was the sort of assignment I could get my teeth into: a call to a model agency, the name of a girl on their books and a trip to her house in nearby Barry.

I have to confess I was none too sure what to expect from a 'glamour model'. Glamour, I suppose, and there was certainly plenty of that – in an understated way, dressed as she was in jeans and shirt – when she answered the door. She was also pleasant, articulate and . . . surrounded by radiators draped in drying nappies.

'Little brother?' I asked.

'Little son,' she replied.

So who was I to make judgements? Who said glamour models couldn't have a family life or, come to that, have a family?

Interview done, photographer arranged, I headed back to the office, wrote the piece, went off to Exeter, came back home to my first byline and found my name changed irrevocably to Bob. 'Where have all the pin-ups gone,' said the strapline . . . 'Bob Humphrys investigates' . . . 'Girls scamper for cover from over-exposure to camera lens'. And there it might have ended, had not a story flashed round the globe a few months later about a Welsh girl who'd become Miss World, a Welsh pin-up to be more precise, a Welsh pin-up from Barry who turned out to have a son and soon found out she didn't have a title.

The Miss World organisers were obviously more puritanical than I'd been when I spotted those nappies back in the South Wales seaside town. 'A *s-o-o-o-on*', you could imagine them wailing in horrified Lady Bracknell tones, and poor old Helen Morgan, Miss Wales and Miss United Kingdom, found her time on the throne five days shorter than Lady Jane Grey. She was truly the Four-Day Beauty Queen.

I kept quiet about the nappies. 'Who'd have thought it?' I tut-tutted with the rest of the hacks over a post-work pint in the Horse and Groom. 'How'd she keep that quiet?' I might have lost my name over Helen Morgan, I was damn sure I wasn't going to lose my job.

My time in 'proper' journalism continued. There was even the odd flirtation with the dark side – sport – though not enough to get anyone excited, even if it did get in the way of finer professional instincts. The case in point involved one Jorge Rafael Videla, then the president of Argentina. It was not a name that cropped up regularly in the contacts books of many of the Welsh media. Worldwide, though, he had a certain reputation, a reputation that anyone who, when he leaves office, is convicted on numerous charges of murder, kidnapping and torture deserves.

In 1977, he obviously felt in need of an image makeover, though quite how he imagined that employing a huge American PR machine to bring over writers from the likes of the *Belfast Telegraph*, the *Northern Echo*, the *Scotsman* and me from the *Western Mail* on a week-long jolly, to meet him and the loyal generals who made his government, was going to improve the rank smell coming from his administration remains a mystery. I remember a swarthy, bushily moustached man, a caricature almost of a South American soldier, a doppelganger for a British character from B list movies who everyone would recognise but few could name, a man who smiled a lot with everything but his eyes.

And what did I ask him about? About '*las madres de la Plaza de Mayo*' – the mothers who gathered outside the Casa Rosado presidential palace in Buenos Aires to demand, in a hugely dignified and courageous way, to be told what had happened to their missing children, many of whose bodies would be found floating mutilated in the River Plate? About the detention, torture and killing of political opponents? About the nine thousand, some estimate up to 30,000 '*desaparecidos*' – forced disappearances – which happened under the iron fist of his nine-man junta?

No. I asked him about the World Cup.

It was not my finest moment. The worst excesses of his regime weren't yet known – it would be the next century before his name was expunged as legal president of Argentina and his picture removed from military school – but, good God, I could have given him a harder time than to ask a question about how his vicious, violent apology for a civilised country was preparing for the 1978 World Cup. Will the stadiums be ready, Mr President? That should have read, who's buried beneath them, Mr President? At least that Dutch magician Johan Cruyff had more balls. He refused to travel with the Holland team to Argentina in protest at Videla's human rights record. I wish I had done the same.

Chapter 3

A Tale of Two Letters

The train trip from Cardiff to Cambridge was long, long but not tedious. Dipping into Tom Sharpe's rollicking South African romp, *Indecent Exposure*, made sure of that. It was strange how at seminal moments in my career that word 'exposure' played a key part: those pin-ups back in 1974, and now, four years later, during what looked like being one of my last jobs for the *Western Mail*. And once again sport was intruding into my life as one of the paper's feature writers.

Cambridge was where the New Zealand rugby team would play the first match on their 1978 tour, a gentle enough curtain-raiser to what was to become their first grand slam tour – matched in 2005 – during which they beat England, Scotland, Ireland and Wales. The light-blues University side wasn't expected to offer much opposition – though it did have a certain youthful E.T. Butler in its line-up before he went on to Welsh captaincy and BBC commentary box – and true to form it didn't: 32–12 the All Blacks won. Looking at their team sheet now, it's remarkable how the demographics of the side have changed. The names from the South Sea Islands, the Sivivatus and Rokococos, Mealamus and Weepus, were nowhere to be seen. Instead it was the Anglo-Saxon Blacks and Bushes, or the Celtic McKechnies and McGregors who dominated, with Robert Kururangi the only nod to either the ethnic past of the Land of the Long White Cloud or the people of Polynesia.

There was another difference all those years ago. They might have been the most famous and successful team on the planet, but you didn't need a raft of accreditation that could also get you into the Oval Office, or interview request forms signed in triplicate and approved by half a dozen line managers before you could approach them. Nor was there a former Prime Minister's spin doctor to open/shut the door for the favoured/not-so-favoured few. No . . . back then the time-honoured way for a young journalist from Wales to find out how the All Black captain, Graham Mourie, was viewing the Welsh leg of his team's tour was to stand outside the dressing room and, er, wait.

He might not have known me from the man who cleaned the Grange Road toilets, but, strangely, it worked. The newly showered Mourie's words were safe in the notebook before it was time for me to make a decision. After all, if there was any city in the country more suitable for taking a punt than Cambridge, I didn't know it.

Those who might have been sad enough to be standing outside the main post office that dank Fenland October afternoon would have had their life brightened by the sight of a young man opening his briefcase, taking out two identical brown envelopes, shuffling them with rather less than the expertise of a Las Vegas cardsharp, then posting one and opening the other. This is what he read:

> Dear Head of BBC Wales Personnel,
> Thank you very much for your offer of a job as a reporter/presenter on BBC Radio Wales. After careful consideration I have decided to remain in print journalism and will not be switching my career path to broadcasting.

I hope you understand that as the result of much heart searching, I will have to turn down your kind offer.
Yours sincerely,
Bob Humphrys

Maths had never been his strong point, but a process of elimination quickly led him to a conclusion.

'Bloody hell,' he said, 'I've taken a job!'

The other envelope, now mixing in the postbox with the birthday cards, love letters and any early incarnation of junk mail, safe from any arm that might want to stretch down and retrieve it, contained a missive similar to the letter in his hand, with a few key differences. The negatives were positives, the rejections were acceptances, and the result was . . . I was joining the BBC.

My new job meant learning a new lexicon of terms. 'Fast forward' was one of them. So fast forward some months to a newly recruited BBC reporter/presenter on the newly launched Radio Wales wishing he'd deployed a different sleight of hand back at Cambridge's head post office. I was pining for print. There was something annoyingly intangible about broadcasting: none of the permanency of picking up a newspaper and reading a carefully crafted piece you'd written – or, more probably in my case, someone else had written. It was also a tad embarrassing to have pronunciations honed in working-class Cardiff savaged by those fortunate enough to be born on the right side of the Welsh-language bed sheet. 'For God's sake, it's not "Pont-Y-pridd", it's "Pont-ER-pridd", you buffoon, "Pont-ER-pridd".' You could tell those of us rowing an English monoglot boat by the scribbled notes on our scripts, spelling out the acceptable phonetic face of the pronunciation police.

And there was time – or rather the lack of it. Print journalism – especially as a feature writer – gave you space to expound and expand, describe and discuss. One page of a newspaper contains considerably more words than a whole half-hour television news programme. If Moses had done an exclusive deal with *The Ten O' Clock News* to unveil the Ten Commandments, our whole lifestyle would be different: 'Look Moses, old fruit . . . ten's a bit much to squeeze into one minute 30 . . . OK . . . one forty-five tops. Can't we cut it down a bit . . . say five . . . and we might be able to squeeze another into the headlines and the "coming up" . . . wodja say, Mo?'

All was not lost though. The editor of the *Western Mail*, an urbane and hugely pleasant man, offered an escape route back: similar job to before, but more responsibility, more travel, more money. I went home to think about it and discovered my house had been broken into. There was no denying the burglars had good taste: the television, the expensive stereo and the record collection had gone – all bar one album, lying forlornly by itself on the floor. It was Roddy Llewellyn's first and only LP, catchily called *Roddy*. In my defence, I didn't buy it. I picked it up at a party that Princess Margaret's then beau held to launch it at the Tramp nightclub in London. The record wasn't memorable. In fact the only thing I do remember about the whole affair is that I interviewed his mother, Lady Llewellyn, largely I suspect because it gave me the excuse to use the line, 'The Lady in the Tramp'. Unlike the thieves who left it behind, I obviously had no shame . . . but while I was holding Roddy's greatest hit (I suppose it qualifies as that on the grounds of lack of competition), the sound of the phone echoed around my newly emptied lounge.

'Bob . . . it's Arwel here.' BBC Wales's head of news and current affairs didn't often ring me at home. 'I know you've been none too happy about the switch you've made, so I wanted to run something by you. We've got an attachment coming up as a reporter on *Week In Week Out* [BBC Wales's flagship current affairs television programme] in the autumn. Thought you might be interested. And we're starting up a new programme. *Sports News Wales* – what it says is what it does – on a Saturday afternoon. I know it's only five minutes long, but we'd like you to present it.'

Sports News Wales. Sports. News. Wales. I could hear the sound of brother John quietly groaning, somewhere far away.

Chapter 4

'There's Been a Murder in Abergavenny'

Sports News Wales, presented by a reformed character now happily reconciled to the BBC and its inherent flaws – namely myself – started one Saturday in the autumn of 1980. I like to think it was an auspicious debut. The next day 5,000 televisions were sold. Those who couldn't sell them gave them away. Not original as lines go, I know, but probably accurate to anyone who might remember those fly-by-the-seat-of-your-pants early days.

It was a programme marked by tension, not on the day – few transmissions with an audience in the hundreds of thousands could be more relaxed – but on the following Monday, when there was the inevitable argument with the news editor about the split between the sports content and news.

'You've got four minutes 45 for the programme, right?'

'Yep.'

'And it's supposed to be split half news, half sport?'

'Yep.'

'So three minutes 15 for sport and one minute 30 for news is half and half, is it?'

'I told you I was never very good at maths.'

But he did have a point. I was being seduced away from the path of news righteousness by the easy familiarity I found in writing and talking about Cardiff City's latest plucky defeat or rugby teams still measuring success in the number of pints they could down at the end of the match. I like to think there was an irreverence about the way I scripted the programme that was unusual in a world where the cliché had become king. The Beeb's powers-that-be might have blanched at the description of a buoyant Swansea City 'rising faster than the unemployment figures under Margaret Thatcher', but I failed to see anything wrong with an early foray into mixing politics with sport.

There was, though, a reckoning to be had one afternoon when time for me stood still. I'd overwritten the sports script, nothing new in that – there was always the director to tell me through my earpiece to ditch the last few stories and go to the news, and as a last resort there was the floor manager to start the clock that told me I had a minute of the programme to go. Wasn't there? As it turned out, no. Basking in self-congratulation at completing all the sport and still having plenty of time to keep old grumpy in the newsroom off my back, I switched to serious mode . . .

'Now here are the main stories in Wales today. There's been a murder in Abergavenny.'

I paused for effect. This provided the gap necessary for the hysterical scream of the director, who was watching the titles of *Doctor Who*, or whatever the next programme was, already running on the BBC throughout the rest of the country, to penetrate my previously malfunctioning earpiece.

'SHURRUP!'

I looked sagely into the single camera. 'Good evening.'

I never did find out who'd been killed in Abergavenny. I never found out why the floor manager had fallen asleep over the clock either, though the beer in the BBC Club might be up there among the suspects. As for the audience, well, they do say leave them wanting more.

Sports News Wales – apart from providing the opportunity to make a fashion statement on behalf of the most appalling jumpers I could find, something that for eight years apparently made for cult viewing (though that could have been a mis-spelling) – was the ideal grounding in studio presentation. But it was sport at a distance: the chance to talk about the major sporting events without actually being able to say, 'I was there.' That changed on the 25th anniversary of the climax of Swansea City's remarkable rise and rise from the old Fourth Division to Division One, thanks to a 3–1 win at Preston North End in May '81.

'Is that, er, *you*?!'

Aaagh . . . if only I had a pound for every time a picture editor working with me on some look-back at famous Welsh sporting moments came out with that little gem, I'd be writing this from some bijou bolt-hole in Barbados. But you can't blame him. After all, he was looking at an image that existed before time dragged me up a dark alley, as it does all of us, and beat the hell out of me.

There I was, locks flowing in the Preston breeze – whereas now it would take a hurricane to find them, let alone ruffle them – standing at the end of a dug-out next to an equally youthful John Toshack *et al* as the Swans went up. I was the BBC's interviewer for the day, and the commentator – should you ask – was no, not John Motson and no, not Barry Davies, but a certain Des Lynam before he headed off to the *Grandstand* studio and subsequently became Carol Vorderman's *Countdown* sidekick.

While the champagne was fizzing in the away dressing room so too was Bill Shankly, there to see his prodigy Tosh come of age as a manager. 'John Toshack manager of the year? Nah . . .' he said in that husky Scottish burr. '. . . he's the manager of the century!' Now why don't all interviewees come out with soundbites like that?

After interviewing everyone who could stand – and a few who couldn't – it was back in the car to follow the team bus, complete with cameraman on board, back to the first pit stop on the triumphal journey down the motorway, Liverpool's Holiday Inn, where sadly the cameraman succumbed to exhaustion and slumped, not to move again, on a settee in the foyer. Not to worry, another was dispatched to the Vetch for the homecoming and the subsequent early-morning celebrations of the newest arrivals in Division One. Yes, it was me.

Not content with having me as an interested onlooker, asker-of-questions and apprentice cameraman, there was also an attempt to turn me into part of an event itself as the commentator. It started off well enough: lunch in a local pub with legendary rugby director Dewi Griffiths and my squash partner cum voice of BBC Wales rugby, David Parry-Jones. 'Nothing to worry about,' they said. 'Couldn't be easier . . . just do your homework, take a look at the players training, get to know them, make sure you can identify them and take it away! Piece of the proverbial!' After another pint of Brains Bitter who was I to disagree with them?

Except for two things: 1, they lied . . . and 2, what happened on the Friday night before the game.

For months before that particular Friday I had been working on a programme about the Welsh troops at Fitzroy in the Falklands War. Forty-eight men – most of them Welsh Guards – died when the troopship *Sir Galahad* was bombed by Argentinian Skyhawk jets in June 1982. The death toll made up a fifth of all British fatalities in the war. Throughout Wales families were left mourning young men who'd sailed off in an outpouring of public patriotism, never to come home again. They accepted that that was a risk they had taken, but what they didn't accept was the fact the *Sir Galahad* had been left helpless on the water for hours while the soldiers waited to be disembarked. When the Argentinian planes attacked, the troops were targets in a shooting gallery.

'Why?' was the question the families wanted answered. 'Why was nothing done to protect them? Why weren't they moved to the relative safety of the land sooner?'

We tried to give them an answer on *Week In Week Out*. A senior British army officer agreed to an interview at the Ministry of Defence in Whitehall. 'The fog of war,' was his reasoning. Yes there had been mistakes, yes they should have done things differently, but these things happened in war. It was probably not what the families wanted, but it was an admission – of sorts: it could have been avoided. It was a powerful programme, one good enough to win an award the following year.

Programme makers, survivors and families of those who had not been so fortunate gathered in the green room to watch the film go out. My brother John, who had joined me for a stint as the programme's studio presenter, was there too. There was no celebration – the subject matter was too sensitive for that – but there was satisfaction at a job we all knew had been done well. The wine went down quickly, too quickly. The early hours of that morning were not the time to be heading for bed, somewhat the worse for wear, before a first-attempt rugby commentary. Which is all very well to say in hindsight.

A Schweppes Welsh Cup semi-final between Newbridge and Swansea shouldn't have been the most exacting of debuts; it was hardly likely to provide one of those Bill McLaren moments – 'He's jinking like a drunken troot!' – or even a Cliff Morgan-like 'What a score!!!' And I did all the right things . . . well, all the things I'd seen proper commentators do. The official programme for Saturday, March 26, 1983 (price 20p) still has the notes I jotted down beside the teams. All very praiseworthy – except the only words I can make out on it now are 'breeze left to right from the river end'. The rest might have been found on the nearest wall to Howard Carter when he opened up Tutankhamun's tomb, such is the sense they make. I'd obviously had rather more glasses than I thought the night before.

I'd had this problem once before, in my newspaper days, when I went to London to interview the Tonypandy born actor, Donald

Houston, who'd starred with Jean Simmons in *The Blue Lagoon*. We met in the White Swan around the corner from his flat in Paddington. Several pints of Courage Directors later, I could have been offering him the lead in a sure-fire Oscar winner such was our new-found friendship.

'Right,' he boomed in his Shakespearean-Rhondda tones when the landlord rang the bell for three o'clock stop tap. 'I've got some good Welsh cawl on the stove. Back to the flat!' He forgot to mention the good Scotch whisky he had to go with the good Welsh cawl. Or the fact that when the landlord reopened the White Swan at half past five we were waiting outside to check whether the Courage Directors had suffered any deterioration in the two and a half hours since we had been so sadly parted from it. When I eventually crawled off the train at Swansea – I should have got off at Cardiff but 'drunken stupor' or whatever the medical term is for such a state had rendered that course of action out of the question – there was a gnawing feeling that something was wrong.

It wasn't until the following morning I discovered that the feeling had been 100 per cent correct. My shorthand, which had been registering the thoughts, words and deeds of one of Wales's most distinguished actors, started off intelligible, passed through a stage of incomprehensible and ended in a vision of a thousand spiders scurrying over the pages after dipping their legs in ink. There was only one solution . . . a second gradual transition from sobriety to intoxication with the shorthand becoming ever clearer as the level of alcohol increased.

Sadly I did not have that option at Cardiff Arms Park. So, when the referee blew his whistle, my brain, battered by all that red the night before, blew up with him. I'd speak, wonder what I'd said, muse on whether it had made sense, consider the next turn of phrase, speak again, regret what I'd said, by which time I was making as much sense as Kenneth Williams on *Just a Minute*.

And that was the good bit. There was some Swansea pressure in front of the posts. The referee raised his arm to the sky. 'Got this,' I thought . . . 'Penalty!', I said with just that bit of authoritative understatement that had you standing out from the crowd. The kick was duly taken and I continued on my stumbling way until half time. 'Er, Bob . . .' said the producer, 'wonder if we could just do one little bit of that commentary again. That penalty . . . it, uh, it wasn't quite a penalty . . . it was more of a . . . penalty try. The kick was a, um, conversion not a . . . penalty. And, just a little point, the score's not six-all but 10–6. Apart from that, great!'

Didn't I say, the match wasn't live? The BBC weren't that stupid.

I watched the highlights the following afternoon, not quite sure why the babbling fool who sounded as if he was being auditioned for the castrati apparently shared my name.

Worse followed in work on Monday. 'Who the hell was that new guy on the rugby yesterday?' asked my editor on *Week In Week Out*.

'Dunno, Jeff. Shit wasn't he?'

I had fared better than my brother, however. After our green-room excess, he'd moved on to a cottage he owned near Carmarthen in West Wales. He put a towel on an electric dryer, sat down and closed his eyes. When he opened them there was no towel, no dryer and scarcely any cottage. There was the local fire brigade, and there was someone offering his less than considered opinion that he was lucky to be alive: 'Could have been toasted in there, you could!'

The moral of the tale . . . sport? Who needs it?

Chapter 5

The Man with the Rubber Face

'The sentence that I impose on you is that of eight years' imprisonment, and an order that you be deported, because this country has no need for people like you to interfere with our way of life.'

Ah, this was 'proper journalism' in all its pomp: the solemnity of Swansea Crown Court in the high summer of 1984, fourteen bewigged barristers, a high court judge passing sentence. The man in the dock, standing in front of the judge with all the uninterested nonchalance of a customer being told his car needed a new windscreen wiper at its six monthly service, was one Soren Berg-Arnbak or, as he was affectionately known by the team on *Week In Week Out*, 'the man with the rubber face'. Never let it be said we passed up an easy tilt at the melodramatic.

As the Danish drug smuggler yawned and studied his nails at the mild inconvenience of a couple of years free board and lodging courtesy of Her Majesty before hopping back to his private island and swollen bank account, we knew we had a humdinger of a television documentary in prospect . . . the story of a gang who'd quarried a huge hole in Seal Bay, a remote West Wales cove, with the intention of filling it with three tonnes of cannabis valued, at early eighties prices, at around six million pounds.

Sadly, however, they hadn't factored in that in Wales you could dig an undercover silo with all the secrecy of a base for extra-terrestrials in New Mexico and there'd still be someone who'd stumble on it with a muttered, 'What's this by 'ere, then?'

Which of course is what happened. Strangers – who, by the standards of that beautiful part of Wales, could have been from a quarter of a mile away and upwards – were spotted. So too was expensive equipment. The reasons given by the interlopers with their pricy outboard motors and the rest, when asked why they were there, had just a hint of the phoney about them. 'Photographing seals,' said one . . . plausible, except that, even if he'd known global warming was on the way, he was two or three months too early. 'Testing equipment for an expedition to Greenland,' said another. 'Funny place to do that,' said one local boatman, obviously unimpressed with the man's dirty hands and fingernails 'bitten down to the quick'. 'Training for a whale-filming expedition,' was another explanation, '. . . but please don't talk about it – certainly not to the press. It's a top secret operation.'

Now this was one person who didn't know the psyche of a West Walian. He might just as well have said, 'Take out a full-page advertisement in the *Western Telegraph*, and while you're about it, phone the newsdesk at the *Sun* and tell them we've got half a dozen page-three girls about to morph into mermaids.'

Before you could say, 'We reckon you're telling porkies', police and locals were being ferried to the cove. As I was to discover when I went there later to film, at Seal Bay the list of things to do is a short one, largely consisting of picking up a pebble and throwing it. To be fair, there is a multiple choice involved. You could a) throw it into the sea or b) throw it onto other pebbles. As luck would have it, a local farmer by the name of Peter Smith chose option two. Up it flew and down it fell with a 'clang' rather than a 'clunk'. Or was it the other way round?

There is absolutely no reason to suspect that the local police said

''Ello, 'ello, what have we got 'ere then?' but if they didn't they missed a rare opportunity because it would have been one hell of a good question. What they 'had 'ere' was a brand new perspex boat-deck hatch leading down into a large man-made chamber supported by timbers and covered by a layer of giant pebbles. Even by the standard of West Walian house prices, a subterranean room on a remote beach accessible only by foot or by sea was not the stuff *Location, Location, Location* was going to leap upon. Someone was up to no good, which might be a cliché to cringe at but does have a ring of truth about it.

That 'someone' turned out to be – among others – our old friend 'the man with the rubber face'. Arrested in West Wales while using the name Sam Spangaard, presumably under the mistaken assumption such an alias would blend in seamlessly with the locals, he was given a fingerprint check and Interpol quickly established this was indeed Soren Berg-Arnbak, wanted drug smuggler, escaped prisoner, all-round bad egg, and, not to put too much of a fine point on it, a bit of a hero back home in Denmark. Eleven years on the run, during which he'd slipped the police net with the panache of a modern-day Robin Hood, had the tabloids turning him into a household name. Or rather names: you could add 'The Chameleon' to 'Rubber Face'.

'The multi-millionaire narco-gangster', trilled Denmark's popular press as they breathlessly wrote about him, his cash and his yacht *Crocodile*, which was almost identical to the Danish Royal Yacht, except, of course, slightly larger. A picture of him, handcuffed to a Welsh policemen after his arrest, had the country's most widely read newspaper, *Ekstra Bladet*, proudly stamping 'Made in Denmark' on his white T-shirt like a side of Danish Bacon. On the streets of Copenhagen he was probably the most recognisable export since Carlsberg. This was a Viking Jesse James or Ned Kelly, with huge reserves of ill-gotten cash. All that knowledge was almost completely denied to the judge and his jury at Swansea Crown

24

Court. When he prepared to sentence Berg-Arnbak to those eight years inside, His Honour couldn't know that this was no foot-soldier but the top man in the organisation. That rubber face had worked again, The Chameleon had blended in, ready to change colour and character – once he was released – for yet another new existence far from Seal Bay.

And that was the story we told. 'The Drug Runner Millionaires' obviously had a resonance well away from Wales, or maybe 'the man with a rubber face' just had a big if unnoticed family all living multiple lives. In 1984 it had *Week In Week Out* picking up the Royal Television Society's Current Affairs Programme of the Year award at the Dorchester Hotel. All that walking up and down Seal Bay, looking for just the right pebble that would go 'clang' – or was it 'clunk'? – and hoisting myself down into the fetid bowels of the drugs chamber as we filmed our reconstructions, had proved worthwhile.

A television programme wasn't all that came out of it. The detective chief superintendent in charge of the investigation, a splendid man called Pat Molloy, wrote a book on it called *Operation Seal Bay* which even now seems to sell for a small fortune on Amazon. It's a hugely detailed account of all that went into a remarkably complicated piece of police work. We couldn't have made the programme without his cheerful co-operation, especially as we pieced together 'The Chameleon's' past in Copenhagen. But what Pat – who sadly died a few years ago – inscribed in a copy of the book he gave to me summed up what the programme was all about. 'To Bob Humphrys', he wrote, 'who took me to the home of lager and supped the well dry! Pat Molloy, 13th March, 1986.'

Who said proper journalism couldn't be fun?

Chapter 6

'Actually ... it's Tony Hopkins'

Lambert Le Roux was sitting in front of me putting on make-up and talking about method acting. He hadn't started the afternoon as Le Roux, a South African newspaper tycoon with all the hallmarks and more of the yet-to-be-disgraced Robert Maxwell. He'd started off as a boy from Port Talbot and had made good. This was the Saturday matinee at the National Theatre and Anthony Hopkins was in the make-up chair, revealing how he transformed himself from amiable Welsh son of a baker into mesmeric stage villain in Howard Brenton and David Hare's smash hit, *Pravda*.

'I think actors are pretty damaged people,' he said, brushing powder onto a face going paler with every stroke. 'People who are a little neurotic. I don't feel I am quite happy with my lot—'

I interrupted. 'You don't feel you need an analyst, like so many other actors though?'

His mouth moved in a way that was strangely reminiscent of a lizard . . . 'Ah, this is the part I like – he becomes . . . a monster . . . that's Hitler's mouth. I had a grandfather, my father's father, who was a pretty extraordinary man, a very forceful personality. He used to do things to frighten me like they do with kids . . .' He pulls another face. '. . . I've based a bit of this on him. That's what

Lambert Le Roux is . . . that's what I hopefully present on stage and it seems to have worked!'

'A composite of all childhood horrors, it seems,' I put in.

'Yes . . . it's a bit like Be . . . la Lu . . . go . . . si.' His voice slips into black-and-white horror movie mode, then effortlessly changes tack to the High Veldt. 'And in Sarrfff Effriken it sounds even more freightenin . . .' With a final check from his dresser, he walks out of the dressing-room door and onto the stage.

If I am brutally honest, all the talk of Stanislavsky and the rest was a little beyond a listener whose acting background had never stretched beyond playing a marmoset press-ganged onto Noah's Ark in an ambitious Cardiff High School production of Benjamin Britten's *Noyes Fludde* in Llandaff Cathedral. Actually I did have a minor starring role with a one-night stand as Noah's son, but a mishap in the middle of my solo, when my voice broke and dropped an octave, caused great consternation to the professional opera singer playing Noah. So it was back to life among the monkeys, where the subject of method acting was seldom raised.

But such was the charisma of Hopkins you could sit and listen to him read out the *Yellow Pages* ('Buildings – Relocatable' to 'Clothes Hire – Men's') and still be riveted. We were making a documentary on his life and work, pre-Hannibal Lecter and the Oscar, but he was still a major star, who in the mid-eighties had decided – for the time being at least – he'd had enough of life in Tinseltown and had bought a house for himself and his then wife in fashionable Belgravia.

'Hollywood isn't anything to do with money,' he told me standing looking out over the Thames near the National during another interview. 'It's about privilege and what your box-office rating is like. If your box-office rating isn't good, you don't get invited to the number one parties. Now, if you take that seriously you can end up in the loony bin, so you learn not to take it seriously. People do though, and they either go mad or hit the drugs because they can't cope with it. But I wouldn't have missed any of it. It's very seductive, it's almost like an insect-eating plant. Before you know it, you get really seduced by it and then you end up years later having wasted your life.

'What is attractive about it though is that it's a very easy lifestyle, the weather is glorious and you can't take yourself too seriously over there. That was something I wanted . . . I went over there and I learned the trick of not taking myself too seriously in this business. If there's anything I've inherited or taken from California, it is that it's all a great game. And that's what I love about acting . . . I enjoy the game! It's better than working for a living and that's why I do it. I don't know what else I could do really!

'I lived a very simple life out there, believe it or not! I didn't socialise much, I didn't know any of the Britons over there – or the Brits as they call them. I've met Michael Caine a few times, but I was very much on my own and I enjoyed it that way. I didn't go to many of the functions, though I went to one of the Oscars awards and that was mayhem. You've got to go there, know the rules, enjoy it and not take it seriously.'

The documentary team watched as he filmed *The Good Man* with Joanne Whalley in London, travelled with him to the street in Port Talbot and the house he grew up in, took him to Margam Abbey where he'd already bought the plot for his grave. It sounds morbid now . . . it didn't then as he talked about his philosophy on life.

'It's all about choice,' he said, 'we make our own hell or we make our own heaven. We make our own paradise or we make our own hell on earth. We can destroy our own lives.'

'Was that insight a flash . . . ?' I asked.

'Yes, I'd say about seven or ten years ago, I had a flash when I was in California, but they're all getting flashes over there. I suddenly woke up one morning and I thought I'd better do something about my life and get on with it, instead of wasting my time with it. I've enjoyed it ever since!'

'Suddenly your life changed?'

'Yeah . . . I have my off moments you know, but I think by and large I get on with it and have trust that everything is OK, that deep down underneath everything is OK.'

'Is that when drink went by the board?'

'Oh that . . . yeah! I got rid of that because I couldn't fool around with that stuff, it wasn't doing me much good.'

'You went through a phase which could almost be described as, what, self-destructive?'

'Well, I just liked the old sauce a bit too much. I had some fun with it and I think it's marvellous if you can have a drink and enjoy it, but unfortunately I couldn't do that. I rather abused it, so I thought "stop" because it's like having a car, you get a nice new car and you pour sand in the petrol tank or you slash the tyres! It's not going to go very far, is it? So I thought, I've got one body and I'd better stop messing about.'

It was cathartic for him to head back to his roots where old men who'd known him in his pretty friendless childhood, when he'd play at one end of the street and the rest of the boys at the other, would scratch their heads, ask 'Still acting are you?' and wonder if he really got paid for going to bed with some pretty young girl on the television. He didn't mind questions like that . . . it showed they weren't taking him seriously. It was how he liked it, the way of a world where he reckoned some kind of mystical force runs our lives.

'I think there's some much greater scale of planning than there is in our puny, finite minds,' he said. 'For example, there was a very strange thing when I was playing Bligh in *The Bounty*. One Saturday morning I was particularly angry because I couldn't get in touch with the producer. He was away and there had been some problems. We hadn't started filming yet, but there had been some re-writing on it which wasn't good enough. I couldn't get hold of anyone and I was so angry about this. My wife said, "There's nothing you can do about it 'til Monday, so forget about it." I couldn't, though, couldn't forget about it, so I stormed out of the flat in Arlington Street about seven in the morning, thinking: I'll have a brisk walk now, then come back and have a cup of coffee.

'I was really steamed up . . . so I walked over Lambeth Bridge and came to a church there, near Lambeth Palace. I looked and there was a tomb: William Bligh and his family were buried there. I went closer to it, looked again, and there it was, "Captain William Bligh", the man I was playing. I started to laugh . . . but I think I was over-awed really. I said to the tomb, "Well, Bill, wherever you are, we're having problems with the film, so help us out!" And I went back to the flat. I really felt much better now, and as I got in my wife said, "Bernie Williams, the producer, just phoned – don't worry about those re-writes, scrap them, forget them!" I thought, well, there you are! Coincidence? Well, it was a little thing, but there have been lots of those in my life.'

Given the material that oozed effortlessly from Hopkins, we had a heck of a programme on a great actor. He was a Welshman, yes, but far from a stereotypical one. Richard Burton might have swapped all his fame and fortune for one Welsh rugby cap, but that is not a wish you could expect to hear Anthony Hopkins make. He spoke of Burton as we were driving along the main shopping street in Port Talbot where his father's baker's shop had stood.

'Strangely enough, after twenty years I met him in New York. He took over from me in *Equus* on Broadway and I remember we got together in the same dressing room I'd occupied. "Good Lord," he said,' – and if you'd turned your head away from the man driving, you would have sworn Burton had taken his place behind the driving wheel, such was the timbre of his voice – '"twenty years and three thousand miles later, here we are." He seemed to be a very nice man. I think it's very sad that he died.'

'You didn't talk about the old days in Port Talbot, did you?' I asked.

'We talked about Taibach. He said, "Where was your father's

shop?" and I said, "Opposite the Co-op where you worked." We knew some of the people that he knew and that was it.'

'That was it!' No cloying sentimentality about him. Far from it.

'Some people say, "Tony Hopkins – he's not really very Welsh." Would you say you're very Welsh?' I asked.

'Well, I don't play rugby, I hated rugby. I don't drink beer and I've never done *Under Milk Wood*, but I suppose I'm as Welsh as I'll ever be. I'm not and I never have been a great Cardiff Arms Park man, I'm not a rugby fan, so I suppose that doesn't make me very Welsh. I remember Ray Smith and Les Roberts, a couple of friends of mine, we were standing in a pub in London and they were talking about "the match". Les said, "Are you going to the match tomorrow?" and Ray said, "yes," and I said, "What match is that?" "What the hell do you mean, mun? England and Wales, mun, what sort of a Welshman are you?" They were very hurt. But that's the way it is!'

The programme with Anthony Hopkins shows I'd so far been successful in resisting the siren songs calling me to sport in my professional life, but what I did outside the BBC was another matter. Ever since college, I'd been involved with amateur football. Nothing serious, you understand . . . how could it be when you turned out for a team called 'Sewage Wanderers' in Division Six of the Exeter University Sunday League? Fellow students claimed we didn't so much play as go through the motions. Those without the luxury of further full-time education simply said we were crap. However, a playing career seriously hampered by a chronic lack of skill, speed and any other ingredient that would normally go into the mix to make a half-decent player meant that running a side rather than running in it was a more feasible option.

I did at first try fighting off the savage assaults of time and lack of talent with some performances at centre back that made the statues in Cardiff city centre look the epitome of athleticism, but I was not helped by being in a side where the combined age of the back four was somewhere north of 160 – nor indeed by playing alongside a left back who showed a stubborn resistance to acknowledging the offside law. It was only on his retirement – probably into a care home for the elderly – that he revealed he'd been deaf in his right ear from his birth many decades earlier. Our calls encouraging him to 'move up, Norman' hadn't been ignored – as we suspected – because of a capricious Geordie liking for resisting authority in any way, especially when it came in the form of an order, but because he couldn't have heard Beethoven's Fifth played by the massed orchestras of the Western World, let alone our increasingly desperate cries already half carried away on the winds of Trelai Park.

It was a dubious Indian meal that finally put paid to any faint resemblance I had to a footballer. As we ate on the night before a cup final against opposition who had already printed the tickets to their winners' disco, those jokes about 'Sewage Wanderers' kept resurfacing – along with the Chicken Ceylon. When the morning came, I was in no fit state to end my career in a blaze of mediocrity, only to stand limply on the touchline croaking pitifully as a bearded centre forward, fuelled on a dozen pints of Brains Bitter and the need to get off the pitch as quickly as possible, scored a match winning hat-trick. Remarkably, he was playing for us, the BBC/*Western Mail*, not the pithiest of names I know but things could only get worse. One shirt sponsor we would later acquire was 'The Out of Town Department Store – Branches at Llantrisant, Cross Hands and Melksham'. Opposition players suffered notice-ably from the boredom engendered by reading our shirts. Even those shirts, though, paled into insignificance against a local rugby team sponsored by 'Tres Chic Unisex'.

We were presented with the cup while the team's resident and remarkably annoying smart-arse was attempting to explain the definition of 'schadenfreude' to an opposing team not noticeably keen on having their linguistic horizons expanded beyond 'How-the-f**k-could-we-lose-to-this-bunch-of-nancy-boy-tossers?!' It was a good time to give away the kangaroo-skin boots that, despite their provenance, had failed miserably to put any spring into my leaden attempts to leap off the ground, and to morph into the supposedly less arduous role of team manager and club chairman, most of which involved getting eleven bodies – preferably breathing – on a football field every Sunday morning.

That was easier said than done. It was remarkable how human ingenuity increased by a factor of ten when faced with finding an excuse to stay in bed on a cold Sunday morning, rather than wade through foul-smelling mud as a disciple of the cult of coarse football. My soon-to-be wife had developed a nose like a pig sniffing out truffles when it came to the call that heralded the ever more elaborate reasons why Tony or Trog, Kevin or Kermit couldn't make the game. Sure enough, the phone rang.

'Hi, is Bob there . . . it's Tony here.'

'OK, Tone . . . so what is it this time?' she said.

'Pardon?'

'Fractured a fingernail so you can't put up the goal nets? Ruptured an eyelash? Bit on the cold side for that delicate constitution of yours?'

'I'm sorry?'

'Or did you just get pissed again last night?'

'Actually, it's . . . Tony Hopkins.'

A strange strangled sound came up the stairs, shortly followed by a woman gulping like a goldfish flung unceremoniously from its bowl. I went down to find the phone dangling by its cord, slowly unwinding like a scene from a forties B-movie. Sport, it seemed, could intrude on even the most unsporting of programmes. Maybe someone was telling me something.

Chapter 7

John and Shades, World Champions

It's early morning in Cwmbran, South Wales in 1980, and the seventeen-year-old is on his new motorbike. He's on his way to training in the town's pool, knowing that in two days' time he'll be named in the Wales swimming team. He's one of the country's most promising young sportsmen.

He's not quite sure why the accident happened – was it the road? was it him? – but the story he told me later was to change all the stereotypes I'd ever held about how a sportsman could be interviewed. The sheer down-to-earth pragmatism shone like a beacon through a catastrophe from which most of us would never recover. He was paralysed from the waist down after breaking his back.

'I suppose it was inexperience on my part,' he told me. 'I came to a T-junction and forgot to stop. The next thing, I'm through a hedge, over an eight-foot wall, into another one, and somebody found me in a brook in six inches of water with a motorbike on top of me.

'There was no real pain or anything. I didn't think there was that much wrong with me: I was chatting the nurse up on the way down in the ambulance. I thought a couple of weeks in hospital and I will be back out . . . but it took a bit longer than that.'

'How long were you lying in the stream?' I asked.

'I'd say I was unconscious for about two minutes. It was really funny because I thought I'd dreamt it all. I can remember waking up and looking up and thinking: Where's the roof gone off my bedroom? The first thing I thought was: Oh, oh, the last training session before the Welsh trials, my coach is going to kill me . . . then I realise I'm in six inches of water, and things started coming to me, and I saw this bloke wading over the stream and I thought: Something funny is going on here, I didn't dream it! Then the ambulance and the police came and that was it.'

'There was no sensation at all, no feeling at all there?'

'No. The bloke asked. I couldn't feel my legs, I knew that. So what happened was the bloke moved me over to the edge of the stream and then the ambulance came. There was no pain, no real pain, nothing like that.'

'How long was it before you realised you wouldn't be able to walk again?'

'They told me after about a week. I felt a bit sad and that was it.'

'How did you feel when the doctor said: "Chris, I'm sorry, you won't have the use of your legs again?"'

'It didn't really hit me or anything. I just accepted it and that was it. I didn't go into a fit of depression or anything like that! I was OK.'

'Is there anything you can't do that an able-bodied person can do, anything you find impossible?'

'Change a light bulb. That's about it!'

'That's the only problem?'

'Yeah. Can't think of anything else!'

'What do you say to people who might just have been put in the same position as you were, after their accident, not being able to walk again? What sort of advice can you give them?'

'Get off your behind and just carry on leading the life you led before. It might be a bit harder, but there's always people worse off than yourself, it's as simple as that.'

'A lot of them might think life is over after an accident like that?'

'It's up to them. It's up to the individual. If you want to give up, then you give up, if you don't, you carry on. As far as I'm concerned, it's not that much of a disability, that you have to give up . . . I don't think it's that much of a disability anyhow. I've seen so many people who are far more disabled than me, and how they're getting on with their lives, so why the hell should I worry?'

Two years later, Chris Hallam, whose vertebra had been found in the exhaust of his new motorbike, was a world champion. He'd won the 50 metres breaststroke at the World Disabled Games. It would be the first title of many. Life might have dealt him a hand that said 'no sport', but he never got round to turning the cards over. There wasn't time.

A few miles north of where Chris Hallam and his bike parted company, John Harris pushed a button for a living, turning out brake parts in the local factory. He was in a wheelchair too. Like Chris Hallam, he'd been a teenager when he'd gone to Minehead in Somerset on holiday – just before his nineteenth birthday. He'd always wanted to go on the big wheel. He did.

'The automatic locking system came undone and I fell something like forty or fifty feet, straight onto a brick wall,' he remembered. 'Someone said the ground broke my fall, but there you go! I smashed my arms as well as my back . . . it's funny, I was lying there and it was the old Marlon Brando touch! I really thought this was the end, I really thought I was dying because everything was just chaos. I was looking at people and it was as if they weren't really there. I could just about manage to look down and all my trousers had burst open. The zip itself hadn't broken but all the stitches had come undone, and I saw this girl looking down at me and smiling! She placed a cardigan over me, and another one put a cardigan under my head.

'I can remember looking at the wall and thinking: Thank God I didn't hit that! I had of course . . . a mate of mine said he tried to catch me, but I just brushed his fingers on the way down . . .'

Fate had done its bit and he was prepared to accept it.

'After about ten weeks I finally decided to ask the doctor what was going to happen to me. Up until then I'd probably been afraid to ask. It probably made everything better for me in a funny sort of way because I said, "How long will it be before I start moving my feet again, doctor?" and he said, "How long is it, John, since the accident?" I said, "Oh, about ten weeks." He looked at me. "I honestly can't see you moving them again, John." I said, "Oh God . . . what does that mean?"' Remarkably he could chuckle at the memory. 'You know what he said . . . he said, "You'll probably never ballet dance again!" Those were his exact words. What can you do but laugh, eh?

'I s'pose at the time I just thought everything was over. I just thought that was the end of my life and I'd be in a wheelchair and that would be it. I thought it would be just down to playing snakes and ladders and draughts! And that's what my life was like 'til I was twenty-eight. I just sat in the pub and got fatter and fatter and drunker and drunker and it was terrific, I didn't mind a bit!

'The will to live is far greater than the one to die. I think that's the easy way out – to top yourself. Everyone goes through phases when they feel like it and I'm no different, I get depressed like everyone else. But, with a disabled person, if you're depressed people automatically expect it of you. They think, "Hell he's a crip, he's bound to get depressed," so now I tend to wear a mask and people say, "What's going on with you, today?" I wear the mask, it's much easier: you can hide behind it and just go home and have a cry then, perhaps.'

When the tears dried, he got on with moving away from the pub to the gym. Push-ups not pints became his reason for living. The need to compete replaced the need to forget himself in a glass, muscle tone that wouldn't have been caused by the monotonous repetition involved in sitting behind his machine at work began to define his arms.

'What's a pair of legs as long as you've still got your brain?' He tapped his head. 'As long as you can talk to people and get on with people, I've always said, the body is just a frame. Skin is something to keep the rain out, to keep your bones from rusting, and these legs are just something to transport you around. It's no great deal walking! I can jump into a wheelchair or get into the car, and if I go into a club, I don't have to pay – *you* do! They'll feel sorry for me, no matter how much money I've got! I can get away with murder, you know – old ladies help me across the road whereas *you* have to help old ladies. When I have to get on a bus, the other passengers all carry the wheelchair on for me, and they get up for me, ninety-year-olds get up for me, pat me on the head and give me a sweet. *You* don't get anything like that . . . I get it all!'

By 1984, he was taking the oath for the British team at a fledgling Paralympics held not in one of the world's great stadiums to accompany an Olympics or Commonwealth Games, but at a hospital, Stoke Mandeville. It was a not so gentle reminder that they might be sportsmen and sportswomen but they were still patients. John Harris was introduced to the Prince of Wales who asked how the discus thrower came to be in a wheelchair. He told him.

'That must have been a very bad fall, Mr Harris.'

'Not really, sir. I got five point eight for degree of difficulty and six for style.'

John Harris went on to win the Olympic gold medal for the discus . . . but there was something absent from his life.

'You know what I really miss . . . putting on a pair of hot socks on a winter's morning. I used to put my socks in the oven to really warm them up, and to feel those going up your legs . . . it was ecstasy! So I miss that . . . and maybe running for a bus. Someone said to me, "Have you got any ambitions, John?" and I said "I'd like to have a heart attack running for a bus . . ."'

The odds would be long on finding two such remarkable characters in a small patch of Gwent, characters who regarded 'disability' as an irritation, a distraction, rather than the reason to curl up in front of a television or head to the local pub. They were athletes, wheelchair athletes admittedly, but, 'Hey,' they'd say, 'what's the difference between pushing a chair around a track and riding a bike in a velodrome? You know what . . . pushing a chair's probably a bloody sight harder!' The blisters and bloodstained bandages on their hands were testimony to that.

'The first big race I did was the Barry half marathon . . . it was only thirteen miles but the last mile was all uphill,' Chris told me. 'I had a police escort and everything, and I couldn't stop because all the crowd was cheering me on. When I got to the top of the hill and finished, I couldn't even see my hands, they were just a mass of blood. I'd just ripped them to shreds. If you didn't use tape you'd just burn through your fingers, and all you'd be looking at would be a piece of bone!'

They didn't conform to the mould of what was then perceived as disabled sport. Despite the self-mocking and the jokes, they didn't want a pat on the head and a patronising, 'Didn't he do well, bless him.' They were ultra-competitive. If they didn't win they let everyone know they were mightily pissed off. It was an attitude that made the blazers uncomfortable. 'It's not the winning, it's the taking part!' Tosh! 'You've done well just to be here!' Baloney! They were winners, pushing themselves and their equipment to the limit. John Harris would spend days walking – or rather pushing – around carrying a discus like some sort of comforter, just so that it became part of him, an extension of his being.

I followed them to the European track and field championships in Brussels. John Harris was the world discus champion but he didn't win there, he didn't even come second, he took home bronze. It was 'crap'. Did he mean that?

'Yes, I'm afraid I do. I just like to win and anything other than that is crap . . . especially because I threw badly anyway and if you don't throw at your best, it's rubbish. I really, really am bitterly disappointed but, hey, get up tomorrow, forget all about it, think about what I did wrong and just train for that through the winter and make sure I win the bloody gold again next time!'

'Was it worth coming to the championships?' I asked.

'Oh they're all worth it, yeah! Every one of them, it's always worth it, it's always memories, another memory for me, isn't it? So I didn't do so well but, hey, I'll forget about that by tomorrow, probably another couple more of these beers and I'll forget about it today.'

'Handsome' Harris – an adjective to be used with a certain amount of scepticism – and Chris 'Shades' Hallam, who was never without a trademark pair of sunglasses, were the trailblazers for disabled sport. Tanni Grey-Thompson, their fellow Welsh athlete, followed closely in their slipstream. Tanni was made a dame, Shades was given the MBE, Handsome Harris appeared on *This is Your Life*. In the true tradition of the secrecy surrounding everything to do with the show, he was auditioned for Eamonn Andrews's big red book at a lunch that followed the 'John and Shades' programme going out on BBC Wales. The producer – there incognito, of course – was obviously impressed by his ability to lift his leg onto the table and play it like a guitar.

They were 'John and Shades, World Champions' . . . and my introduction – on television at least – to how sport and journalism were not mutually exclusive. We three became friends and I became ever more astonished at how they were able to swat off disability like a fly at a summer picnic. Each Christmas Eve we would go for a drink, either around their haunts in Gwent or mine in Cardiff. Shades would drive . . . and drive and drive around a car park looking for a space left by the last-minute shoppers. It took *me* to say, 'You stupid bastard!' and point to a disabled space he'd already passed several times. 'Disabled' . . . that was for someone with a touch of arthritis, not someone who was Rambo from the waist up and 'Pinocchio' from the waist down. One Christmas he fell from his chair playing pool in the pub. It wasn't until a few days later that he discovered he'd broken his leg in several places. No feeling might mean no pain, it didn't mean no infection.

The programme we'd made together helped, but it was their own personalities and passion that pushed them towards celebrity. Shades, after that bloody start in Barry, would win the London Marathon twice, and he'd set countless records on the track and in the swimming pool. Handsome Harris made his name in the field events: the discus, the javelin and pentathlon . . . but it was the easy eloquence with which he spoke on a subject many still felt uncomfortable to talk about that gave him a role as the voice of disabled sport, unrivalled until Tanni Grey-Thompson came along with her world record haul of Paralympics medals.

He was given a place on the 'Walkway of Heroes' at the Millennium Stadium. The inscription on his paving stone is 'Disabled kids need heroes too'. With Shades he became the public face of a charity, 'People versus Handicap' (PvsH), working to build a dedicated sports centre for the disabled in Cardiff. It was an idea hatched over a beer on a trip to the United States where John and Shades were researching the latest techniques in wheelchair sport as part of a programme we were filming about Welsh entrepreneurs taking advantage of the American market. Along with the editor of *Week In Week Out*, Jeff Iverson, I became one of the vice-chairmen of the charity, headed by Ewart Parkinson. Our involvement largely involved encouragement from the other side of a glass containing some sort of alcohol. John and Shades put rather more of themselves into it, twice pushing around the entire coastline of Wales to raise nearly £60,000 for the centre which finally opened and is flourishing. Harris might have been introduced at the start of one of those pushes in Wrexham as a 'former world *disco* champion', but those days of disabled games being held in the grounds of a hospital seem a long time ago!

Out of anguish, came achievement. W. Somerset Maugham wrote a short story about a man who was sacked as the verger of St Peter's, Neville Square when a new vicar discovered he could neither read nor write. On his way back to his lodgings, he needed a cigarette. The road he was walking along had no tobacconist. With the help of his sympathetic landlady – later to become his wife – he opened one, then another, and another until he had a chain of ten shops across London. The story ends with his bank manager asking what he would have been if he had been able to read and write. 'Easy,' he said, 'the verger at St Peter's, Neville Square!'

Ask John Harris, the John Harris who's set world records, won gold medals, travelled the globe and become an ambassador-extraordinaire for disabled sport, what he'd be now if he'd never gone to Somerset that summer, never stepped onto the big wheel, never plunged onto that wall and he'll look at you . . . 'Easy,' he'll say, 'I'd be pushing a button at a car-part plant in Cwmbran!'

It goes without saying that John and Shades are two of the most inspiring people I've ever met. If you can't make good television programmes about the likes of them, you may as well pack up and go home. However, *Week In Week Out* was changing. Jeff Iverson left and with him went a maverick influence always prepared to stand up to BBC personnel superior in title but vastly inferior in the ability to make programmes people actually wanted to watch. I applied for his job, not because I particularly wanted it, but after ten years at Cardiff's Broadcasting House it was expected of me. 'Enough of that gallivanting around reporting. Time you grew up and got some quality management-time in. You've a career path to follow,' you could imagine the ghosts of personnel-officers-past saying. So a decade after I'd gone for my first BBC board – Beeb-speak for an interview – and had been left with those two letters outside that head post office in Cambridge, I went for another.

I got the job. Well, I sort of got the job. I wasn't actually the new editor of *Week In Week Out*, I was actually the new acting editor of *Week In Week Out*. I think. Nobody seemed terribly sure. Whatever I was, it was welcome to that nether world of the BBC meeting where people who could no more make a television programme than take on Einstein in a debate about the theory of relativity would sit and pontificate about what viewers wanted and how we could give it to them . . . usually at a greatly reduced cost. If in the land of the blind, the one-eyed man is king, in the world of the bland, the meeting is king . . . with many a job justified by how many boardroom tables you could sit around and the amount of inconsequential waffle you could generate.

I wasn't very good at it. Like an actor addicted to greasepaint, I wanted to be out on the street or in the countryside, wherever, interviewing people, writing scripts, voicing programmes. I didn't want to be in a soulless room talking about it while other people did it. The politics, the infighting, the empire building, the back-stabbing, they were for others much more talented at them than me.

My mother's death at the end of 1988 proved the catalyst for change. I was off work over her funeral. When I went back the dynamics in the office had subtly altered. A cameraman in his nudge, nudge, wink, wink way had already told me of one programme producer, steeped in the time-honoured BBC Wales tradition of stirring things up behind your back, whose public long face at hearing of my departure from *Week In Week Out* would mask a private polka of delight. Several awards as the Welsh Current Affairs Reporter of the Year and that Royal Television Society Current Affairs Programme of the Year for 'The Drug Runner Millionaires' meant there wasn't quite a Henry the Second moment as the Head of News and Current Affairs railed, 'Who will rid me of this turbulent priest?', but I was cast in the Thomas à Becket role. What to do with me?

'We've been thinking of revamping the sports coverage on *Wales*

Today, said EWNCA or whatever the acronym was then for the department's head honcho. 'And we want a sports correspondent dedicated to the programme. You're the obvious choice, Bob . . . it's a chance, a chance to combine your hobby with job!' I'd heard that before somewhere. Either that or I'd hear it somewhere in the future. But, whatever the motives for offering it, the opportunity was an interesting one. John and Shades had proved to me that covering sport didn't preclude providing quality.

'OK!' I said, after I'd fought off the temptation to write two letters. It might have been an underwhelming response, and it had taken a quarter of a century, but my brother's words came back to me. I WASN'T a proper journalist.

Chapter 8

A Carnival for Welshmen

They stood out from the other passengers milling around Cardiff Airport that August Sunday afternoon. They were taller, fitter, better dressed . . . not that that was any great sartorial feat among the eighties T-shirts and sandals of holidaymakers decamping to all points sunny. I was decamping too, although a partner with an Australian passport didn't mean there was a guarantee of sun where we were going with our baby daughter – Jersey, our idea of an overseas holiday (along with the Isle of Wight) – before she was given permanent right of residency in the UK.

It was a last week-long break before tuning the journalistic antenna into sport, but the young men at the airport set it twitching early. They were rugby players, well known Welsh internationals – but with that summer's British Lions tour long since over and a new five nations tournament five months away, what were they doing with their suitcases at the airport? It might have sent Poirot's little grey cells into overdrive but did I really care? Not really. Time to fly out for seven days of Mary Ann beer and claustrophobia. Nobody had told me Jersey was so small! Or that a child so little could cry so loudly when you shared a room!

I had started a diary.

You might have thought that the world of Welsh sport would have welcomed me like a long-lost suitor who had developed a nervous tic at the thought of taking the plunge, someone to be welcomed into the fold, while studiously avoiding anything that might frighten him off. There'd be a cup of tea and a digestive biscuit, a little chat about taking your time to settle in and making yourself at home, and no story more contentious than Glamorgan cricket club declaring ten overs earlier than the octogenarian in the panama hat sitting in the members' enclosure thought they should. There was only one thing wrong with that utopian scenario, one thing and two words: 'Welsh sport'.

Cardiff City were living up to their billing as the sleeping giant for whom the word 'catatonic' could have been invented. Manager Frank Burrows was quitting to take over as number two at Portsmouth . . . and just so he wouldn't be lonely in his new South Coast surroundings he was taking the club's top scorer, Jimmy Gilligan, with him. Not to be outshone, Cardiff were making loan signings from those giants of the game, Notts County, and were playing in the old Third Division in front of crowds of three and a half thousand. The club's chairman was having the windows of his travel agency smashed by irate supporters who saw this as an ever-so-subtle hint that his presence at the club was no longer required. It all added up to the fact that the club would make its worst start to a season since the team first stepped out onto the reclaimed rubbish tip that was Ninian Park when it opened for business in 1910.

Swansea City weren't doing much better, Wrexham were doing worse, old internationals were lining up to lambast the Welsh football team as it looked like missing out on yet another World Cup finals, and Welsh rugby was battening down the hatches to fend off the approaches of predators from up north who were eyeing up fresh recruits to add to the thirteen top players who'd already be doing their bit for Widnes and Wigan rather than Wales. Bridgend's powerhouse centre John Devereux was the latest name to be added to a *Who's Who* of exiles that included Jonathan Davies, David Bishop and Paul Moriarty. Why, it was all so humdrum, you could yawn.

And then there were always those well-dressed young men from the airport I'd seen a couple of weeks before. Elementary deduction might have suggested they were waiting for a charter flight to Manchester before heading along the motorway to new, well-paid billets in Warrington and St Helens, Bradford and Leeds. However, further fields were awaiting them, further fields and games that would leave the talent drain to rugby league shrinking into insignificance. The rugby writers could sense the headlines already. Welsh rugby would soon be facing its biggest crisis in sixty years. I'd been an unwitting and mildly curious witness to the start of it. Now I was catapulted into the middle of it.

As I'd jetted – if that was the right word – off on the 50-minute flight to St Helier, the ten Welsh players were taking the first step on a much longer trip to South Africa. This, however, was not the South Africa of the twenty-first century, this was a country where Nelson Mandela was still some months away from freedom, and F.W. de Klerk had just taken over as president of apartheid-era South Africa, succeeding P.W. Botha who'd been a staunch advocate of racial segregation. There was nothing – apart from conscience – to say the players shouldn't go to play in the centenary celebrations of the country's rugby board, they'd been sanctioned by the International Rugby Board, but the repercussions were huge.

Early in August, it had seemed the tour was dead. Top Welsh players Paul Thorburn, Bob Norster, Robert Jones, Mike Hall and Tony Clement, had turned down the invitation to go. Thorburn, the Wales captain, spoke for them.

'The players involved have been speaking to each other, but there was no way one of us would go if the others weren't,' he said. 'There were a number of factors involved: we have all been on tours this summer, so there was not only the fact of getting time off work but also the pressures the anti-apartheid movement would be putting on us and the respective councils about playing on their grounds.'

And it wasn't just the Welsh players. New Zealand said no All Black player would be going on the tour; star Australians like Michael Lynagh turned it down – 'I would have been honoured to join the World XV side, but unfortunately it is to South Africa,' he said. The British Lions and England hooker Brian Moore said 'No', despite confirming he'd been offered a substantial sum for his services. A couple of weeks before the first game was meant to be played the *Independent* was predicting that 'the best for which the hosts can hope is an unprepossessing Franco-Australian combination'.

Or not. By the time the first test came along at the end of the month, not only had the five Welsh players who'd originally vetoed the idea had a change of heart, they'd been joined by five others – Mark Ring, Paul Turner, David Pickering, Phil Davies and Phil John. The ten-strong contingent brought the travelling party up to the thirty players the South Africans had wanted. Not to be outdone, half a dozen members of the Welsh Rugby Union joined the Welsh players.

It was not Welsh rugby's finest moment. Councils across the country were appalled, there were threats to stop the Union using their training headquarters at the South Wales Police owned Waterton Cross in Bridgend. 'We've accommodated the Union in the past, but with a number of committeemen and wives going on a free holiday to South Africa, and with players saying they'll go privately but not admitting it publicly, the web of lies has got people's blood boiling,' fulminated the chairman of the South Wales Police Authority. 'It's been deceitful and a disgrace to the people of Wales.'

Neil Kinnock, leader of the Labour Party, had his two-penn'orth. 'Kinnock calls for "mercenaries' ban"', shouted the *Sunday Times*.

'Their mentality is that of the mercenary,' said Kinnock. 'The rugby unions should recognise that fact and tell the players they are no longer eligible to play the amateur game.'

You could almost hear the long-suffering sigh coming from the secretary of the Welsh Rugby Union, who'd only been in the job for eight months and who before that was the highly respected Chief Constable of South Wales Police. 'I had just started to get excited about the future, but now I feel very flat,' said David East.

So there it was . . . the welcome mat for the new sports correspondent of *Wales Today*.

Lesson one for the new boy . . . news and current affairs coverage come from the same stable, but they are different animals. A Shetland pony and a shire horse might share a common ancestor, but evolution has decreed that one wouldn't necessarily choose the other for a romantic night out. Current affairs programmes were usually well planned in advance. A researcher would set up a filming schedule and the producer, reporter and film crew would attempt to stick to it. 'Mr Jones? We're making a programme on the effect rising cereal prices are having on farmers in Wales and wondered whether we might pop along to your farm and do a little interview with you?' the conversation usually went. 'No, we won't be there long. And, of course, we won't get in the way, though perhaps you wouldn't mind if we filmed you doing a little bit of what you farmers do? Feeding the sheep or whatever. You're a dairy farm? Well, cows have to eat too, don't they? Right, shall we say half past two on Thursday?'

And at half past two on Thursday the producer and his assistant would drive up a narrow lane in some remote part of the Welsh countryside, turn into a gate and head up the track to a farmhouse. Just behind them was the reporter in his car . . . and just behind him the cameraman and his assistant in their car . . . and just behind them the sound recordist in his car . . . and just behind him the lighting man in his car. Usually the local village wouldn't have seen such traffic movement since the rehearsals for D-Day. By the time Mrs Jones had tripled her shopping budget for the week by supplying tea and biscuits to the television invasion force, the price of cereal had normally tumbled on the world markets and the crisis in Welsh farming was no more.

The news operation was leaner: usually just the reporter, a cameraman and a sound recordist. It was also more flexible, or, more to the point, done on the hoof. When a 'crisis in Welsh rugby' was unfolding, you didn't ring up to arrange an interview, you got what you got.

Which is why I spent most of that first week in September 1989 standing at the top of the ramp leading into the old National Stadium on Westgate Street in Cardiff, waiting for someone at the centre of South Africa-gate (no one actually called it that then but, hey, give it a couple of years and the title would have been nailed on) to throw me a morsel of information which I could pass on to the waiting viewing public of Wales. What the waiting viewing public of Wales mostly got was a shot of me scuttling down the ramp in valiant pursuit of WRU secretary David East when he headed off for lunch or to pick up his dry cleaning.

'Mr East . . . Mr East . . . what action are you going to take over the Welsh players in South Africa? And what about the committeemen who've gone with them, Mr East? Have they let you down, Mr East? What's this done to the image of Welsh rugby round the world, Mr East? And what are you going to do, Mr East? Do you plan to resign, Mr East?' And with little more than an enigmatic smile and a 'Can't say anything, now!', David East would leave me and the perspiring crew behind. Another interview gone west!

8.9.89 *WRU Press Conference 10 a.m.*
Wales woke up that Friday morning to a headline probably not replicated in that typeface and sombre black underlining since the one fifty years ago that week saying 'War Declared'. 'East Out'

Early days: (*right*)
With his friend
Stephen Jones;
(*below*) Captain of
Marlborough Road
School baseball team

BY DAY 19-year-old Marion Kear works as a telephonist for a car sales firm in Pontllanfraith. At night, she is a pin-up—one of the few remaining photographic models in Wales.

The pretty faces and tantalising bikini poses that once launched a thousand dreams are no longer big business for Welsh photographers.

Prohibitive printing and processing costs have turned pin-up photography into an expensive hobby, and publishers who constantly demand more revealing poses no longer have space for girls in swimsuits.

At one time when a low neckline or a high hemline was considered daring, photographers relied upon pin-up shots for a large part of their income.

Many ran model "stables," churning out glamour pictures for scores of magazines.

But that was 10 years ago. "Now anything goes, and girls in South Wales are very apprehensive about taking off their clothes," photographer Mr. Adam Lee, of Clive Road, Cardiff, told me.

Embarrassment

An amateur like Marion Kear, who lives with her parents in a terraced house in Tredegar Street, Cross Keys, certainly does not pose for the money.

On rare occasions an evening's modelling can bring her £3, and for Marion, the cold, scantily-clad hours in front of a prying lens are a labour of love.

Often she asks for nothing more than copies of her photographs, an insurance, she says, for a happy dotage.

"When I am old and grey and lined I will have something to look back on, something to remind me of what I once looked like," says Marion.

She says people have been taking pictures of her almost as long as she can remember. Huge boxes

Girls scamper for cover from over-exposure to camera lens

of photographs around her home testify to that.

Her mother is delighted that she models, proud that her daughter should be in demand by photographers.

There is no embarrassment at all that many of the poses should be in the near-nude.

"I don't like to pose entirely unclothed. I always like to have something around me, even if the shot makes it look as if I have got nothing on. Some fully nude shots can look horrible," Marion says.

If a boy-friend objects to people seeing her semi-clothed, then that boy-friend has to go. Experience has shown her that men usually become possessive — and nothing is going to interfere with her modelling.

Unlike Marion, 21 - year - old Helen Morgan, of Port Road, Barry, is a professional model, working for the Pat David agency in Cardiff.

Much of her work is fashion modelling, but she too spends a lot of time in front of the camera.

A one-time bank clerk, she took up modelling because she felt life had become over-regimented.

She likes her work to be varied and interesting, and modelling seemed the perfect answer.

Now she can earn up to £8 a day, though she counts herself lucky if she works two or three times a week.

"The only place a model can really earn money is in London, but at the moment I am quite happy at home," she said.

Home is with her parents, though she does intend to buy a house with her boy-friend. What does he think of her modelling?

"He doesn't have much say in it. Anyway, there is no real difference between modelling in a bikini and modelling in clothes, except that when you are fully dressed you don't need such a good figure," said Helen.

In fact she finds it flattering that men should think her attractive enough to look at her pictures. It would take a lot of money however before she agreed to nude photographs, though if a chance of fame came through the pages of *Playboy* she would certainly consider it.

Fame for a model in South Wales is rare. Photographers say both Marion and Helen are a dying breed in this area. Models are becoming as scarce as the clothes they are expected to wear.

Camera clubs in Newport and Cardiff have difficulty in supplying models for their classes. Now they concentrate more on landscape and pictorial subjects.

● 19-year-old Mar

phonist w

Starting out: (*left*) The first 'Bob Humphrys' byline – Marion Kear and Helen Morgan, soon to be the 'Four-Day Beauty Queen'; (*below left*) In the dugout with John Toshack at Deepdale as Swansea City clinch promotion to the old First Division; (*below*) Taking part in a charity cricket match (Max Boyce is among the players)

Cross Keys, is a tele-
‡ modelling.

● 21-year-old Helen Morgan, of Barry, is a professional
model. She likes horse-riding and chess.

'Proper Journalism' 1:
With the *Western Mail*
(*top left and left*)

'Proper
Journalism' 2:
(*above and left*)
With brother
John at *Week In,
Week Out*

Sir Galahad: *Week In, Week Out*'s powerful investigation into the disaster became famous

BBC publicity photograph

'Welsh Sport!': (*above*) Rugby triumph – Max Boyce at the Opening Ceremony of the 1999 Rugby World Cup; (*left*) Rugby farce – Mike Ruddock at Sophia Gardens, just days before his resignation as Wales coach

Award-winner: (*above and left*) Welsh Sports Journalist of the Year; (*below*) With Chris Needs at the 2006 BBC Wales Sports Personality of the Year Awards

trumpeted the *Western Mail*: 'Welsh Rugby Union secretary David East last night quit after storming out of a meeting called to discuss the controversial South African trip.' The press conference was called to put flesh on the bones of his departure from the meeting along with the WRU president Clive Rowlands 'who looked angry and grim-faced as he drove away from the gathered newspaper reporters and photographers without a word'.

When it came, the word was: 'Like any other person, I have the right to choose for whom I work. I regret that I have been placed in a position whereby I no longer wish to remain in the employ of the Welsh Rugby Union. Whilst I am contractually bound to serve three months notice, I hope the committee will make it possible to leave at their earliest convenience.' Now that was a first. A WRU secretary actually telling it like it was. You could obviously take the policeman out of the force but you couldn't take the force out of the policeman. WRU president Rowlands, who'd turned down his invitation to the South African jamboree, also quit, and it was he who came up with the most telling description for the whole sorry affair. It was, he said, a 'carnival for Welshmen'.

The aftershocks hung around for a while longer. Rowlands was eventually persuaded to reconsider and returned to his post of president; a special general meeting was held; and a few weeks later a 6'5" policeman and recently retired Wales second row forward, Steve Sutton, revealed he'd been offered a substantial sum by a member of the Welsh Rugby Union to go on the tour. 'The rumour was that players were being offered between £30,000 and £50,000 to tour,' he said. 'I didn't want to risk losing my job for two or three years' wages and I turned it down on the spot.'

What happened during that first week in September 1989 set the tone for a decade of change that would see rugby union almost unrecognisable at the end of the nineties from the sport that went into them.

*

On the Friday night after *Wales Today* had dissected the story with grim relish, the head of news and current affairs who'd offered me the chance to combine work with hobby asked me into his office for a gin and tonic. At least he had the gin and tonic. I had a beer.

'Not bad,' he said. 'Been in the job a week and so far we've lost one WRU secretary, one WRU president and one WRU senior vice-president . . . rugby's very own night of the long knives and you've been in the middle of it bloody all. Not bad, not bad at all. I bet they wished you'd stayed in current affairs.'

And at least I'd had a warning right at the off of just how careless Welsh rugby could be with the people they employed to run it. It was one that would serve me well as the years went by.

Chapter 9

The 5.30 to Paddington

1.2.06 *London. Peter H., Sian, John and Rhod*

The 5.30 a.m. train to Paddington didn't, of course, run smoothly. A lorry somewhere near Swindon had driven into the side of a bridge over the track. While the railway officials waited for the engineers to study the damage, before coming out with a considered, 'Mmmm, don't like the look of that!' or 'Nothing wrong with that, it'll last another 100 years!', passengers already bleary-eyed from the early start stared out into the Wiltshire darkness, wondering when they'd get to London and whatever awaited in their day.

For once, my filming schedule had been carefully planned, down to a specially hired cab to ferry me around to do interviews with four ex-pats. It was nearly a year since Wales had won rugby's Grand Slam, their first since those days of the seventies when there seemed an umbilical cord between the Welsh team of Edwards and Bennett, J.J. and J.P.R., and success. If there was a seven in the year, a Triple Crown or Grand Slam was likely to be heading to Cardiff. But famine followed feast, failure trudged gloomily after triumph, and by the time 2005 came along it had been twenty-seven years since 'Calon Lan' had been sung with much other than melancholy.

It wasn't so bad if you lived in Wales. We could wallow in our shared trough of self-pity, and the gloating of those who'd crossed

53

the border to live amongst us was muted, either by sentiments of sympathy or self-preservation. We developed a black sense of humour, a resilience that meant record scores against us and humbling defeats didn't have us staring into the watery depths of the Taff or the Towy contemplating a watery end to it all, but instead saw us almost smiling at our own ineptitude. We did 'inept' better than most.

So, lose to Western Samoa at the National Stadium in the world cup of 1991 and once the initial shock at being beaten by a Polynesian nation with a population considerably smaller than Cardiff's, a land size that would have it looking up to Rhode Island as a big brother, and a captain rather bigger than the pianos he made a living shifting, soon gave way to rueful resignation: 'Never mind, could be worse, could have been playing the whole of Samoa!' And there was always the memory of Arthur Emyr's attempted drop goal to chuckle at if things got really bad.

The pain of days like that was lessened because it was shared. Not so for those who lived outside Wales. For them it was magnified. While we had the safety of numbers, they could be picked off one by one, in pubs, at the coffee machine, in the office or while washing their hands in the toilets. They had to smile and listen to the estuary tones of the Arsenal season ticket holder who'd become a 'Jonny' fan for the weekend, and who was happy to explain at extraordinary length and with the certainty only profound ignorance can bring why 'Woody' had got his tactics right, and why Wales were a miserable bunch of misbegotten, no hopers who'd never again beat anyone more powerful than Portugal, and only then if they were suffering from debilitation brought on by a dodgy sardine.

A degree of come-uppance was probably due. Welsh fans of the seventies had not been known for their 'Bad luck, boys . . . you were the better team and really deserved to win' approach to the Scots, Irish, French and, especially, English who'd travelled to Wales for their biennial beating. If with national pride came a certain amount of that less attractive trait of 'rubbing their noses in it', then so be it, it came with the territory. And so did a certain amount of retaliation when Welsh rugby turned sour, but, apart from the odd shaft of sunlight that penetrated the gloom every now and again, the Welsh exiles living in London had been in the firing line of the Twickers rugby triumphalists for too long.

Until, that is, a February afternoon in 2005 at the Millennium Stadium when a tan-in-a-bottle player, who'd made his debut four years earlier but had since lost his way in international rugby, etched his name on the national consciousness. I'd spent my usual schizophrenic Six Nations afternoon: first half at the game in the stadium's less than spectator-friendly press box, a dash to a waiting taxi at half time, and a quick trip through deserted streets to the office to write and voice a report that would appear on our truncated Saturday bulletin minutes after the match ended. When I'd left, the game was close – Shane Williams had scored a try that had Wales eight points to three ahead – but there was still a feeling of inevitability. History told you that England would come back to win; after all Wales hadn't beaten them in Cardiff twelve years. That feeling became stronger when Charlie Hodgson kicked a couple of penalties that had England 9–8 up.

'Normal service was resumed,' I wrote in my preliminary script.

Then, with a nonchalant swing of his boot, Gavin Henson, who'd already had the crowd wincing with a couple of dump-truck tackles on a hapless Matthew Tait, sent the ball arcing through the English posts, and four minutes later Gareth Thomas's toothless grin into an obliging BBC camera was visual confirmation that a bogey had been banished.

'Normal service' it was not. The script was rewritten and Henson, maybe more than Wales's win, became the story. The following day when the press turned up at the team hotel for Sunday afternoon interviews with nominated members of the Welsh squad, there was only one target for the questions. 'Tell us about the kick, Gav . . . did you ever think you'd miss it?' 'Nope!' Remarkably you believed him. And with a shameful disregard for the proprieties of my profession, I got his autograph on the match ticket – for my teenage daughter, you understand. Well, it was pre-Charlotte Church.

The Henson phenomenon was up and running. In newsrooms up and down the country there was no controlling it, certainly not on *Wales Today* where the next day we produced a celebrity profile rather than a sports report, heading back to his old Brynteg school in Bridgend to talk to the teachers, pupils and presumably the lollipop lady who'd seen him safely across the road. Mention the 'Gav' word and the ears of programme staff who didn't know a conversion from colonic irrigation pricked up in breathless anticipation of another piece on the tanned one.

There was no denying though that that kick was one of the main reasons I was sitting, a year later, somewhere outside Swindon, waiting for the train to lumber back into motion. The 11–9 win over England had given Wales the impetus and self-belief to make a clean sweep of the rest of the Six Nations teams and the bragging rights were back with those who'd stayed over the border to endure the jibes that years of underachievement had brought. One Welsh émigré, Rowan Williams, the Archbishop of Canterbury, had in a most Christian way turned down the chance of some gratuitous gloating, but others had not been so reluctant. First up, after the 5.30 had eventually negotiated the shaken but obviously not stirred bridge and I'd made it to the Whitehall home of the Welsh Office, was the then Secretary of State for Wales, Peter Hain.

'One of the best Cabinets I've been to,' he said, remembering his first meeting with his government colleagues after the Grand Slam win. 'There was a real spring in my step, I was smiling and they were all looking pretty sheepish – especially the Prime Minister. I think that showed the wave of euphoria that swept right across Wales, and even up the M4 into the Cabinet room.'

He pointed to the giant picture behind him of the Welsh squad spraying champagne as they celebrated their win. 'I had a bit of an argument with the fuddy-duddies here at Gwydyr House as to whether we should replace the picture of some ancient parliamentarian that had been here for decades. I said we've got to put it here because this is the new Wales! Everyone who comes in now has to walk right past it and salute the new Wales. If they don't salute it, they don't get up the stairs to see me!'

My second interviewee was BBC presenter Sian Williams, who has a giant red and white hat, presented to her by colleagues on the *Breakfast* programme settee. Despite confessing to two teenage sons who support England, she told me she had looked forward to going to the local pub after the match and finding another ex-pat to celebrate with if Wales won, or to console her if they lost – though she was still a little confused by the competing emotions of one who'd managed to cry all the way through Wales's win of the previous year.

When I went to meet brother John, of the *Today* programme and *Mastermind*, he was musing over whether the Welsh had an inferiority complex when it came to their relationship with the English.

''Course we do!' he said in his understated way. 'We are the Welsh sitting next to the English! They're bigger than us, there are more of them than us. They may not be as clever as us or as literate as us or as musical as us or as nice as us, but there are lots of them and they go around invading countries and things. They haven't invaded us for a while I grant you, but of course we've got an inferiority complex . . . though deep down we know we're better! By the way, can you have an inferiority complex *and* know you're better?'

I didn't see why not.

At the Comedy Store just off Piccadilly Circus, one of Britain's best up and coming comedians, Rhod Gilbert, wasn't sure if Welsh success on the rugby field had given him any psychological edge in dealing with English audiences showing their talent for original heckling by making sheep noises.

'When I'm standing up there, in front of four or five hundred of them who've been drinking, it seems to me they're not very keen on us! I think they reckon we're a bit weird. Mind you, my act is a bit weird, except for when I go back home to Cardiff or somewhere and play the same character, the weird character . . . then I'm one of them, one of the gang. It's a bit, er . . . weird.'

For all four, during the previous twelve months, they'd been on the front foot, even Rhod the beleaguered comic who liked to do his act swinging metaphorical punches at the audience from the back of the stage. Wales had been in the ascendancy. It wasn't to last.

Chapter 10

The Voice from the Angel

3.2.06 *London Live*

Two days later I was back on the train. Same journey, different destination. On the Friday night before Wales again played England, the great and the good of London Welsh society were all in one place: the plush surroundings of the Grosvenor House Hotel on Mayfair's Park Lane. It was the sort of affair I had always done my best to avoid. Paying a small fortune to squeeze into a dinner suit to eat uninspired food while receiving an injection of *hiraeth* via the tape of great Welsh tries of the seventies playing on a loop on the big screens dotted around the ballroom, was not my idea of a good night out.

Fortunately, none of that was for me that night. I was there to prise a couple of the guests away from the pre-dinner canapés to preview the game on *Wales Today*. Gareth Edwards, who could remember the days when losing to England at Twickenham or Cardiff Arms Park was enough to have the players slinking home slightly more shamefaced than if they'd been the main topic of conversation in a *News of the World* exposé, was there to make the case for Wales continuing the success of the previous season's Grand Slam with a first win at HQ since 1988; while, from somewhere up near the roof, the 6'10" Martin Bayfield – the former policeman, also used for the long shots of the half-giant Hagrid in the Harry Potter films – appeared for the defence, England's defence.

Presenting the live interviews with the guests was the easy bit. Waiting for them to turn up was altogether more nerve racking. If they didn't, three minutes live 'filling' on air awaited, which might not seem very much, but offer three extra minutes to a man going to the electric chair and he would bless you for offering him eternity. The dinner's organisers had promised to provide the contributors, seemingly believing that everyone's ambition was to appear on Wales's leading news magazine.

Gareth Edwards, ever the professional, walked down the long corridor from the ballroom to where the camera was set up in the hotel foyer in plenty of time; Jeremy Guscott, who was meant to be in England's corner, was somewhere in the bowels of the hotel, lost between room and rendezvous.

It wasn't the first time it had happened to me. Athlete Christian Malcolm is one of the nicest guys on the Welsh sporting scene; he's also one of the most laid back – two traits that, when they complement each other, create an enviable character cocktail in a person. When it comes to a television programme, however, the two don't make the best of bedfellows.

I had phoned him when he had headed back to his home in Newport – go there, his mother makes the best Caribbean chicken I've tasted – after winning gold at the European indoor championships in Belgium in 2000.

'Hi Chris, well done, mate . . . can you make it into the studio tonight for a quick interview? We'll send a taxi for you, say about six?'

'Aww, Bob . . . do I have to? . . . I'm shattered, man!'

Aha . . . a problem . . . Plan B.

'Don't worry, mate, you'll be done and dusted by ten to seven . . . back home in bed by seven fifteen . . . couldn't be easier!'

'Sure? OK then . . . but don't bother sending a taxi. I'll bring the car.'

For one of the fastest men on the planet, Chris could show a remarkable burst of tardiness in his timings. If it wasn't a tenth of a second shaved off his personal best he wasn't interested. The alarm bells rang. I erred on the side of caution.

'You've got to be here by six fifteen though, Chris . . . you're OK, but you know how long it takes me in make-up, they put the Elephant Man's make-up on in less time. Mind you, the result was probably better looking than me. So six fifteen . . . see you then! And bring the medal with you!'

At five past seven, programme over, I was thanking former Olympic hurdler Nigel Walker for his last-minute stand-in spot on the programme, after hijacking him from whatever piece of business had originally brought him to Broadcasting House, when Chris Malcolm, Colin Jackson and assorted friends wandered down the corridor to the studio.

'I've brought the medal, Bob!'

'Thanks, mate . . . but put it this way . . . in athletics terminology, you've just missed the start of the Three A's final by 20 minutes. No Olympics for you!'

It was a lesson I'd learned early in my broadcasting career. Miss a deadline and there was no going back, two seconds late was as bad as two minutes, two hours or two days. Wales coach Graham Henry fell more towards the latter category. My phone rang as I drove through Cardiff one Tuesday afternoon. The word 'Coach' flashed up.

'G'day, Bob,' the clipped New Zealand tone was unmistakable. 'I think I've got a bit of an apology to make.'

Surely I was hearing things. The man they called the 'Great Redeemer' saying sorry. This could not be!

'Didn't I say I'd be on the programme with you last night. Sorry, mate . . . got stuck in a team meeting in the hotel. Clean went out of my mind. Switched the phone off and everything!'

Didn't you just, Graham! Which is why at a couple of minutes notice when all hope was gone – excluding a familiar figure beaming down next to me from the starship *Enterprise* – I had to become an expert on the synthetic surface being used at the squad's new indoor training centre at the Vale of Glamorgan and how it would help transform Wales's playing abilities in the great outdoors. How convincing I was, only others can tell. Suffice it to say the programme editor phoned on my way back . . . 'You were meant to have someone with you, weren't you?' she asked as if considering whether it had always been my lifetime ambition to spout forth on the merits of various forms of artificial grass. 'Ah well, I don't suppose anyone noticed!'

Hopefully they didn't notice the night the Rugby World Cup came to Cardiff in 1999 and Wales played Argentina in the opening match, either. It probably doesn't register with most people just interested in watching the action which channel is showing it. That's not the case if you're involved in covering it! For the World Cup, ITV had the broadcast rights, we on the BBC and our colleagues on Sky were the little boys with our noses pressed up against the sweet shop window. While ITV was cosseted cosily inside the Millennium Stadium we had our satellite vans over the Taff on an embankment only marginally less wet in the driving wind and rain than the river below. It could have been worse. My good friend Derek Brockway, who was standing on top of an open air double decker bus parked at the bottom of St Mary Street, saw his umbrella take off like Mary Poppins with an Exocet under her coat in the middle of his live weather forecast. Quite where it landed, we've never liked to ask!

Our problem? The cast of thousands we'd arranged to trek over the bridge to mark the start of one of the biggest sporting occasions ever to come to the city, Graham Henry – who's the common denominator here? – Max Boyce, Jonathan Davies and all couldn't move because of combination of the crush of the crowd and the climate.

Broadcasting rivalry went out of the window. Who Sky had, we borrowed. Who we had, Sky snatched. It was the biggest exchange since the Berlin Wall came down. Everything that was planned didn't happen and everything that wasn't planned did! The result? 'Excellent programme! Summed up all the World Cup means to Wales,' said the powers-that-be. Strange job, broadcasting.

Even the simple can be complex. A live interview with the greatest rugby commentator we've heard on the night before he retired should have been the proverbial walk in the Millennium Stadium. Bill McLaren was in Cardiff for an emotional, valedictory broadcast on the following afternoon's Wales game against Scotland. Bill had always been the most approachable of professionals, a man not touched by the fame that coated him almost by accident. Meet him by the side of the muddy training field as he put face to name, or vice versa, for some obscure front row forward called up from Newbridge or Neath – ready to be immortalised on his legendary crib sheets – and there'd be a rustle in his pocket as he pulled out his tin of 'Hawick balls' to offer to the chosen few.

Whenever we met, I was reminded of an old-school *Daily Mirror* reporter, Tom Lyons, meeting Sir Matt Busby for the first time as a young, up-and-coming sports writer in the North West. At the end of their interview the Manchester United manager turned to him and said in his Scottish burr, 'Young Tom, if you ever need me for anything here's ma home number . . . any time, lad.' Tom was surprised . . . why was one of the most pre-eminent football figures of the day giving him his number?

'Because, lad . . . if I can do you a kindness on your way up, perhaps you can do me one on ma way down!'

It was the sort of line I could imagine Bill McLaren saying, and not just because of the shared Scottish accent. Neither, though, would need such favours; neither slid down the pole.

Bill had promised to leave his evening of pre-match preparation in the Angel Hotel to wander across to the touchline of the

Millennium Stadium for a chat about his long career and what Wales and Welsh rugby meant to him.

The programme headlines tempted the viewers with Bill's presence and I waited.

'With you in ten minutes, Bob!' said the programme director in the studio gallery. Well, at least someone would be with me because as sure as 'they'll be drinking on the streets of the valleys tonight', Bill McLaren wasn't.

'Ring his room,' I asked a researcher who'd come down with me, 'just to be sure he's left.'

'Hello . . .' said the voice from the Angel. For a man in his eighth decade, Bill McLaren would have to show a remarkable turn of speed.

As I looked into the camera and said with more hope than conviction, 'and joining me now . . .' a lightly perspiring figure walked down the players' tunnel into the Millennium Stadium. He didn't miss a beat!

So, having someone who was already 6'4" at the age of twelve – prompting parents at under 13s-games he appeared in to enquire why the team he was playing for had the coach driver in their side – coming in as a late replacement was not unusual in the world of live television where the maxim was 'If anything can go wrong, then it probably will.' The imposing figure of Martin Bayfield was not to be argued with. It was a sensible policy as it turned out. Gareth Edwards, ever the optimist, ever one to let heart rule head, figured Wales could repeat their win of a year ago. Martin Bayfield read the runes differently: there was only one winner for him – England. He was right.

Chapter 11

One Man's Misfortune

6.2.06 *Wales v England Wash-up, Brent Cockbain*

'One man's misfortune is one lion's dinner' reads the caption on a picture of an airman parachuting from a crashing plane – and landing next to a smug-looking king of the jungle. The 'misfortune' was Brent Cockbain's. He'd been one of the leading lights of Wales's Grand Slam season: a rampaging second row who put the 'n' into nasty when Wales's opponents adopted intimidation as the best way of pouring water on the oil of the smooth-running Welsh machine. Every team, they say, needs an enforcer, someone to add grunt and grind to the glide of the backs – forwards win games, backs decide by how many – and Brent Cockbain, a naturalised Welshman, born and brought up in rural Queensland, was the epitome of the in-your-face play needed in any side.

He was also the perfect example of why you should not let someone's on-field persona colour your perception of them off the field. The Cockbains – Brent and his wife Kate – had been hit by personal tragedy when their thirteen-month-old son died of a brain tumour. They set up the Toby Lloyd Cockbain Foundation to raise money for charity, and the way Brent promoted it marked him out as an unusually articulate contributor on television and radio. A match against Fiji, in the autumn internationals that followed the Grand Slam, saw one of those knee injuries that had you turning

65

away in your own pain when it was shown again in slow motion. That was his 'misfortune'. Our 'lion's dinner' was the fact that *Wales Today* took the uncertainty out of who would be our studio guest to look back on that season's Six Nations matches by signing up Brent as the pundit for all five of them.

Previously, on the Monday morning following a game we had to have a quick roll call of former internationals to see who was available for a couple of minutes' live TV at six forty-five in the evening. J.J. Williams? With his son at an athletics meeting in Portugal. Ieuan . . . heading to a business meeting in London. Jonathan Davies? Away for a couple of days' break. Andy Moore? Busy with his building company, but able to re-jig his diary! See you then, Andy.

Now we went for continuity. There's always a danger using a current player to comment on the people he was packing down next to. He was – is – their mate. One of the boys. He's hardly likely to say, 'Martyn Williams should never be allowed close to a Welsh shirt again' when he's got a pint – or should that be a large glass of high energy drink? – scheduled with Martyn in his diary for later in the week. Actually, he's hardly likely to say that anyway, on the grounds that Martyn Williams is usually about as close to undroppable as an aitch in a conversation between Henry Higgins and a reformed Eliza Doolittle in *My Fair Lady*. Even when he retired the indefatigable Williams couldn't get dropped.

Cockbain, however, could now give valuable insights into why game plans had worked well or gone horribly wrong, how players might react to success or adversity, and answer the occasional question which producers like so much, sent in by Mr Cliff Jones of Abersychan – 'Evening, Cliff' as they like us presenters to say in our informal, all-inclusive style of broadcasting – who wants to know what changes Mike Ruddock might make for the next game against Scotland.

And there was plenty to talk about after that first post-Grand-

Slam, Six Nations game against England. For all the optimism – for all the hope that London Welsh society might have another year of saying, 'All that money, all those players and you still can't beat little old us!' – 'Disgruntled' of Tunbridge Wells could put away his pen dipped in vitriol, forget his letter to *The Times* demanding the defenestration at best of English coach Andy Robinson, and bask again in the knowledge that the rightful order had been restored to his red-rose tinted world.

Two tries from Mark Cueto and Lewis Moody seemed to put England in command. Martyn Williams hit back to make it a manageable 15–10 deficit at half-time, then turned from saviour into sinner when he was sin-binned – a moment Welsh coach Mike Ruddock singled out as 'crucial' – giving England the impetus to run in another four tries. Eccentric refereeing by New Zealander Paul Honiss – who gave a passable imitation of a New England Patriots linebacker to set up one score for Laurence Dallaglio and missed a knock-on picked up by those in Row Z – made the scoreline crueller than it should have been, but as the BBC report said, 'Wales were missing half a dozen players through injury or suspension and in the end their lack of strength in depth was brutally exposed.'

'Brutally exposed, Brent? Can't we cope with losing players?' was probably the gist of the first question asked in our *Wales Today* wash-up on the game. With that delightful yet extraordinarily elusive talent known as hindsight it should probably have been, 'Is this the beginning of the end for Mike Ruddock, Brent?' That Monday, though, it would have been unthinkable. The honeymoon was still going on. Results and performances in the autumn had not been hugely impressive – heavy defeats by New Zealand and South Africa, leavened by a narrow win over Fiji and a much more heartening first success over Australia since 1987, suggested that the Welsh team was still a work in progress, one that required a fair wind and a reasonable dollop of good fortune to see off the very best of opponents. However, after so long in the wilderness supping on the most meagre of rations, the country could afford to be patient.

The country didn't know, though, that events in London on the Saturday night had set in motion a process that wouldn't stop until Welsh rugby had slipped into . . . a word which would have had to be invented to accommodate it if it hadn't already been in existence . . . 'turmoil', definition: 'a state of extreme confusion or agitation; commotion or tumult'. If I had been given money for every time I either said, wrote or heard, 'Welsh rugby is in a state of extreme confusion or agitation; commotion or tumult', I'd be as poor as I am today. If I'd been paid piece-rate for every time I said, wrote or heard, 'Welsh rugby is in turmoil', Beavis the butler would be polishing the Bentley outside while I was on the phone booking a night out eating snail porridge and sardine sorbet with Heston Blumenthal at the Fat Duck in Bray.

When you look at what happened, the grievance that soured the relationship between Ruddock and his players was hardly in the league of John Wilkes Booth getting into high dudgeon with Abraham Lincoln over plans to extend voting rights to recently emancipated slaves. It was all over a night out, or, in rugby vernacular, a 'piss-up'. In his autobiography, the Welsh captain Gareth Thomas wrote that many of the players had wanted to follow up their defeat by England by heading into Central London for an evening arranged by the English scrum half Matt Dawson, a popular figure especially with Welsh players who had gone on the Lions tours. Thomas should have recalled that, where defeat is concerned, the Welsh public can be a contrary bunch. A former captain, Colin Charvis, had inadvertently been caught on camera smiling as his team were slipping to an embarrassing 30–22 defeat by the Italians in Rome in 2003. He'd rapidly been installed as the second most unpopular person in Wales . . . sandwiched between Osama bin Laden and Saddam Hussein. Now I've met neither. Nor am I likely to, especially as far as Saddam Hussein is concerned. I have, though, met Colin Charvis many times and tend to think that when he said, 'It shows that people in Wales sometimes lose a little bit of perspective where rugby is concerned,' he was putting it rather mildly. As it was, he was no longer captain and out of the team when the side to play England in the next match was named.

Gareth's political antenna now picked up that a night on the razz in London as Welsh fans drowned their sorrows might not be the most astute move he'd ever make. 'Even though I was intending to go, I did not think it was a particularly good idea,' he wrote, so he wanted it laid on the line by Ruddock that the players couldn't go into town. And that's what Ruddock did, except the captain had wanted it done in the team room, while the coach decided to scotch the party plans from the front of the team bus. Not authoritative enough, thought Thomas. And sure enough, when they got back to the team hotel, Ruddock became the focus for the disaffected in the squad who reckoned they were grown-ups and should be treated as such. Discipline crumbled, the players split into factions and squads and there was just one common factor . . . no one was happy. And all for a night out.

When rugby teams so reliant on the team ethos and watching each other's backs fracture, the omens are not good. On a July night in 2001, I'd sat on the top deck of a Monday-night ferry from Manly to Sydney Harbour with several of the British Lions who'd be playing their final and decisive game against the Wallabies the coming Saturday. Not only were they all English, they were all from Leicester, including the captain Martin Johnson. Hardly conclusive as polls go admittedly, the Lions who travelled to Australia might have shamed the Von Trapp family singers when it came to togetherness, but it was indicative of the 'we knows what we likes and likes what we knows' philosophy. Squads have factions, and the Lions coach, Graham Henry, probably paid for that with his job as the Wales coach when he returned.

He'd already suffered in Australia, particularly from the diaries of Austin Healey – ghost-written by Eddie Butler in the *Observer* and the *Guardian* on the occasions he could escape from 'Stalag 8' (Butler's words) – and of the same Matt Dawson whose night out was to create such problems for Wales five years on and 12,000 miles away. An unwitting saboteur in white, perhaps.

Healey was fined around £2,000 for bringing the tour into disrepute with his comments, despite reckoning he neither wrote, said nor agreed – slightly remiss for a column which is being splashed under your name – with what was in an article describing the Australian second row Justin Harrison as a 'plod' and a 'plank', a little bit of alliteration that might just have inspired him and his teammates to a match winning performance in the final test. Such is the power of the ghost writer . . . not that Butler was apologetic, saying that week after week he'd meet with players who'd roll their eyes and describe the tour as living hell. 'Living hell?' Well, maybe 'a prep school from the 1950s – a junior boot camp!'

Dawson also found himself out of pocket after 'Dawson's Diaries' in the *Daily Telegraph* talked of players so fed-up that they wanted to leave the Lions tour early.

The Lions coach got his retaliation in with his own book, *Henry's Pride* . . . 'it really was an age-old story. Betraying trust, and betraying your mates for 30 pieces of silver'. So maybe not quite the togetherness of the Von Trapp family singers, then.

The ramifications rumbled on long after life with the Lions. Graham Henry's relationship with the Welsh players forced to play bit parts down-under never quite recovered. Less than a year later he left his job as the Wales coach.

If the seeds of Mike Ruddock's downfall had been sown in Australia, his fate was probably sealed in the front of that Wales team coach in a Twickenham car park.

Chapter 12

Texts and Same Size Nuts

8.2.06 *Wales Team Announced (v Scotland)*

I had some bad news to break to Mike Ruddock. For the last couple of seasons the Welsh team had been announced 'exclusively' by the Welsh coach and myself on BBC Wales. Why the inverted commas? Am I suggesting the event wasn't quite the seminal broadcasting experience it should have been, with the public salivating by their TV or radio for the first indication of who'd beaten off the competition to the tight head prop slot? I suppose I am – after all, various media outlets had no compunction about playing fast and loose with arrangements made between the Welsh Rugby Union and the BBC who'd paid a small fortune for rights to both the Six Nations and Welsh domestic rugby. OK, so the newspapers would dress up their preview as 'Probable Wales team to play Scotland', 'probable' being their code for 'Take it from us, we might not be able to say so officially, but this is as gospel as it gets!' And you knew damn well somebody had been on the phone, leaking the chosen names like a colander.

The Welsh rugby supporters' website, Gwlad, would have someone, presumably from within the Welsh camp, posting the side name for name, often while I was sitting by the computer on my desk, waiting for the Welsh team's media officer, Simon Rimmer, to e-mail it to me. And on my way to film the announcement, I would switch on Radio Wales to hear one of our sports depart-ment's rugby pundits tipping their line-up: 'Breaking news . . . Wales coach Mike Ruddock is expected to stick with the team well beaten by England on Saturday for the game against Scotland at the Millennium Stadium at the weekend. The only changes could be on the bench where Blues scrum half Mike Phillips is set to replace Gareth Cooper, who's out with a dislocated shoulder, and Bath back row man Gareth Delve, who could come in for the Scarlets' Alix Popham.'

Note the key words, 'expected', 'could', 'set to': the broadcaster's equivalent to the newspaper's 'probable'. It roughly translated to 'We know it and you know it, but hang on a bit because we'll soon be able to tell you that what we knew and you knew was absolutely . . . spot on!' So by the time Mike was wheeled in front of the board crammed with sponsors' names on the first floor of the Welsh cricket centre after a morning training session at Sophia Gardens, the only person who hadn't worked out who'd be lining up against the Scots was probably still fighting his way out of a Burmese jungle, unaware that the war with Japan had ended in 1946.

But least we were able to dot the 'i's and cross the 't's with never a 'probable', 'expected', 'could' or 'set to' passing our lips. It might not have been dynamic, but it was definitive . . . the team from the coach's mouth, with a two-minute interview to follow explaining just why a side that had right royally cocked it up at Twickenham had escaped with minor tinkering to its fringes, when much of Wales would have been in with the pruning shears before you could say 47–13.

The official WRU response had always been decided beforehand in a discussion between the coach and his media adviser, who'd have checked with me what lines I wanted to cover. So, while he might like to say, 'That's a bloody stupid question, Bob . . . you know as well as I do that we're down to the bones of our arse with injuries and that completely over-the-top suspension of Gavin

Henson by those incompetent nincompoops on the International Rugby Board . . . and the one thing we don't have is any strength in depth because there are too many overseas players clogging up places in the regions!' – what he actually said was, 'We think these players have a chance to dispel the demons of that loss [against England] and show what we are really capable of. Just as we were confident we could win last week, we think these players have the talent to put on a show against Scotland and get us back where we belong . . . on a winning run!'

Now, version two is admittedly not so much fun as version one, but such is the broadcaster's lot. At least with Mike, I usually managed to have a bit of fun. I'd known him for a long time before he became the Wales coach. Many an afternoon in those days before spin doctors and saturation coverage that came with the world of professional rugby, I would head down to rickety old St Helen's rugby and cricket ground to film a preview of Swansea's up-coming game. There was no posh Ospreys training headquarters at Llandarcy then, no warm-ups, warm-downs, and, for all I know, warm-in-betweens. You'd get there as the players were arriving from their day jobs, and hope to film the interviews you needed before the training started. Otherwise, you'd risk being stuck shivering at the edge of Swansea Bay until they'd finished at nine o'clock or later, on a cold winter's night. Experience had taught me, and a variety of cameramen I worked with, that that was not a fate to be recommended.

Mike and I faced each other on either side of a camera so many times that we were comfortable with each other. It was a relationship undisturbed even after the last Welsh cup final to be held at the old National Stadium before it was knocked down, when his Swansea team was beaten by a Nigel-Walker-inspired Cardiff, the side I'd supported from way back in the sixties when I would sit in the Arms Park, watching my soon-to-be brother-in-law, Elwyn, play in nearly four hundred appearances for the club.

Elwyn's mother had eight sons. All of them played for the self-styled greatest club in the world, and two of them also played for Wales, one being Bleddyn Williams, the so-called Prince of Welsh centres. Splinters in your backside from the wooden benches of the old main stand were a small price to pay for the half-crown Airfix construction kit and six-penn'orth of chips my sister would buy me on our way home. Bribed I may have been to keep her company, but following Cardiff was a loyalty that stayed with me long after the badly painted plastic Spitfires had met their end on some rubbish dump.

Support for a team doesn't disappear when your job is reporting on them. It just gets buried so that, I hope, no one can tell what part of the rugby or football divide you come from. So, as I stood in the bowels of the stadium that would soon be no more, ready to interview a visibly hurt Ruddock after a few expressions of sympathy that would probably not have stood up to a polygraph test, it didn't help that one of my radio colleagues stuck his head into the interview room and said, 'Oy, don't talk to him, Mike. He supports K-a-a-a-r-ddiff!'

Thanks a bunch, I thought. 'Don't worry,' Mike said, 'could be worse . . . not much worse, true, but you could support Llanelli.'

The working relationship survived through his time in Ireland with Leinster, the spell at Ebbw Vale when he came back to Wales, and his incarnation in charge of one of the four new regions at the Newport Gwent Dragons. Then, when he was given the Wales job, despite the world and his dog waiting for the white smoke coming out of the WRU chimney to magically form the name of Gareth Jenkins, we developed communication by text, which for a technological Luddite such as myself, who thought 'Internet' was a team in Italy's Serie B, was quite a feat.

It started when I texted my congratulations after Wales's first win of his reign against the Barbarians. I wasn't really expecting a reply. When it came, my son opened the message. He learned several words which apparently he'd yet to encounter in the lower reaches of Whitchurch High School.

On another occasion, Mike was the guest at Jamie's Rhiwbina presentation night for the under-12s rugby team. The club's nickname was the 'Squirrels'. If the person handing out the trophies was a player like Martyn Williams or Iestyn Harris, with young children, as a thank-you gift we'd give them a cuddly toy squirrel. If he was a coach, like Graham Henry or Mike, whose kids were long since past the need for stuffed animals, we'd present them with a stone squirrel for a garden ornament. The following day, a text arrived: 'I've named the squirrel Bob. A definite likeness my wife thought! Same size nuts I thought!'

During the Grand Slam games, I'd send a message of good luck, and he'd joke back about how I'd helped pick the team we announced on *Wales Today*. As for the tactics for the deciding game against Ireland . . . 'I can't trust u on those . . . tictacs suit u better.'

Our text banter extended to the television where, just before he'd read out the names of the team, he'd jokingly thank me for my help in selecting it. It was a level of informality that appealed to the audience.

But no longer, it seemed. When I headed off to meet Mike for the announcement of that side to face Scotland, I was under orders to end the joke about our 'joint' selection. It had run its course. That bit of banter was to be no more. I explained the producer's thinking to Mike before he listed his side. 'No problem,' he said, and got on with it: 'Thanks, Bob,' he picked up as usual from my introduction . . . 'Number 15 and full back, Gareth Thomas; on the wings, Mark Jones and Shane Williams; the centres Hal Luscombe and Matthew Watkins . . .'

There wasn't the usual sparkle. Something about him, and the players milling around ready for the press conference, was different. They were polite, but the atmosphere was charged. Even the friendliest of players, like Martyn Williams and Dwayne Peel, seemed more distant than usual. 1 put it down to reaction to the defeat by England and their determination to put it right against Scotland, but I couldn't stay any longer to find out. I had to get back to the office to lay the pictures of the chosen players – the graphics we called them – over the names as Mike Ruddock read them out, and edit his reasoning behind the team selection down to the time allotted in our lunchtime programme's running order.

It was only later that I learned of the real reason for the tension. The players had refused to attend a press conference while my BBC colleague Graham Thomas – who'd ghost-written the Gavin Henson autobiography that had caused so many waves inside and outside the Welsh camp a few months previously – was there. They'd also been upset by an article he'd penned for the match programme at Twickenham. The coach was left to face the press while his captain Gareth Thomas, supported by the rest of the players, boycotted the event.

At best, it was an embarrassment for the Wales team management. At worst, something seismic was happening. That team announcement would be my last with Mike. The joke certainly was over.

Chapter 13

'Say It Ain't So, Mike'

13.2.06 *Wales v Scotland Wash-up*

'Sorry, sir!'

There was something so quaintly 'rugby' about it – a 6'6", 17-stone second row forward towering over the referee who's just shown him a red card for kicking his opposite number, and saying 'Sorry, sir' as if a teacher had just reprimanded him for running in a school corridor. (That image of Roy Keane and his Manchester United teammates surrounding referee Andy D'Urso for having the temerity to award Middlesbrough a penalty against them came to mind. Testosterone ruled Old Trafford; local accident and emergency units were put on high alert, waiting for an influx of young millionaires in red shirts suffering burst blood vessels. Somehow you got the impression Captain Keane and his merry men were not saying, 'Sorry, sir.')

Scott Murray's apology befitted the Sunday afternoon on which the game was played. You could imagine him showering, changing and heading straight off to take the local Bible class, where the special subject would be, 'contrition in the face of adversity'. His simple yet dignified reaction to what must have been gut-wrenching disappointment was the abiding memory from what had been a strangely unsatisfactory game. Wales had won, as Mike Ruddock had predicted they would in the week leading up to the

77

match, but, despite two tries from captain Gareth Thomas and a 28–18 scoreline skewed by a couple of late Scottish scores, the swagger of the previous season seemed to have dissipated into the Cardiff night air.

What would Brent Cockbain make of it? He arrived early for his slot with me on Monday evening's *Wales Today*. As we walked along the corridor towards make-up and the C2 studio from where the programme went out live, I asked him whether there was any basis for my feeling of the previous week that all was not well inside a Welsh camp that had previously been considered a watchword for togetherness. Despite his injury, the Ospreys second row was one of the senior members of the side, a player who, along with Gareth Thomas, Stephen Jones and Martyn Williams, the young bucks in the set up would look up to. He was one of the conduits between the players and team management.

'So what do the players make of Mike as a coach?' I asked him.

Brent's answer surprised me. I wasn't expecting a gushing tribute to Mike as the man who'd transformed no-hopers into grand slam winners – the Australian's laconic style didn't lend itself to that sort of conversation – but I expected more from him.

'Aw . . . you know, Bob, we don't really see too much of him on the training paddock,' he said. 'He seems to spend a lot of his time sitting in one of the vans.'

I wondered if this was confirmation of what many suspected, that it was Scott Johnson who was the key figure in the team's training and tactics, not Mike.

'He's not under pressure, though, is he?'

'I wouldn't have thought so . . . he's got other strengths, hasn't he?'

'Well, yeah, he's great with us, the media,' I said. 'So you mean as a sort of figurehead?'

'I suppose I do . . . something like that. We need someone who's a good front man.'

It was hardly a ringing endorsement. We did the programme, looking back at the Scottish game, looking forward to the Irish game, and then went for a pint and a chat in my local pub on our way home. There was plenty of banter with the Monday night regulars of the Dynevor Arms, but never was there any indication, and this was from someone as close to the team as you could get without actually packing down with them, that within twenty-four hours Welsh rugby would be facing its own version of Armageddon.

14.2.06 *Mike R. Resigns*

St Valentine's Day, and my day off. I was in the car. I pressed the button to turn the *Drive* programme on Radio Five Live on to Radio Wales's *Sportstime*. I could tell by his voice that the presenter, Rob Phillips, never one to use one decibel when ten will do, was excited. This time the breaking news wasn't who was 'expected' to be in the Welsh team to face Ireland at Lansdowne Road in ten days' time but a 'major announcement due from the Welsh Rugby Union at the Millennium Stadium' later in the evening. Hamish Stuart, one of the sports department's senior journalists, came on with a hastily put together voice report suggesting that Mike Ruddock was 'expected' to stand down from his role as Welsh coach. I knew they would never have run with the story unless it was true. It was too big for conjecture, however informed.

In the time it normally takes for the amber light to turn green and the car behind to blow its horn, my mobile phone rang. 'Bob, you listening to Radio Wales?' It was the office. 'There's a press conference down the stadium at nine. We've got a crew booked. Can you get down there?'

Days off, even St Valentine's Day off, don't count for much when one of the most high-profile men in Wales had seemingly fallen on his sword. I pulled into a car park by the side of the road and punched a name into my phone. R, U, D, D, O, C, K. I pressed the green button, the number rang . . . and rang. No answer. I wasn't surprised. There was the text . . . the last message on my inbox had been from Mike on the day before the Scotland match. 'Thanx Bob,' it read. 'Thanx 4 the team advice.' In the dark of the car park, our joke seemed a long time ago.

For some reason, don't ask me why, the story of an illiterate baseball player from Pickens County, South Carolina came into my head. 'Shoeless' Joe Jackson was one of the stars of his day; some of the batting records he set for the Chicago White Sox in the 1910s still stand today. In 1919 his team were odds-on to beat the Cincinatti Reds in the final of the World Series. Unaccountably, they lost. Eight of the White Sox including Jackson were accused of throwing the series. A year later a grand jury was convened to investigate.

Outside the courthouse, a group of boys was waiting as 'Shoeless' Joe Jackson walked in. 'It isn't true, is it, Joe?' asked one. 'Yes, boys, I'm afraid it is,' he said.

By the time it reached the West Coast of the United States, the report had become, 'Say it ain't so, Joe!'

I changed one word for my text: 'Say it ain't so, Mike!' I pressed Send.

There was no answer. If there had been, it would probably have read, 'Yes, Bob, I'm afraid it is.'

Chapter 14

Crisis Management at Its Best

I should have been used to Welsh coaches being fired or resigning or simply deciding they had better things to do. It was a job that started – usually – with an undetermined period of approval from the great Welsh public. The team would win. Canonisation should surely follow! Then the team would lose. The ardour would cool, no sainthood for you yet, boy! Another World Cup would slip by. A Six Nations tournament would end with furrowed brows or, worse, a wooden spoon and defeat to England. Eventually, inevitably, just like Canute, the current incumbent would recognise that the turning tide was on its way to drown him.

Nine had come and gone while I'd been on *Wales Today*, including John Ryan who'd been in charge when I took over in 1989. Three I would have counted as good friends.

When Graham Henry's time came, I rang his home, the Coach House in Marshfield near Cardiff. Its name no longer seemed quite so appropriate. His wife Raewyn answered.

'Rae, it's Bob.' We knew each other well enough for surnames to be unnecessary. 'Is he all right?' I didn't need to say any more.

'He's having dinner, Bob.'

'Is he talking?' Raewyn was canny enough to know that meant:

Can I bring a camera around and ask why he's left? The sub-plot was: Did he jump or was he pushed?

'You know better than that, Bob . . . he never talks with his mouth full.'

It was an elegant way to tell a reporter doing a job who also happens to be a friend that the time for intrusion has not yet come.

Alan Davies had viewed his departure differently. He found himself surplus to requirements just before the 1995 World Cup in South Africa. The year before, he'd brought the then Five Nations Championship to Wales but that wasn't enough to save the man known as ABCD, nor his management line-up of Robert Norster and Gareth Jenkins, from the impatient push of the WRU towards whatever they considered to be progress. Davies and Norster would be missed, not least because they made an engaging and amusing double act. After a 10–9 win over England in 1993 the burly former Wales second row forward, whose nose still shows the marks of battles past, was asked if the dressing room had been an emotional place to be.

'Emotional? said Norster. 'You know me . . . I burst into tears every time *Little House on the Prairie* comes on the telly.'

It was one of his better one-liners. Personally I preferred an aside to the Canadian team's female physiotherapist who was sitting in a press conference not long after the Wales team had beaten a physically challenged Japan. Norster was staring intently at her rather large earring. Finally he spoke. 'I don't mean to be personal,' he said to her, 'but that wouldn't happen to be the Japanese scrum half abseiling from your ear, would it?'

When he was ungraciously deemed surplus to requirement, Alan Davies invited me to his house for an exclusive interview to explain why he went, an act which didn't endear him to my counterparts on ITV Wales news but gave him the platform he wanted.

His sentiments could have been: 'Regrets . . . I've had a few, but then again, too few to mention', if they hadn't already been purloined by Frank Sinatra, but as you might have expected from someone who cocked a snook at the usual sartorial standards of the international coaching scene by wearing a bow-tie to press conferences, he gave an articulate insight into the demands placed on a Wales coach even in the pre-professional world.

Mike Ruddock was the third of those coaches I'd call a friend. For a journalist, that might sound as if it should make your job easier. It doesn't; it makes it harder. My editor and producers at the BBC knew our relationship went beyond that between a reporter and his contact. Understandably, they wanted what was best for their programmes, something that would make them stand out from our rivals on the other channels. I couldn't blame them. They were in thrall to the viewing figures when they arrived on the desk in the morning. A good story equalled good viewing figures equalled happiness . . . so call in a few favours, Bob, see if Mike will do something with us. And me? I was torn. Of course, I wanted to do my job well, be professional, but someone I liked no longer had a job. He was hurting. Why add to the hurt? But if I didn't probe and pry, someone else would . . . no, *everyone* else would. Why not give him the option of at least someone he could trust. One quick cut to lance the boil.

But that would be for another day. First there was the press conference.

At five to nine on St Valentine's Day, I drove into the under-ground car park at the Millennium Stadium. Paul Rees, the *Guardian*'s rugby writer and someone I often asked to be an expert pundit on *Wales Today*, was walking towards the lifts. I said something banal: 'They never cease to surprise,' something like that. But maybe not so banal after all. This was a new one, even for seasoned watchers of Welsh rugby: a coach going before he had to play Canute and turn back the tide.

Upstairs in a suite usually used for corporate hospitality, the coffee was poured, not quite what I expected to be drinking tonight of all nights. The press waited. It had all happened too suddenly for many of the London-based correspondents who normally travelled down the M4 for major stories, but several of the game's big hitters in the media world, those who lived in or near Wales, were there. And all the local reporters. The television cameras and the newspaper photographers – the snappers – jostled for position at the front of the desk. Nine o'clock came and went. Nothing unusual there. The day a WRU press conference started on time was the day I'd get up on stage and sing the lead role from *Cats*. People started looking at their watches. Everyone had deadlines. Mine was the 10.25 p.m. bulletin that followed the main ten o'clock news on BBC One, but I'd have to be back in the office well before that to cut a piece and get ready to appear live on the camera we had in our newsroom.

Several times the sound of the lift doors opening came into the suite. The chatter died . . . only for a latecomer to come in.

'Ladies and gentlemen, if you could all take a seat now and make sure your mobile phones are turned off . . .' finally, the Union's media officer signalled the wait was nearly over. Two sheets of paper were handed round.

> WRU chief executive Steve Lewis today announced that he had been notified by the Wales head coach Mike Ruddock that he will not seek to renew his contract at the end of his current term.
>
> As a result it has been agreed between the WRU and Ruddock that he will stand down with immediate effect. In his absence, Scott Johnson will take over as head coach for the remainder of the RBS Six Nations Championship.
>
> Ruddock, who took over from Steve Hansen two years ago and was at the helm for Wales's first Grand Slam for

27 years last season, has decided to leave the post for family reasons.

WRU chief executive Steve Lewis's statement said:

Mike informed me today that he will not be seeking to extend his contract as Wales' national coach.

His announcement, and the timing of it, has obviously come as a shock and will be a blow to Welsh rugby as a whole. It is public knowledge that we have been in contract negotiations with Mike for some time in order to agree an extension through to the 2007 Rugby World Cup and beyond.

We had reached agreement on the terms of the contract, but clearly Mike has indicated reasons for not signing which are beyond those which are capable of negotiation and I understand his position.

It is disappointing that Mike has not been able to commit himself to a new deal and we now have to respect the decision he has reached about his future and his reasons for it. The role of head coach to the national team carries immense pressures, and the expectations of a nation and Mike, with a young family, has found these and the commitment required of the position over the next two years, unacceptable.

His place in Welsh sporting history is already assured for what he has done for Welsh rugby in such a short space of time. He will leave with our blessings and the heartfelt thanks of Welsh fans around the world and we wish him the best of luck for his future endeavours. I hope that the press will leave him to the privacy he requires.

As a result of Mike's decision it has been agreed between us that it would be inappropriate for both him, and for the team itself, for him to continue to prepare the team for the remaining games in the RBS Six Nations Championship and I have asked Scott Johnson to assume that responsibility for the games against Ireland, Italy and France.

There is still all to play for in the championship following our win over Scotland last weekend. Scott, in conjunction with Clive Griffiths and the rest of the National Team management, is dedicated to delivering further good results and performances.

The most successful head coach to lead Wales for the last thirty years is leaving the top job in Welsh sport with the stated intention of putting his young family first. Ruddock's statement read:

After consultation with my family, I have made the decision to stand down as National Coach.

On that basis, I have decided to withdraw from the contract talks to take Wales to the 2007 World Cup in France. This has been a tough decision to make but I have decided to put my family first.

What I have found during my two years as a coach is that this position is 'more than a job'. That has meant I have spent long periods away from my family, in camp and on overseas tours.

As a consequence, I felt the intense build up to next year's World Cup would mean more time away from my family. That is something which, on reflection, I would like to avoid.

Therefore, I have taken the decision to stand down as national coach. I would like to thank the WRU for providing me with the opportunity to coach my country at the highest level.

I would also like to thank my fellow coaches, my support staff and the players for their contribution and support in what has been a very enjoyable couple of years.

I must also place on record my sincere appreciation of the role the Welsh public has played. Quite simply, they have been outstanding in their support of the Wales team and myself and I must thank each and every one of them.

I wish the WRU and the Wales team the very best in the future. There are another three fixtures left in the Six Nations and I firmly believe we can win them all to give us a chance of retaining our title.

So there we had it. The definitive story as spun by the WRU.

The president, David Pickering, Steve Lewis and Scott Johnson took their places behind the table.

'This,' said David Pickering, 'has been crisis management at its best!'

The day had started like any other, but that had all changed in the afternoon when Steve Lewis was told that Mike Ruddock had decided to quit and would not renew his contract when it expired at the end of the season.

The dam had been breached, but at the moment the little boy still had his finger in the hole. The plan was for Lewis and Ruddock to meet later in the week, the following day was favourite, to decide how the news was to be managed. David Pickering was away from his office, but he would be able to get to the WRU early in the evening.

At the meeting, Pickering and Lewis were joined by, among others, Paul Sergeant, the Stadium's chief executive; Tim Burton, who'd been negotiating Ruddock's contract; press officer Liz Jones; and Rob Cole of the Westgate News Agency. The room where they met wasn't the most discreet of venues. They were in the full glare of those staff who hadn't been invited.

Initially, they talked about how they should handle a number of issues caused by the bombshell that had landed in their laps. Who'd talk to the players who were still in their training camp? Who'd liaise with the WRU board? And what about the media? As far as they were concerned, this was a matter purely between coach and employer. They were wrong.

The little boy now found that a finger wasn't enough to staunch the flow. The calls started to come in from different journalists. Is it true? Has Mike Ruddock quit? Why? How? What's going on? This is too big to keep quiet!

It's strange how things work in the incestuous world of the Welsh media. One of the calls was from a friend of a friend who was working on the printing press for the following morning's *Western Mail*. The *Mail* was running an exclusive 'Ruddock: I Quit' story. It was a sensation. The paper was coming out all guns blazing. This was one story he couldn't keep to himself until the paper hit the newsstands.

Those in the WRU meeting quickly realised there was no keeping this genie in the bottle. The press officer's mobile was ringing frantically as she fielded more and more calls. Each and every one was the same. It was Ruddock, Ruddock, Ruddock. A couple of the WRU's board had joined them, but what to do? Liz Jones tried to contact the man at the centre of it all. Like everyone else that night, she reached his answerphone. The coach had gone underground.

Ruddock had told the WRU he was going, but that was it: nothing had been decided about how it would be managed. The 'world exclusive' given to the *Western Mail*'s rugby writer Andy Howell had left them in what they thought was an impossible situation. At seven o'clock, just as I was receiving that first call from the office, they came to a decision. Ruddock wouldn't be allowed to remain until the end of the Six Nations. He would go, and go now. As far as they were concerned, his position was untenable. Both Pickering and Lewis now tried to contact Ruddock. They couldn't. The die was cast: 'Press conference . . . nine o clock'.

Crisis management or seat-of-the-pants management? Maybe they're one and the same.

Chapter 15

'On Holidays'

15.2.06 *Mike R. Goes*

'On holidays' said the text that preceded the familiar name of Ruddock on my mobile. That was one way of putting it, I suppose . . . but these holidays were being taken in Swansea, not in the early spring sun of the Costas. They were the coach's way of saying that now was not the time to be appearing on a television news programme, fanning the flames of a story which had already been given the ultimate appendage of a gate. 'Ruddockgate' was in full flow.

It was a term I now disliked with an intensity burning on obsession. I hadn't felt so strongly a couple of years earlier, when the England flanker Neil Back had indulged in blatant gamesmanship to deny Leicester's opponents Munster a chance of winning the Heineken Cup final at the Millennium Stadium. It was roundly condemned in the media, but, try as I might, I failed miserably in my one-man campaign to have it dubbed 'Backgate'. I am still hopeful though that former Goodie, Graeme Garden, might become embroiled in the scandal that will give us 'Gardengate'.

'Ruddockgate' was evidence that the WRU's 'crisis management at its best' should make us thankful that we hadn't seen crisis management at its worst. Their St Valentine's Day statement was an attempt to stop the conspiracy theorists in their tracks. Nothing wrong with that. But any hope – and it must have been a forlorn one – that a story as big as this could be contained by telling a slavering press a few core truths surrounded by a sea of claims that had even the most malleable of hacks muttering, 'You've got to be joking', was naive in the extreme.

The *Western Mail* was at its never-knowingly-undersell-anything best with a banner headline that took us back to 1989 and 'East Out'. 'Ruddock: I Quit' were the three front-page words its readers woke up to, followed by the apocalyptic proclamation that 'Ruddock's news is one of the biggest bombshells in the history of Welsh rugby and will rock the game here to its core.' There was a whiff of sour grapes about their coverage. The paper had been hoping to celebrate a major scoop that morning by exclusively revealing that Ruddock would be stepping down at the end of the Six Nations. Somebody should have told them to tell the people who worked in their print room to keep schtum and not phone their friends.

The *Mail* went on to say: 'But extraordinarily the WRU spin doctors called a press conference at the unheard of time of 9 p.m. after hearing that Ruddock had spoken to us. It was a clear attempt by the WRU to get their retaliation in first.'

Ouch! Whatever else the WRU's night-time press conference had done, it had scotched the *Western Mail*'s hopes of a 'scoop'. They were smarting.

But that was their problem. Ours was to make some sense of the confusion and tell the viewers not just what had happened but *why* it had happened. It was a long-standing tradition that I phoned the newsdesk at eight minutes past eight on each morning I was working, and I'd discuss with the producer what sports stories we should be covering that evening. On some days there would be virtually nothing, on others there'd be a long list. Unusually, today's main news programme had been planned well in advance because it was the tenth anniversary of the *Sea Empress* going aground at Milford Haven.

I remembered the day well. The evening before, I'd asked Tony the producer if there was much on. 'Not bad, but we're short of a lead,' he said. A few hours later 72,000 tons of crude oil were being discharged into the seas around South West Wales and Tony had his lead story, not just for that night but for weeks afterwards. Ten years on gave us the chance to see how and if Pembrokeshire had recovered from one of Wales's biggest environmental disasters, so the programme was already full of pre-filmed items. The only available shot was a 'newsdesk' – the least important part of the programme, 20 seconds of news read by the presenter in studio and covered by pictures. 'Ruddock going! Newsdesk?' I said. It was a joke. In newspaper terms this was a 'hold the front page' moment. The *Sea Empress* was going to have to accept lesser billing.

It's self-evident, but a television programme can do nothing without pictures. Newspaper and radio journalists can paint their own with words, but we had to have the shots that would add to the story being unveiled to the people watching the flickering set in the corner of their living room. Fortunately for us, the Welsh squad was attempting to keep to the schedule laid down before 'one of the biggest bombshells in the history of Welsh rugby' had been detonated.

Each morning before the players began their training proper, television cameras were given access for ten or fifteen minutes to the session. Then they were told to bugger off before the team began the sophisticated business of line-out calls and the rest – perish the thought that we should show six seconds of those on the news, and give away secrets to the Irish, French and Italian spies monitoring the airwaves to gain a scintilla of advantage. That morning's training window was a godsend for us, allowing us to film and gauge reaction in the faces and body language of the players as they went about their business under the watchful eye of a new man.

Where a few days ago it had been Mike Ruddock overseeing preparations, now it was Scott Johnson. If we had been expecting any trade-union tub thumping by militant props carrying placards demanding 'Give us back our Coach' or 'Justice for the Grand Slam One', then we were to be disappointed. My script for our lunch-time bulletin started, 'It couldn't be business as usual . . . not when a popular grand slam winning coach has sensationally quit' – but anyone wandering into the Vale of Glamorgan's indoor training centre that morning would have been hard pressed to notice any sense of unrest.

The lunchtime press conference was another matter altogether. By now the massed ranks of the national media had mobilised and the advance guard had swept down the motorway to revel in another of those peculiarly Welsh bouts of bloodletting. Mike Ruddock might have been sticking to his 'family reasons', but they were having none of that. 'Family reasons?' Not sexy enough by a long way. There must have been more to it than that. Even if there wasn't, there would be. By the time the room had emptied and the new coach and the new captain Michael Owen had done their interviews and made their excuses, I was almost alone, waiting to do a live interview into the 1.30 news programme. A senior member of the Welsh management made his way over to me.

'Surprised?' he said.

'Yep.'

'You shouldn't have been. We've had to talk him out of going before.'

Enigmatic . . . but confirmation all was not well in the Welsh camp. The conspiracy theories had already begun.

Chapter 16

Professor Plum Dunnit!

16.2.06 *Cluedo*

One of the reporters in our morning news conference had a good idea. Normally I didn't go to them – the time spent chewing over what should go into the evening's programme usually ate calamitously into the period actually spent filling it; I preferred my early morning phone calls to sort out what my input would be – but two days on there was no sign of people's interest in the story waning. Quite the opposite. 'Ruddockgate' was still wide open.

Another 'No comment for the moment' text from the deposed coach still ruled out him appearing in front of a camera. His solicitor was advising silence. However, WRU Chief Executive Steve Lewis – the man most people regarded as public enemy number one when it came to Ruddock's going – took the opposite position. He had offered a live interview at the Millennium Stadium to update us on how the 'crisis management' was going. That would be a seat of the pants job for me, totally dependent on how well I was able to divert Lewis from his pre-planned answers and shed some light where previously there had been darkness. A favourite definition of 'news' is that it's what other people don't want you to know. I had to try to find out what *he* didn't want me – or the audience – to know.

We also needed to make the various conspiracy theories as clear as possible for those whose interest in rugby and rugby politics was no more than passing. When you are in the middle of a huge story, there is the danger of believing that everyone is as consumed by it as you. A rule of thumb told us we had done our job well if the man in the brown jumper at the end of the bar in the pub was talking about the story we'd put on air that night to the guy standing next to him. The fact that I felt it was part of my job to carry out the essential research needed to establish that, yep, it was a favourite topic of conversation in the Dynevor or the Royal Oak or the Maltsters was irrelevant. Someone had to do it.

The aficionados could get their fix by reading the rugby correspondents of the broadsheets – the *Guardian*, *Times* and *Telegraph* – who could (and did) use a small rainforest in explaining over a couple of acres of newsprint their take on what had happened. The anoraks would log on to the websites, where posted message after posted message would offer ever more outlandish and, sometimes, ever more libellous, views on events. The occasional rugby follower could turn to the 'red-tops' – the tabloid newspapers – for their more condensed versions of events. We, however, had to make those events comprehensible for a complete novice who'd just sat down in front of the TV for a relaxing cup of tea after making the kids their evening meal of turkey twizzlers and chips.

'So why don't we set it out like a Cluedo board?' said Nick at the morning meeting. 'You know, get the graphics department to create the background and we can have our own Colonel Mustard, Professor Plum and Reverend Green as the suspects for who might have done the dirty deed!'

The idea had a simplicity that should appeal to the viewer who didn't know his Welsh Rugby Union from his Welsh National Opera, or alternatively, his hymns from his arias. So when it went out that night, I said something like, 'There are conspiracy theories a-plenty, with fans across the country still wondering "Who dunnit to Ruddock?" Well, let's take a look at some of the main players. The man who publicly broke the news of Ruddock's departure was the WRU's chief executive, Steve Lewis. He was in contract talks with the coach, but Ruddock pulled out of the negotiations at the beginning of the week. So did it all come down to money?

'Or was it down to the man who's now acting Wales coach, Steve Johnson? He's extremely popular among the players and credited by many as being the man behind the team's all out, attacking style of play . . . did the WRU want him at any cost?

'The phrase "player power" has been at the forefront of this whole controversy. With the players rumoured to be critical of Ruddock's coaching style, could the real authority have shifted from the touch-line to the pitch? Are they dictating who they want as their coach?'

In a 50-second-long nutshell, there we had it, not in the finely argued prose of the broadsheet maybe but enough to grab the attention of Sarah in Skewen or Tom in Treorchy.

That was a recorded insert in the programme. Next up was the 'live' with Steve Lewis. The cameraman and the links van – which would send the interview up to a satellite, ready to be bounced down again into Broadcasting House just a couple of miles away as the crow flies – were already there when I arrived at the Millennium Stadium. It's a strange place when it's empty: a theatre which seems to take on a life of its own when it's throbbing with the sounds and emotions of more than seventy thousand fans, but it can seem a soulless and echoing place when it's empty. I was used to it. If any sporting venue was my second home, the Millennium Stadium was it. Celebration, crushing disappointment, I'd run through most of the emotions there, but this was a different sort of occasion: one on one, interviewer and interviewee.

I watched Steve Lewis come out of the players' tunnel and walk around the perimeter of the pitch to our camera position. He wasn't alone. Liz Jones of the WRU's communications team was with him. That was to be expected. The stadium's chief executive, Paul Sergeant, was also there. That was less usual. Lewis could be a difficult subject to interview, not one to react well if he felt he was being misunderstood or manoeuvred into a place he didn't want to go. Paul Sergeant was more urbane and measured. He was the man who'd taken on the task of organising a Tsunami Relief concert at the Stadium with just a couple of weeks' notice and turned it into a money-spinning triumph. His multi-coloured sweater, picked up in the duty free of an Australian airport, had become a trademark. So had his ability to think on his feet in live broadcasts. The time he'd spent at Wembley Stadium before coming to Wales had been an effective grounding for working with the media.

I gave Steve Lewis the outline of what I wanted to talk about . . . as usual our 'touchy feely' relationship with the viewers was reflected with a couple of questions people had e-mailed in to the programme. Lewis and his colleagues talked quietly among themselves as we waited to go live into the programme.

'Two minutes to you, Bob,' said the programme director.

I gave the camera a thumbs-up.

'Everything OK, Dave?' I asked the cameraman. 'Tie straight? Hair tidy – what's left of it? Don't need a comb any more . . . I make do with a chamois leather.'

He had the good grace to chuckle at a line he'd probably heard me use a hundred times before in exactly the same circumstances.

I gestured for Steve Lewis to join me.

'We've got a bit of a surprise for you, Bob . . . an exclusive . . .' he said.

There was little time to expand before the voice of the programme director came through my earpiece. 'Cue, Bob!'

'So it's been just about the most traumatic forty-eight hours in Welsh rugby I can remember,' I said to Sara Edwards, who was presenting the programme in the studio. 'And the man who's very much at the centre of it all is the WRU's chief executive, Steve Lewis . . . well, Steve, we've asked our viewers what they think about Mike Ruddock going and they're very unimpressed with the way the Union handled it, particularly about why he had to go now! Mrs Thomas from Neath says, it's "wicked" the WRU has denied Mike Ruddock the opportunity to see the season out. Why didn't you let him finish after the Six Nations as he wanted?'

'Well, with all due respect to Mrs Thomas from Neath . . .' began Steve Lewis, insisting that the job of coaching Wales had become a burden to Ruddock. This was interesting but not incompatible with what he had said about 'family reasons' being behind his going. Then the interview began to take on a life of its own. The real bombshell was the timescale of the coach's going, with Lewis revealing Ruddock had told the newspapers that he was going *before* he spoke to his employers on the WRU. It put a new perspective on the affair. The time allotted for the interview – an already (by *Wales Today* terms) generous three minutes – came and went. It wasn't just me enjoying myself . . . Lewis's 'Now let me finish, Bob' over my interruptions made it good knockabout stuff for the audience.

As a joust it was probably honours even, but it had provided invigorating television as well as a new revelation to the story. As I walked away around the deserted stadium, I remembered an encounter my brother had had with the Conservative government minister Kenneth Clarke on the *Today* programme. It came shortly after the soon-to-be disgraced MP Jonathan Aitken demanded John's head for having the temerity to interrupt the Chancellor something like seventy-six times in one interview. The next time they met on air, John pushed a pocket calculator across the table to him.

'What's that for, John?' asked Clarke.

'I just thought that every time I interrupted you in the interview, you could add it up, so that at the end we can see if we've broken our record.'

'That's very kind . . . but perhaps you should know that I might be the Chancellor of the Exchequer but I've never learned to use one of these bloody things!'

We wouldn't need a calculator, but it would be a long while before Steve Lewis had finished with interviews.

Chapter 17

Never Let the Truth . . .

20.2.06 *M.R.; Gareth Thomas;* Scrum V

My mobile phone rang as I had my usual Sunday evening pint. It was the manager of my son's rugby team, a friend who shared the vicissitudes of following the Cardiff Blues' fluctuating fortunes, where the immutable law is, 'If you think it's going to be bad, don't worry, it'll be worse.' It must have been serious. Normally all communication was through a Ruddock-esque sharing of texts. Like e-mail, it saves an awful lot of small talk.

'Are you watching this?' Bob said.

'If you're asking, am I watching a pint of Brains bitter swirling seductively in a glass, I suppose the answer would be "yes",' I said.

'No . . . the television?'

'Ah, you mean the hits of the eighties! Did you know that Big Country had a hit with "Steel Town" which was the number one album for a week in October, 1984? Either that or it was Steel Town had a hit with "Big Country". Either way, I don't know why anyone would want to write a song about, or call themselves after, Port Talbot.'

The pub – or rather its bar staff – had a habit of playing fast and loose with the 'television only for the watching of sport' rule. If you want to brush up on the names of obscure bands you've never heard of, and then discover why you'd never heard of them, the Maltsters in Whitchurch is the place to be.

I could sense Bob wishing he'd stuck to a text message.

'No . . . are you watching bloody *Scrum V*?'

'Are you telling me that "bloody" *Scrum V* can compete with The Smiths singing "Meat is Murder"? Number one in late February, 1985, by the way.'

By now he was losing the will to live.

'Gareth Thomas!' the two words came out like the last croak of a strangled swan. 'I've heard of car-crash television, but this is motorway-meltdown stuff!'

'Can't be worse than Five Star singing "Silk and Steel". Can't believe it was top of the album charts for a week. No taste some people.'

'Have you got it taped?'

'Why would I want to tape T'Pau's recording of "Bridge of Spies", for God's sake?'

The phone cut off.

I did have *Scrum V* recorded, but Bob was wrong. It wasn't motorway-meltdown television. It was worse.

The words 'player power' had swirled around the Mike Ruddock affair ever since the story had broken, and not just because of the usual journalistic attraction to alliteration.

A few rugby writers whose antennae were normally to be trusted had reported the breakdown of trust between the coach and his senior players even before he quit. What snippets had come out from Mike Ruddock since his immediate reaction had already breached the dam that had been built to hold in 'family reasons' as the be-all and end-all of his going. The fact that the contract negotiations had been suspended was now deemed to be *much* more than just a postponement of a new contract, one that the world and his dog had been told was done and dusted, to allow him to concentrate on repeating the success of his previous Six Nations campaign.

But as for the full story . . . the word 'conjecture' could have been made to fit it. Tantalisingly, an interview to reveal 'Ruddock, the Coach's Story in His Own Words' had been pencilled in for Friday. I'd gone as far as jotting down a list of questions to ask when we met. It seemed we'd finally have the authoritative account of his going . . . then the long arm of the lawyer intervened once again.

Instead of having Mike talking to the media and through them to the rest of Wales and the extended rugby world, which had been fed so far on a diet of rumour and innuendo, our final programme of an extraordinary week was in lyrical mood . . . 'They do say, breaking up is hard to do − but on this, Day Four of the drama, former coach Mike Ruddock has told the Welsh Rugby Union that they don't know the full story!' So what was new in that? the cynical might say.

Ruddock now reckoned the time had come for the board of the WRU − the new slim-line management forum that had been the brainchild of the recently departed chief executive David Moffett − to be given his version of events as quickly as possible. Quite whether he'd have been so sanguine about who awaited him if he had shared the drink I'd had years ago with Vernon Pugh − the former chairman of WRU and the International Rugby Board who'd died in 2003 − is another matter.

The QC from an Amman Valley mining family was a genuine high flier in a world of rugby administration usually populated by dodos. He was a son of the grass roots, coach of Cardiff High School Old Boys on the muddy rugby fields in the north of the city where he'd played as a centre of limited ability − as he happily acknowledged − and where he'd become best known, according to a former secretary of the Old Boys, for his reluctance to part with his weekly £1 sub.

As a barrister, he'd investigated the tour to South Africa that had brought so many casualties and so much disrepute to the Union in 1989. His report was not the usual bundle of platitudes painted in the bland colour of whitewash but a damning critique of the players and administrators involved. And there was more: one final section which the Union had neither asked for nor expected. It said simply that the Union wasn't up to running the game in the commercial era. This was not what the WRU wanted to read – or, more to the point, what the WRU wanted others to read. It was kept under wraps until 1993, when it was leaked to the BBC and the *South Wales Echo*.

As an exercise in self-preservation, the tactics were understandable. They were also futile. Pugh's lone voice of criticism was joined by another, then another, until there was a choir of protest demanding change. They got it. A vote of no confidence saw new committee elections with Pugh eventually persuaded to stand. He became the new chairman. The rest, as they say, is history. With the miner's son to the fore, the march to professionalism was unstoppable.

He was one of the most powerful figures the game had seen, one it was always worth having a drink with when he came into the studio for an interview. It didn't really matter what the subject was – if he said something was going to happen, it tended to happen. He was the very definition of 'newsworthy'.

'So, Vernon. A question!' We were chatting as he sipped his bottle of Pils in the BBC Club after an exchange on *Wales Today*. 'You're the chairman of the WRU, the WRU's a multi-million-pound business, and it's got a cast of thousands running it in the shape of "the committee". Now let's say you were the chief executive of a major company, and that "committee" is your board of directors, responsible for the running of said company and making a profit . . .' I paused for effect; his studious QC's demeanour must have been contagious. 'How many of that WRU committee would you employ?'

'How many? If I wanted it run professionally, if I wanted it to operate smoothly and if I wanted it to make money, how many of them would I employ?' I didn't realise it, but we'd invented a version of *The Apprentice* years before Donald Trump and Sir Alan Sugar. 'I think I'd employ . . . er . . . one. Maybe.'

I thought it best not to ask his identity.

The WRU 'committee' was now an 18-strong WRU board. Its personnel had changed, and the great Wales and Lions wing of the sixties and seventies, Gerald Davies, who'd become something of a synonym for probity, had been elected on to it. He was a totem for the calibre of people it might attract *in the future* – people who had achieved on and off the pitch, rather than those who'd simply served their time on the committees of district rugby clubs. So it was to this group that Mike Ruddock wanted to give a full run-down of what had happened.

Others though had had a chance to get their retaliation in first.

The Welsh captain Gareth Thomas – or Alfie as he was known to the rugby world – had been back in France with his club Toulouse when the brouhaha of Ruddock's going broke. Sensible man, you might conclude from that, cocooned as he was from the nigh on hysterical media reaction back in Wales. Except, of course, that in the communications-conscious world of the twenty-first century there is no such thing as being 'cocooned'. He could be stranded in an igloo somewhere close to the South Pole with just a hungry husky for company and he would still be able to access the latest opinion piece coming off the presses of the *Western Mail* almost before their rugby correspondent had finished writing it. *Wales Today* was just as available on a satellite channel on the banks of the Garonne as it was back in the Garw Valley.

So, after an initial phone call from the Wales team manager Alan Phillips telling him, 'Mike's leaving', and a somewhat incredulous, 'What d'you mean? Why?', he could still follow the 'conjecture and opinion, speculation and tittle-tattle'. As he said in his autobiography, 'I don't think it would have been knocked off the front pages had a volcano erupted underneath the Millennium Stadium.' It was an interesting thought.

However, there was to be no Welsh Vesuvius that day or the following days, just tittle-tattle that was leaving Alfie fuming not-so-quietly in the Midi-Pyrenees. One story – that the players, their captain in particular, were jealous at the fact that Mike Ruddock had been awarded an OBE in the New Year's Honours – he reckoned was especially deserving of derision. England's cricketers might have collected OBEs en masse for beating the Aussies and winning the Ashes – even those whose minimal involvement would later bring the dismissive sledging of Shane Warne at slip – but the Welsh players were apparently more than happy that their coach had received the gong on behalf of everyone who had been involved in the Grand Slam.

Thomas says he took Ruddock to task for not telling the squad to their faces that he was going . . . and says he had a text back telling him Mike was quitting because of a breakdown in communications with the WRU over the renewal of his contract. Most annoying to the captain, though, were those pesky couple of words that just wouldn't go away: 'player power'.

But, maybe, just maybe, there was a way out of it. BBC Wales's weekly rugby programme *Scrum V* had been searching all week for a new angle on the story, one that hadn't been done to death in the newspapers or on daily news outlets. An exclusive interview with the Wales captain ticked the boxes admirably. If the man-at-the-centre-of-it-all was taking the fifth amendment on the advice of his lawyers, then the man-some-said-caused-it-all would be a damn good second best. When Alan Phillips phoned *Scrum V*'s producers on Friday night, saying Thomas wanted to present the players' case in the face of some pretty hostile accusations against them, it's fair to say they didn't need their arms twisted too far up their backs before they agreed – and set about trailing it on every occasion they could.

Eddie Butler – one of the programme's presenters – reported that Phillips told BBC Wales on the day before the interview, 'You'd better watch out tomorrow! Alfie is really up for this!'

Thomas arrived at Broadcasting House at half past five, along with his parents and, bizarrely, Rupert Moon, the Llanelli and Wales scrum half who was then working for the Union's commercial department. According to Butler, Moon said, 'Don't ask me why I'm here. Seems everyone else is away. They [the Union] phoned me and asked if I'd come along. And don't ask me what he's going to say. You know what he's like. As if anyone could ever tell Alfie what to say . . . !'

Just when a good experienced bruiser from the press office was needed they were all on a day off. Of such things are broadcasting legends made. Whether it was an accident of set-design or a cunning set-up, Alfie never had a chance.

In front of him sat Gareth Lewis, a useful radio presenter but an inexperienced performer on television. He had been drafted in to replace regular anchorman Graham Thomas, Henson's ghost writer and apologist, who had already felt the captain's ire when Alfie had singled him out as the reason for boycotting the press conference at Ruddock's last team announcement. To his left was Jonathan Davies, the cheeky chappie of rugby broadcasting. And to his right was Eddie Butler, the undisputed heavyweight champ of the pundits, opinionated and self-confident. Gareth Thomas sat in the middle of the V, the prey caught in a pincer movement that would have left the Eighth Army hanging on for an early armistice if Rommel had come up with it in the Western Desert.

Davies, with his affectionate 'Gar' and general air of embarrassed discomfort, played the 'good cop'; Butler, the Cambridge graduate and writer for the *Observer* was the 'bad cop'. Lewis was the 'honest broker'.

The early skirmishes were promising but hardly conclusive, with Thomas being offered a few medium-paced balls he could bat away with the usual passion he showed in interviews. He might not have been the most refined of speakers – deconstruct his sentences and any professor of English would probably wince – but there was an honesty and earthy robustness about his answers that was rare in a time when interviews were becoming ever more anodyne. Ask any of the two, three, four or five players put forward by the Union's media people at a press conference the same question and you would get very little variation – give or take a few words – on the same answer. Alfie was different. He might not be sure where his tongue would lead him, but he wasn't afraid to let it off the leash. It was a maverick stance that didn't guarantee any prizes for popularity but made a refreshing change.

On this occasion there wasn't just passion, there was a sense that he was aggrieved. 'I'm telling you the truth,' he could have said, 'why the hell can't you accept what I'm saying?' It was that palpable.

The crux of the matter came down to the coach's relationship with his senior players . . . had they backed him or had they betrayed him? If you believed the conspiracy theorists, Thomas had called a meeting with the WRU chief executive Steve Lewis to demand the sacking of Ruddock. 'Sadly for the would-be Hollywood script writers,' he later wrote, 'it was nothing like that.'

The senior players – Thomas, Stephen Jones, Martyn Williams and Brent Cockbain – Alfie said, *had* met Lewis, but largely to find out whether they were sufficiently covered by insurance. The scrum half Gareth Cooper had injured his shoulder in the game against England at Twickenham, and Thomas made it clear that unless they were given assurances that they were covered for the worst injuries imaginable on a rugby field, they would consider 'withdrawing their services'. Butler saw the threat of a strike – not the first in Welsh rugby history: a plane to Australia had been missed a couple of years before as they sat and discussed a pay offer in a motorway service station – as evidence of 'player power'. Thomas saw it as sensible working practice.

They had had their minds set at rest about the insurance before Thomas then brought up the subject of the coach, claiming he wasn't taking enough responsibility in the running of the team. This supported what Brent Cockbain had told me. The chief executive's answer was that it was an issue between the players and Ruddock who had the Union's full backing. If they had an issue with the coach, they should speak to him about it, not the WRU. 'Fair enough,' thought Thomas, and the meeting came to an end.

That was Thomas's reading of it. For Butler, 'This was an important revelation. Lewis had been heavily criticised all week for being, at the very least, contradictory about how deeply he was involved in Ruddock's departure . . . As for the players Lewis dispatched back to their Vale of Glamorgan base, it was now difficult for them to deny the accusation of muscle-flexing when they had just admitted to threatening their chief executive with strike action in the week before a Test. And that was a few days after they defied Ruddock, who had instructed them not to go on the town after the England game at Twickenham.'

Car-crash television it most certainly was: uncomfortable, even a little distressing, to watch, but watch it you must, with Thomas demanding Butler reveal his sources and Butler refusing. It wasn't the sort of elegant confrontation he was used to but it ended amicably enough with handshakes all round.

The following day, there was one topic of conversation in the BBC. 'Did you see . . . ?' There was no need to complete the question. Mid-morning, I had a call from one of the staff who worked in 'newsgathering'. It's a job which does what it says on the box. They're responsible for making routine calls to the emergency services to check if anything untoward has happened in Wales, and they are the first port of call when a member of the public phones in with what they consider a story. Nine times out of ten, it's thanks but no thanks. This was the tenth time.

'Bob, we've just had a call from someone saying Gareth Thomas has been admitted to the Princess of Wales hospital in Bridgend. We've put in a call to them, but they're not saying anything. Can you check it out?'

The team's press officer answered his mobile after just a couple of rings. You can usually tell from the tone of reply whether the person at other end is being guarded or trying to hide something. This time I didn't sense it.

'I haven't heard anything . . . I'll check with Alan Phillips and come back to you.'

He did. 'Apparently Alfie's had a bad migraine. He did go to hospital, but he's home now. And we don't know yet how this will affect his chances of playing against Ireland at the weekend.'

Knowing the press officer as I did, he was probably telling it as he knew it. The truth turned out to be slightly different.

After he'd left the BBC, Thomas had gone home and he and his wife Jemma waited for the *Scrum V* programme to begin. 'He couldn't sit still. He was pacing from corner to corner and was very red in the face,' she later told reporters. 'Ten minutes into the programme, he started shouting, "No, no!" and said he couldn't feel the left side of his body and his vision was blurred. He kind of slid off the chair . . .'

'I thought I was going to die,' said Thomas. 'I was looking round the room at my family, thinking this was the last time I was going to see them all.'

The Wales captain had had a mini-stroke, not as a result of the programme – though that made for another conspiracy theory – but as a result of damage to an artery in his neck caused in a game against Narbonne on the Saturday before the *Scrum V*.

Gareth Thomas was the latest casualty of Ruddock-gate. As was another less tangible, more esoteric one . . . the relationship between the Welsh Rugby Union and BBC Wales. The organisation that had shown such a blasé approach to their volatile skipper's appearance on what they knew would be a highly charged programme that they had sent a high-profile but inexperienced figure from the commercial department of all places to hold his hand, was now incensed. 'We had been to see the BBC and reached an agreement on how the interview was to be conducted,' the WRU chairman David Pickering told a radio programme later in the week. 'The BBC reneged on the deal. This matter will be taken up at the highest level.'

All this mayhem, yet still all was quiet on the Ruddock front.

Chapter 18

The King is Dead

21.2.06 *Wales Team Announced (Wales v Ireland)*
It was quiet, too quiet, as Gary Cooper might have said as he peered out from behind his upturned chow-wagon at the deserted moonlit plain. In the black and white western, his observation would have been ended with the wail of a coyote that was obviously the local Cheyenne loosening up their larynxes before launching their dawn raid on the plucky settlers cleaning their six-shooters. At the Welsh rugby squad's training headquarters in the Vale of Glamorgan, there wasn't even the sound of a mis-hit six iron bouncing off the roof from the nearby driving range to break the silence. It was quiet, too quiet.

Seven days on from the St Valentine's Day massacre – well, the passing of time leads to exaggeration – it was evidently getting to me. It should have been the first sign of an orderly transfer of power. Scott Johnson, the man many labelled 'public enemy number two' after Gareth Thomas for his perceived role in Ruddock's departure, was due to arrive any minute to announce his team to play Ireland the following Sunday. Gareth Thomas wouldn't be in it. Doctors had ruled him out of the rest of the Six Nations after examining the results of an MRI scan. They hoped he'd be able to resume training in ten or twelve weeks. Hopes that he'd be able to travel to Dublin to play an inspirational role had also been dashed. The damaged blood vessel needed time to heal.

No Gareth Thomas then . . . and still no Scott Johnson. I rang the press officer. His number shouldn't have needed any dialling, my mobile should have put me through as a matter of course after the number of times I'd contacted him in the last week.

'Bob, where are you?'

'Where we said!'

'Where's that?'

'The Vale.'

'The Vale?'

'The Vale.'

Give or take a question mark this was getting repetitive.

'What are you doing there?'

'The team announcement. Ireland. Small matter of a match this weekend!'

'It's not there!'

'I was beginning to get that impression. So where is it?'

'Cardiff Arms Park. In the hospitality suite off the car park.'

'When?"

'Er . . . now!'

This was not a good start to a relationship with a new coach – even if he was a stand-in who was meant to be heading back to Australia at the end of the season. I broke it as gently as I could to the cameraman that we were in fact due in the centre of the city, ten miles or so away, like about five minutes ago. He'd been at the BBC long enough not to be surprised. He rolled his eyes, a bodily function devised and honed to perfection by the BBC's technical staff over the ages, sighed and got into his BMW. I got into my Hyundai.

A couple of speed-camera flashes later I was listening to Scott Johnson laying down the rules of engagement: no jokes this time about me picking the team, no questions either about anything other than the personnel chosen to head across the Irish Sea. The restriction said a lot about what had happened, but it didn't worry me too much – that's why I was there – even if the guy from Radio Five Live was less enamoured with it. The Welsh public were presumably still interested in who'd be wearing the red shirt in their last-ever visit to Lansdowne Road before it was knocked down and rebuilt. Shane Williams joined Gareth Thomas on the injured list, but the *wunderkind* himself, Gavin Henson, was back on the replacements' bench after the ludicrously long suspension imposed on him by the International Rugby Board for an indiscretion against Leicester in an Ospreys Heineken Cup match before Christmas. Was it only a few weeks ago that Mike Ruddock was texting me with a bit of advice as I camped on Dublin's St Stephen's Green for the result of Henson's appeal hearing? 'Go down the pub and wait!' he'd sent, followed by, 'Is Charlotte there?' then 'A long wait means good news I reckon.'

So little time had passed . . . so much had changed.

The team announcement was only the hors d'oeuvres to the main event of the day. I was now listening to Sara Edwards reading her link in the *Wales Today* studio: 'Good evening. A week ago he told his bosses he was quitting. Tonight he's been facing the Welsh Rugby Union again, this time to give what he's calling the "full story" about why he resigned. Former Wales rugby coach, Mike Ruddock, had asked for a meeting as speculation has grown about why he left. And tonight he got it. And there's been another dramatic development – the captain of the team, Gareth Thomas, has been ruled out of the team against Ireland on Sunday. And he's set to be out of action for up to twelve weeks. Let's go straight to the Millennium Stadium now and join our sports correspondent, Bob Humphrys . . . Bob . . .'

I was standing on the ramp leading up to the stadium entrance. It was a case of suck it and see. The former coach had headed into the underground car park off Westgate Street at four in the afternoon with a smile and a wave – but no words – for the cameramen and reporters he'd got to know well. A press conference had been scheduled for after his meeting with the WRU board. But what form would it take? Would he respond to questions? In a perfect world, where mankind existed to pour bounty on hard-pressed reporters like me, he'd do one-to-one interviews with the various broadcasting outlets. Experience said that this wouldn't happen. So would he just read a prepared statement and, in the never to be forgotten words of the *News of the World* reporter, make his excuses and leave? For the betting fraternity among the assembled hacks, that was apparently six to four on.

Waiting for a meeting to end and a press conference to begin is a strange affair. This one was being held in a glass-fronted suite at the Stadium. People filled in their Sudoku grids, read the newspapers or chatted idly. No one really concentrated. Each time one of the Union's spin doctors wandered in there was a stir, cameramen moved towards the prime spots where they'd parked their tripods, notebooks were opened . . . only for another false alarm to go down on the list. For broadcasters like myself, the uncertainty gnawed away at you.

The 18.30 *Wales Today* running order was the way the producers hoped the programme would pan out. It was a wish list, based on the untoward packing its bags and heading off on holiday for the day. The events at the Millennium Stadium were the first items in the programme . . . the titles would run, the studio lights would fade up, Sara would read her handover to me at the Stadium, I'd pick up and link into shots of Mike Ruddock and the WRU committee arriving earlier in the afternoon, then I'd go to the team announcement I'd filmed with Scott Johnson at Cardiff Arms Park. Probably the press conference would be over by the time we went on air at six-thirty, so the plan was to have shots of Ruddock sitting in front of the media, followed by a clip of the man himself talking. It would be rounded off by an interview with our rugby correspondent Gareth Charles, who would put all that had been said into context and read the runes for what it meant for Welsh rugby.

That was the plan. The imponderable was that the most up-to-date pictures had to be sent via satellite from the Stadium to Broadcasting House, edited and given to a suite from where they could be transmitted. The staff operating in the corridor where the edit and intake machines were based were used to tight turn arounds and regarded them as a challenge rather than a problem. Most of them would give Olympic sprinters a run for their money over a three-yard course and drown a town crier with their shouts of 'Gerrout of my f*****g way' as they barrelled through, American-footballer-style, with the videotape to the transmission point. Anybody in their way would be scattered like skittles. No offence meant, none taken. It was a matter of pride that the story made its slot. It almost always did.

All that, however, depended on Ruddock's meeting with the WRU board not lasting much longer than expected. There were no guarantees, it was all in the lap of the gods.

For once they smiled down on us. At about six o'clock a familiar figure walked into the room and sat down in front of a line of microphones and mini-recorders. A week's silence was about to come to an end.

He started to read a prepared statement:

> I've had a meeting today with the Board of the Welsh Rugby Union which has given me a full opportunity to give a detailed and factual account of events over the last few days, which I appreciate.

> I have explained my position and given my personal views in my own words, which I hope has been useful to the board and avoids any further unnecessary speculation or any false impressions, which could undermine my personal position or that of the Board.

It is now a matter for the Welsh Rugby Union Board to consult with the Districts and Constituent Clubs of the WRU and decide on their next steps.

The Board members have been provided with a copy of my statement and copies of other relevant documents, which I hope will help their deliberations without the risk of misinterpretation or confusion as to my exact position.

The most important message I would like to convey to Welsh rugby fans and to the media is to focus their efforts and energy on getting behind Wales for their big match against Ireland.

My message to the team itself is to concentrate on the next game and to carry on the brilliant performance against Scotland. My issues are unimportant and insignificant compared to the challenge they face on the pitch.

I wish them all the luck in the world and I believe they can go on and win all their remaining games.

I would also like to express my thanks for all the messages of support I have received.

I will not be making any further comment at this stage and would appreciate the media's respect for my position in this matter.

Mike Ruddock
21st February 2006, 6.30 p.m.

Well, that was the one-to-one interview out of the window. In fact the sound that greeted the statement was predominantly that of jaws dropping and hitting chests at the sheer banality of what was on offer. Admittedly we hadn't been expecting something on the scale of 'Four score and seven years ago our fathers brought forth on this continent, a new nation, conceived in Liberty, and dedicated to the proposition that all men are created equal', but even if Ruddock's statement had, as was likely, been scrawled on the back of an envelope twixt meeting and press conference, something, *anything*, more profound should have come after a week of silence. Gettysburg it most certainly wasn't.

Still, at least the elements we had wanted were there for us to fill *Wales Today*. They may not have been as dramatic or controversial as we would have liked, but at least we could fill the programme.

There was a final text from Mike to me, before his WRU-issue phone went back to the Union, after I'd made one last plea for an interview on the momentous events of the week: 'No mate it's over to d clubs.'

The day, however, wasn't over yet. It could still end with a ramification that would make the coach's going almost pale into insignificance. It could go out not with the Ruddock statement but with the bang of a mass resignation. Welsh rugby, in the beloved words of the headline writers, was facing meltdown.

Chapter 19

Exterminate

It's 2012. My son and I are in an underground silo, five miles beneath Salt Lake City in Utah. Henry van Statten, a crazed, billionaire – well, if you've got that much money who's going to complain if you're a bit off your rocker? – collector of alien artefacts, receives a visit from a battered police box and a familiar theme tune. Impressed by the visitor's knowledge of things extra-terrestrial, not to mention his vehicle's ability to materialise at will, without so much as a 'by your leave', halfway to the centre of the earth, he takes him to see the 'Metaltron', a creature the billionaire reckons is the last of its kind.

Which indeed it would be if the visitor, otherwise known as the Doctor, had his way. It's a Dalek!

The Doctor is not in conservationist mode. Oblivious to the need to preserve endangered species – and they don't come much more endangered than a tin can with lumps, tethered by straps – he tries to kill it, only to be pulled off by the billionaire's guards.

But where brute force has failed, maybe a little bit of tender, loving care can help. Enter Rose, now recovered from the claustrophobia caused by sharing an 8' x 3' blue box for the last eight trillion miles, who, moved by the Dalek's fate, defies 'Item One' on the time traveller's list of what-not-to-do-on-encountering-strange-alien-life-forms: Do Not Touch. She leans over to stroke its casing.

117

You'd have thought it would have been grateful! But no. Did it use its voice like a rusting gate hinge to say, 'How nice to find someone with a smidgen of human kindness round here. You're an all-round good egg, Rose Tyler.' Did it, heck as like! It did what any ingrate bent on the mass extinction of the human race would do. It stole her DNA.

Well . . . apparently, when you have your DNA pinched you don't know that it's gone – not until the Dalek experiences the same feeling as Popeye swallowing his spinach, breaks free of its ties and, despite the best efforts of a couple of guards emptying their revolvers into it, glides off to do the maximum amount of harm to the maximum amount of people. Surprisingly, the beady eye that closely resembles the plunger from my shower misses the man and the young boy with the ear plugs, sheltering behind the firing guards, as it goes on its way . . . 'Exterminate!' . . . 'Exterminate!' . . .

I was thinking of the afternoon Jamie and I had spent, courtesy of a friend on the production staff, watching the making of the first series of a new *Doctor Who*, as we headed towards the second press conference of the day. The concrete subterranean corridors of the Millennium Stadium, usually the province of the police, stewards and members of the media going to their underground press room – it wouldn't do to have them on show to members of the public and corporate guests – made an ideal location for the raft of sci-fi productions the BBC had brought to Cardiff. If you wanted to create a stand-in for a silo deep below the deserts of Utah, the netherworld of the stadium was the place to do it.

That night though the only alien life forms there were working for television and the tabloids. Mike Ruddock's distinctly underwhelming statement, leaving the matter in the hands of the clubs, was only part of the story. He'd had his say to the WRU board, the board would now have the chance to have their say about what they thought of 'crisis management at its best', in particular the role in it played by chief executive Steve Lewis.

The concrete blocks of the press-conference room ensured it was never the most welcoming of places. With Arsenal playing Real Madrid in a Champions League match on televisions everywhere but there, it seemed less attractive than ever as a place to wait for the latest – and possibly final – chapter in the former coach's drawn-out departure. There was, however, something that struck me as odd. The men most in the firing line were those who'd announced Ruddock's going seven days before: Lewis and chairman David Pickering. That night, though, all the main movers and shakers in Welsh rugby were there, present and correct, waiting for 'Lewering' – as the fans' message boards had christened the duo in a deft combination of their names – to arrive.

Paul Sergeant, the stadium's chief executive, stood at the back wall alongside Rupert Moon from the commercial department. With them were several more members of the stadium staff not normally seen at such events.

A week almost to the minute from the first bombshell, in came Lewering Act Two.

They looked out at the press as the cameras rolled and the mini-recorders waited to capture their words. For the second time that evening, a statement was read. For the second time that evening, no questions were taken. For the second time that evening, it was all about as dramatic as a school concert where year-12's troublemakers have been given the afternoon off.

The WRU board had gone through four hours of interviews, which included those with Ruddock and his solicitor Tim Jones as well as Wales team manager Alan Phillips, Steve Lewis and the WRU's Head of Group Services, Tim Burton. This name had many of those there scratching their heads and asking 'Who the hell is Tim Burton?'

The result of the board's deliberations? David Pickering slowly read out the words which somehow surprised no one . . .

> The Board is satisfied and unanimously supports the actions of its executive staff and in particular Steve Lewis and Head of Group Services, Tim Burton.

> The Board discounted media speculation that senior players had met with the chief executive to discuss Mike Ruddock prior to his resignation.

So it was the media whatdunnit! It had been a very Welsh crisis. Welsh rugby, we'd been telling everyone all week, had been rocked to the core – but who was at fault? Why . . . nobody!

Pickering later added some flesh to the bones of the statement:

> There were some pretty cynical Board members going into the meeting who wanted to ask some hard questions about this whole affair. They needed convincing that the unanimous verdict they had reached on the issue last week [when the story had first broken] was correct in every fashion.

> This time, of course, they had the benefit of hearing directly from Mike Ruddock and his representative. Yet still, and having brought with them the concerns of many of the clubs that they represent, they returned the same unanimous verdict.

> The Board has now heard all the facts from both sides surrounding the contract negotiations the Union was undertaking with Mike Ruddock. In that respect they are very much in the minority in Wales, yet have been able to make a more balanced and non-emotive decision than many.

As far as the WRU Board is concerned a line has now been very firmly drawn underneath this whole process. We will of course be keeping our clubs fully informed and hope to get information to them before the week is out.

But it is now time for Welsh rugby to move on to its next important date – the Six Nations clash with Ireland in Dublin on Sunday.

It was, he reckoned 'a tough day in a tough week for Welsh rugby'. The 'Red Zone Road Show' – so called after the phrase 'entering the red zone', coined by the Welsh players – was now ready to roll, as Lewis and others in the WRU hierarchy prepared to travel from Aberavon to Ammanford, Carmarthen to Colwyn Bay, explaining to all 245 clubs in the various districts of the Union what they had outlined to the board. They would tell them just why they had taken the decisions they had. The meetings would be 'open, honest and frank'; they were also to be 'entirely private and confidential'. The more cynical might have thought the two were mutually exclusive.

'They will be hearing the facts direct from source, so there can be no confusion or misunderstanding based on hearsay. I'm looking forward to getting the truth out there to the people that matter – our members who are the grassroots of Welsh rugby,' said Lewis.

All well and noble. The truth was on its way . . . but would it be 'the truth, the whole truth and nothing but the truth'? The answer to that was, no. Much more had been afoot that day than had been dismissed by a simple press statement.

The actual truth goes something like this.

The WRU had completely underestimated the reaction that was unleashed by the departure of a popular coach so soon after delivering the Grand Slam. Day after day had seen a relentless media battering of those deemed culpable. Countless column inches and interminable television broadcasts had heaped opprobrium on the Union's hierarchy. They had tried damage limitation, bringing in a public relations expert to try to stem the tide of negativity. Journalists – including me – were given individual briefings by officials genuinely nonplussed at why they were being condemned so widely as the bad guys in the whole affair. Nobody it seemed had wanted to print or broadcast the WRU's side, partly because neither Pickering nor Lewis wanted to go public with the issues behind why they had wanted to make Ruddock go before he was ready. Both of them had wanted to respect their former coach's privacy, no matter what it might cost them.

They'd also made an enemy of the *Western Mail*. The Union recognised that and put it down to two things: that they'd spiked the paper's guns when it came to publishing maybe its biggest-ever exclusive, and the fact that Ruddock was on good terms with its rugby writer Andy Howell, who'd been central in its original story of his going. They met with the *Mail*'s editor several times, but it was clear this was an editorial line not for turning.

Steve Lewis, in particular, had become 'public enemy number one', pilloried from just about every quarter. He was the pantomime villain for the press pack and the fans – not helped by his hectoring attitude in interviews – but, more damningly for him, he also began to become a scapegoat for those who professed to be supporting him: the WRU's board. Some of the so-called blazers within the WRU sensed this was the chance to turn on a chief executive who'd gained more enemies than friends in his time at the top table of Welsh rugby. Part of that was the fault of his abrasive and often confrontational style, when he showed little or no patience with the political games they played. He was more interested in getting grassroots rugby in order, for what he considered to be the long-term good of the game.

Lewis wasn't close to many of his colleagues in the day-to-day running of the union, but – like David Moffett before him – he had a respect that was solid and supportive. A lack of finesse occasionally upset people, but – along with his fellow chief executive, Stadium boss Paul Sergeant – he kept the staff onside despite the one-way tide of criticism washing in the WRU's direction. In a way, that helped. It developed a siege mentality, galvanising a workforce that had grown weary and suspicious of what was going on around them. They weren't, however, immune from the rumours and gossip that were everywhere; they heard them and they listened to them. One thing in particular got through to them . . . they were not getting the support they expected from the 'blazers'. The WRU board was keeping its distance.

It was time to close ranks. When Mike Ruddock walked down the ramp towards the Millennium Stadium and his meeting with the board, neither he nor they realised that Welsh rugby was on the brink of open warfare.

The staff had been briefed by Lewis, Sergeant and Tim Burton. Their reading of the situation was that Ruddock was being hung out to dry by the people who should be supporting him. They also knew that Steve Lewis's job was on the line and they came to a decision. If he went, they all went.

Lewis, they reckoned, was being railroaded by a board that put self-preservation above everything. That instinct was about to be put to the test. While the chief executive was putting his case to his peers, the people who were the professional arm of the WRU were holed up in a hospitality suite at the stadium, waiting for the outcome. As one told me, 'We were all fully aware that this was likely to be our last day in their employment. But, such was the immense passion about supporting what was right, we were steadfast behind the cause, so much so that each had spoken to their wives, husbands, boyfriends and girlfriends to tell them that by the end of the day we could well be out of a job.'

Why such a hardline stance? Most of them remembered the gravy train that had existed when the WRU was committee-led. They had no wish to return to what had been. They hadn't been press-ganged: each and every member of the management team had made up his own mind. But, for all of them, the memory of what they called the 'dark days' was too strong to do nothing.

These were not minor personnel of little account. They were highly paid professionals, charged with running every aspect of rugby in Wales from the Stadium to coaches to referees. If they had walked out that night, the game would have been in chaos. Welsh rugby would have been a laughing stock. More than that, the WRU was just achieving some success in restructuring its debt. How would the banks have looked upon the mass resignation of what they saw as a skilled, knowledgeable and respected team? They'd grown used to working with them, they trusted them. If they'd quit that night the financial plight of the WRU would have suffered a setback it could have taken years to recover from.

Only one board member was aware of the sub-plot and its possible backlash: the WRU chairman David Pickering. The level of emotion and commitment among his staff took him by surprise and left him with a massive dilemma: how could a multi-million-pound business function with no management? As it was, he didn't have to find a solution because the board backed Lewis. However, the whole play-within-a-play was the answer to the question of why there was such a delay between Ruddock's statement to the press and the response from Pickering and Lewis. It seems Pickering in particular had other business. Like stemming a revolt. He went to the staff, to where the entire management team were holed up. It was a clever move. It was a show of strength, a sign that the board had to act fast to regain control and avoid the tail wagging the dog. He had learned much about the art of self-preservation.

It stood him in good stead a couple of months later, when an EGM called by a handful of clubs failed in a vote of no confidence, but succeeded in having the decision – made by David Moffett when he stepped down – to have two chief executives in charge of Welsh rugby deemed unconstitutional. This paved the way for the autumn installation of a New Group Chief Executive: Roger Lewis, a man who had been with Pickering when he climbed Mount Kilimanjaro for charity. It also marked the beginning of the end for both Steve Lewis and Paul Sergeant. A week before Christmas 2006, Roger Lewis called a press conference to announce that Steve Lewis and Sergeant were on their way. It was couched in the usual management speak . . . mutual consent, off to meet new challenges, all predictable stuff.

'So, Roger,' I asked in a question that must have been inspired by the time of year, '. . . are you telling us we've finally found two turkeys who really are willing to vote for Christmas?'

Paul Sergeant, who was soon to be given the MBE, smiled. Roger Lewis's answer was lost in the convoluted lay-preacher's language for which he's become known.

The cards of Steve Lewis and Paul Sergeant had inevitably been marked when they stood up to the board that dramatic day when Ruddockgate was at its height. This time there was no one to save them.

Chapter 20

Mr Anon

The delivery of the post within BBC Wales is not the best. It's a big place. There are too many spots where it can be dropped off by the people from the post room and left to gather dust. Many is the time I have had to write shame-faced to the organisers of various charities to apologise for ignoring their pleas for a personal appearance. Turning up to play Santa Claus in the middle of March is probably not what they have in mind when they ask you at the end of October if you would don the red coat and white whiskers.

Strangely, whenever a listener wrote to tell me how much he/she enjoyed my show, and could I play Kiri Te Kanawa singing 'Bailero' from *Songs of the Auvergne*, it was always on time. It was only when I sent the request on to its rightful recipient, the opera singer Beverley Humphreys, who shared a building and an employer with me, but not a Christian name and an identically spelled surname, that it became late.

Even by BBC standards, the letter I picked out of an in-tray in the newsroom in the bright midsummer of 2007 was spectacularly tardy. It was dated 17/02/2006, well over a year before. '*Dear Mr Humphries*,' it said. (Well, at least it didn't go to Beverley.) '*Re your interview with the CEO, WRU Steve Lewis. It provokes me to send you important background details concerning Mike Ruddock's dismissal. I must apologise for not giving my name or address but it is to ensure that anything I write could never be traced back to me. I am too close to the WRU administration though I am retired. I hope you will accept this.'*

Normally I wouldn't. If someone could not trust me enough as a journalist to give me information on an off-the-record basis, knowing that I would protect the source it had come from, then I could not trust information supplied without a name. In this case though, so much had been said and written about 'Ruddockgate' in the sixteen months between the letter being sent and my opening it that normal rules didn't apply. It also sums up pretty accurately what I believe caused Mike Ruddock to jump ship in the middle of the 2006 Six Nations.

Let's piece it all together.

> *As you know Mike Ruddock was appointed coach instead of the firm favourite Gareth Jenkins. The latter was unacceptable because as head coach he wanted (demanded) full autonomy/ control over the immediate coaching team. He wanted this incorporated in his job description and in those of the team manager and skills coach. The WRU declined this and offered the post to Mike Ruddock who accepted the terms.*

Hindsight, with the twenty/twenty vision that comes with it, meant you couldn't argue with what Mr Anonymous of Anonymous-shire had written. When Gareth Jenkins lost out to Ruddock, with every publication from the *Western Mail* down ready to anoint Jenkins as the new coach in the spring of 2004, a presentation he'd given to the WRU outlining his vision for the way Welsh rugby should be run was considered the main reason why he didn't get the job. It wasn't because the case he outlined was slip-shod or badly thought out, it was because it put too much control in the hands of the man who would be coach. The WRU is not a body to cede the power it has easily.

Ruddock inherited the back-up staff previous coach Steve Hansen, and before him Graham Henry, had bequeathed. Scott

Johnson was the skills coach, Andrew Hore looked after the conditioning of the team while Alan Phillips acted as the team manager. Ruddock decided against any great reorganisation.

'I do not regret not insisting on my own coaching team because I liked the way Wales played in the World Cup and the WRU wanted minimum disruption,' he said in the 2008 book, *Resurrection Men*. 'I was used to coming into fairly settled environments and working with coaches I had never teamed up with before, notably with Wales A, Ireland A and Ireland where I worked for a short time with Brian Ashton and Warren Gatland . . . I only brought in Clive Griffiths and that was because defence was an area we needed to improve on.'

This sowed the seeds for dissent. Ruddock reckons his appointment of the former Wales rugby league coach caused a split in the Welsh camp, with the players torn between Ruddock and the assistant he'd inherited from Steve Hansen, Scott Johnson:

'What I didn't appreciate at the time was the extent of the resentment some of my management team felt towards Clive after his time with Wales between 2001 and 2003,' said Ruddock. 'He had been moved on to the Dragons after the World Cup because the Welsh management group at the time did not want to work with him. I'm not sure why Clive and some of the other members of the coaching team had fallen out previously, but even though Clive and I tried hard to make things work, there was just too much of a divide.'

It was all very different when Gareth Jenkins's much delayed rise to the top happened a couple of years later. He was helped by the fact that Johnson and Hore had headed back down-under to Australia and New Zealand respectively to take up other jobs, but in came his own rookie back-up team of Nigel Davies, Rowland Phillips, Robin McBryde and Neil Jenkins. Clive Griffiths was off to Doncaster, en route to jumping on the back of the tandem again with Ruddock at Guinness Premiership club Worcester, while Phillips proved to be the great survivor in staying on as team manager.

Ironically both paths would prove equally dangerous. Ruddock's because he was undermined by too much experience; Jenkins's because he was let down by too little experience.

The letter went on . . .

> *After two years in that post, he* [Ruddock] *has come to realise that Gareth Jenkins was right. He is shackled by his lack of control over Alan Phillips and Scott Johnson who can attend meetings etc. when, and if, they like, and bypass the head coach.*

What he wrote was uncannily borne out by Ruddock's own words a few years later:

> Would I have done anything differently? I don't regret taking the job and no one can expunge the 2005 Grand Slam from the records. But perhaps it would have been better if I'd had my own coaching team given that I had underestimated the ill-feeling in the coaching group that my bringing back Clive, who had been moved on by my predecessor Steve Hansen after the World Cup, provoked.
>
> To this day I don't understand why there was such ill feeling towards him.
>
> I don't regret not being stricter or more of a disciplinarian. I felt that to get the best out of the players they needed to play and train in a more relaxed manner. I wanted a greater emphasis on them being able to express themselves, rather than being directed by an iron fist and being heavily programmed each step of the way; getting away from the Jail of Glamorgan mentality if you like.
>
> To some it seemed to be undermining what Steve Hansen had developed but I never meant it to be interpreted that way. Looking back, I came into a settled

management environment and brought in only Clive, a man whose coaching ability I rate very highly. For some reason Clive's arrival split the management team and because of my friendship with Clive I think some always saw me as an outsider; ultimately you are not going to get anywhere if you are divided.

The weight of trying to keep everything and everyone together became a major difficulty and because of that the players did not see the best of me in 2006.

My letter writer was now in full flow:

Mike Ruddock's contract problem <u>*is not about money as reported, but is one of control*</u> [He obviously didn't want me missing the point]. *He wanted this put in his new contract, as Gareth Jenkins wanted. The WRU typically have dragged their feet for much of the past six months hoping that Mike Ruddock would give in and sign the contract given him. In that they completely misjudged the man. Undoubtedly, Mike R. now realises the demands placed on him and his family life as head coach which following his disenchantment over his contract terms reminded him what was most important in his life.*

Ah . . . the contract. It was an accident waiting to happen. That much is acknowledged by a source even closer to events than my anonymous letter writer. I was told:

The whole Mike Ruddock saga started months before the now legendary Valentine's Day massacre when the WRU and Mike Ruddock failed to agree terms for a new contract. Why the two main protagonists Steve Lewis and Mike Ruddock never got their heads together to thrash out the key terms themselves, God only knows. As it was, the WRU couldn't concede on key issues because it had to consider the business as an entirety and these issues were incredibly niggly. So, as we know, before the start of the Six Nations it was agreed to park negotiations until after the conclusion of the tournament.

Those negotiations of course would never be completed.

My letter writer was not finished.

> *Returning to Steve Lewis.* [How could we have forgotten him?] *As you realise one has to ask him carefully phrased questions so he cannot avoid the question.* [Ah, memories of 'Let me finish, Bob!' came flooding back.] *A question I would like to pose to him in public would be, 'Why did you have an informal meeting at a gathering of some of the Wales team, held before the England v Wales game last month, at the Monks' Castle (Castell y Mynach) public house?'*

'Questions about players' insurance and issues about Ruddock's coaching which Lewis had point-blank refused to discuss' would have been the public answer to that. But my contact obviously suspected there was more to it. And I think he was right, a fact confirmed to me later:

> It wasn't a happy camp, especially after the mauling by England at Twickenham and there were a few issues with some of the players who decided to defy the coaches' curfew that night and hit the town. A few days later, captain Gareth Thomas asked to meet Steve Lewis privately with a few other senior members of the squad as the whole relationship between the players and some members of the coaching team was at breaking point.

The meeting began in a pub close to the Vale [the Castell y Mynach, just as the letter said] but with so many high-profile people involved they had to move to the Miskin Manor [a nearby country hotel] for a bit of privacy. The meeting was never minuted and was always said to be about insurance issues and contracts but everyone knows there was much more discussed, namely how the coach had lost the dressing room and the players were on the brink of mutiny.

For me that was game, set and match when it came to the veracity of my anonymous correspondent. With a parting shot at another senior player whom he accused of being the 'principal stirrer', he signed off his letter with the guarantee that 'all the above is completely accurate and true. I would ask you to believe that'.

Mr Anon, I do. But then I'm always willing to be flattered by being called a reporter in which someone has full confidence!

Chapter 21

'Send Three and Fourpence'

It might not be the pinnacle of investigative journalism to quote from an unsigned letter, but I do because Mr Anon, formerly of the WRU, hits almost all the right notes. His assertions, written at the height of the storm, were subsequently confirmed in the calmer months that followed by a variety of sources, in particular by the one I've quoted in confidence, who I trust implicitly. Also, once the hysteria had died, once the conspiracy theorists had sated themselves on a feast of delicacies, other less dramatic postings started to appear on the rugby message boards, which, to the chagrin of many journalists, often lead the way when it comes to breaking news or influencing opinion.

Sometimes, however, they can be dangerous. The old chestnut of the word-of-mouth relaying of the instruction, 'Send re-inforcements, we're going to advance', only for it to become on the sixth retelling, 'Send three and fourpence, we're going to a dance' presents one problem. A perfectly accurate statement at the top of a website thread can be corrupted out of all recognition by the time it reaches a few readers further down. He takes it as gospel and a new urban myth, or something more sinister, is born.

A totally fallacious story can be posted which, because it's there in print, is accepted as fair and accurate. One football message board in South Wales, which often branches out of matters sporting into the political arena, spoke breathlessly about how studies on the Holocaust were to be suspended because of pressure from the Muslim lobby in Britain. Right-wing elements leapt into the fray, not to check its veracity but to heap abuse on the crazy political correctness of modern-day society. It was only when a measured response from someone who actually knew the subject he was talking about poured scorn on the original premiss, that people calmed down. Was it too late by then though? Had other posters gone on to other websites and other threads to promulgate the same bilge? Was it on its way to becoming accepted cyber-fact? Who knows?

They also take themselves too seriously. A failing football manager or rugby coach can attract stinging criticism from a fan who maybe has an agenda or simply doesn't like the way his target smiles in the press conferences he sees him in on the television. A couple more like-minded souls join in the pouring of vitriol, a few more add their dollop of abuse, and suddenly the little ball of ice that broke off the glacier at the top of the mountain has become an avalanche that engulfs the valley. The fact that it is only a handful of people is irrelevant as they convince themselves they wield power out of all proportion to their number. A newspaper might run an opinion completely contrary to them, one shared by the vast majority of the club's support, but, hey, these are the elite among fans, the manipulators at the top of their game.

Twenty-first century technology, then, can have its downside – but treated with caution the message boards can be a rich seam of information. After all, why not? Just as for my letter writer, there is a veil of anonymity. That message-board posting could be by the best friend of the character at the centre of the story, or by the wife of the character at the centre of the story . . . hell, it could be by the character at the centre of the story himself. If you want to put right a false impression, what's wrong with using a message board to do so, especially when the media-savvy among the posters know there is a good chance that what they say will be picked up by the mainstream local press – if that's not a contradiction in terms – to be spread over a much wider audience. Is that any worse than a bona-fide journalist basing his facts on the time-honoured, un-named 'source close to the club'?

Some posters on certain sites get reputations as responsible and reliable. Others come up with rumours destined to remain unsub-stantiated for ever and a day. So, when one of the regular posters on the respected Gwlad site weighed in with the suggestion that in Mike Ruddock's case: '"Player power" is a major red herring. Hopefully those who lambasted the players without evidence will hang their heads in shame. Also, the idea that [Scott] Johnson had anything to do with Ruddock's departure is totally untrue. Family reasons and contractual wranglings are the reasons, nothing more conspiratorial or underhand than that', you take notice.

Everyone had an opinion and everyone wanted to voice it through whatever medium was available. A picture is built up until it's finally ready for its unveiling.

So why did Mike Ruddock leave? Until recently, he's remained quiet after he met with the WRU the week after his going. He received a pay-off – though not the hundreds of thousands of pounds bandied around by those who claimed to be in the know – and part of that was to guarantee his confidentiality. Sure enough, during his time coaching first home-town club Mumbles in the lower reaches of the Welsh leagues, then Worcester in the Guinness Premiership, he's never gone into detail over his departure. Occasionally, the odd tit-bit has been dropped to add more evidence to the various theories. When the BBC asked him for his reaction to the second Grand Slam in four seasons, inspired by a coaching team of Warren Gatland, Shaun Edwards and Rob Howley, his reaction was telling: 'What could create difficulty is if it breaks up from within and the coaches don't pull together. That certainly happened in 2005.'

Gatland, like Gareth Jenkins before him, had the pick of his own back-room staff. Ruddock didn't have that luxury. I felt he was perturbed by the closer bond that his senior players had with his assistant Scott Johnson than with him. Then again, it would have been naive to expect anything else. The NCO is always closer to the troops than the commanding officer – he can provide the shoulder to cry on, the outlet for the venting of frustrations or grievances. The ultimate responsibility is not his. He can afford to play 'good cop'.

In each of Mike Ruddock's squads there would be thirty or so driven individuals. They were grateful to the head coach for their inclusion, but each would have had his own agenda. Some would have liked Ruddock, others would have tolerated him, a few might have been dismissive of him. Bizarrely, the man on the back of the number-seven bus looks at a squad and presumes, because it is playing under the banner of Wales, that its members are all pulling in the same direction. That, too, is naive.

Before the British Lions left for their ill-fated tour to New Zealand in 2005, I interviewed Martyn Williams and Shane Williams live on *Wales Today*. 'Of course you'll want the Lions to win every game they play,' I said, 'but what about those rivals for positions in the test team, will you want them to do just a little less well than the rest of the side?' Now, Martyn and Shane are too wily and experienced to be caught off guard by any attempt to bush-whack, and came out with the diplomatic responses you'd have expected of them . . . how they'd be busting a gut to make the test line-up, but if the other guy was better than them on the day and it worked out the best for the Lions, well, that's the way it is.

Until the camera was switched off. 'Bloody 'ell, Bob . . . what sort of a question was that? What do you expect us to say . . . that we want him to play like a three-legged dog?'

The inference was clear. Of course, they wanted him to play like a three-legged dog! Just so long as the Lions won too!

We shouldn't expect anything different. Players are not

automatons, they have the same ambitions and self-interests as any other person. They respect some people more than others. Gareth Thomas went on record as supporting Ireland against Wales as a means to an end: the end of Graham Henry. One top player was, privately, openly scornful to me about the Gareth Jenkins/Nigel Davies partnership taking over Wales. For him it was a disaster in waiting. Read his quotes in the newspapers and the second coming would have paled into insignificance compared to the pair from the Scarlets.

For six weeks in the spring of 2005, however, everyone was pulling together. Those on the outside, who thought privately they should be in the squad instead of X or Y or Z, kept their counsel. There was no market for the mutterings of the disgruntled as win followed win. And on a magical March afternoon it came to glorious fruition. The smiles, the hugs, the celebrations, the drinks, the hangovers, were all shared, the camaraderie was genuine – but these were still different men with different agendas, and for many of them Johnson was their man rather than Ruddock.

Mike knew that, and in the immediate aftermath of his going Scott Johnson and his chief lieutenants among the players were hardly top of the Christmas card list in the Ruddock household. Even before that, however, during the autumn internationals – when results and performances against the All Blacks, where they were on the wrong end of a 41–3 hammering, the Springboks who beat them 33–16 and Fiji where a late drop goal helped them scrape home by a single point in an 11–10 win, hardly mirrored the derring-do of the previous spring – Ruddock was twice on the edge of stepping down.

Conflict in the camp there was, then, with the players much more culpable than their captain has painted. Also, the contract was an issue. Ruddock and his lawyer did ask for extra clauses to be put into it, safeguarding his position. Some of the clauses Ruddock wanted about his terms and conditions, the WRU considered unworkable. Despite that Grand Slam success, he did feel he was on trial virtually game by game, especially when the Welsh Rugby Union suspended negotiations for the period of the Six Nations.

And Ruddock is a family man. The pressure-cooker world that goes with being Wales's rugby coach may have been part of the territory for *him*, but when it spilled over on to his children, it was never a situation he was going to be easy with. The ingredients were there. Mix them together, and the cocktail was powerful enough to send Welsh rugby into that crazy tail-spin.

You could choose the melodramatic to describe Mike Ruddock's going. Words like 'betrayal' and 'disloyalty' tug at the emotions – but they would also be overstating it. Mike Ruddock, for a combination of the factors, believed it was time to go – though the time he thought was right was the end of the Six Nations not mid-way through. The WRU was caught unawares by his plans to reveal his decision in the morning newspapers. Their macho response may have been what they considered 'crisis management at its best', but it led to events spiralling out of control and becoming the conspiracy theorists' delight.

It was an oddly Welsh affair!

Chapter 22

'My Son . . . Bridgend'

There was one bizarre postscript to the Ruddock affair. The whole business could have played out eight years earlier.

8.5.98 *Kevin Bowring Goes*
For once I was not there to read the last rites on another coaching casualty. My mother-in-law had died peacefully twelve thousand miles away in tropical Australia two days before, leaving me to look after my children while my wife made a visit to Cairns for the funeral. When the former schoolmaster at Clifton College called time on his 29-game spell in charge of Wales, I was busy arranging flights and ferrying her to Heathrow. Surprise, though, was not an emotion that came immediately to mind when I learned that the Welsh Rugby Union had turned down Kevin Bowring's demands for increased powers in the job – powers he felt were needed to move Wales up from the distinctly mediocre level they'd lived at during his time in charge – and that he'd fallen on his sword.

Bowring had never quite been able to leave his old profession behind. Perhaps he was never allowed to. There was a distinctly frosty response when he was asked, after an exhaustive – not to mention, exhausting – press debrief on his first season in charge, how he would rate himself: six out of ten, or seven out of ten. His strangely piercing eyes seemed to yearn for the opportunity to send this particular, impertinent jackanapes to the headmaster's office for the sort of short sharp retribution that wouldn't be popular with the 'say no to corporal punishment' brigade.

I did have one favourite memory from the three years when he was in the role, one that had little to do with events on the pitch and everything to do with an exchange with one of the great characters the game of rugby has thrown up. Phil Kingsley Jones played in the seventies for Ebbw Vale and Abertillery, two prosaic Gwent rugby clubs where locals tend to think 'charisma' is December the 25th. But this was one Jones the others couldn't keep up with. When he wasn't stepping out on the muddied turf of Eugene Cross Park, he was treading the boards as a stand-up comedian. He won the London Palladium's *Search for a Star* and a heat of *New Faces* before heading off to New Zealand, where he encountered the physical phenomenon that was Jonah Lomu and became his manager. It must have been the way he told them!

Working with the likes of Lionel Richie, Neil Sedaka and Cliff Richards and the Shadows might not have seemed the logical preparation for looking after the world's most famous rugby player, but Phil Kingsley Jones was a twentieth-century incarnation of 'renaissance man'. We met shortly after the 1995 World Cup in South Africa that had etched the name of Lomu on rugby's, and in particular England wing Tony Underwood's, psyche. He was back in Blaina visiting his son, also called – with a lack of originality you would not have usually associated with Kingsley senior – er, Kingsley. If that was a subtle challenge to step out of his shadow – a 'boy named Sue' moment – it worked. Kingsley Junior went on to captain Wales, coach Sale and develop a nifty stand-up routine of his own.

A stage background, where dealing with hecklers is a key part of the entertainer's CV, made Phil one of sharpest interviewees you could have. You'd serve the question, he'd belt the answer back and before you knew it the umpire was saying, 'Game, set and match, Jones' – except for one occasion when it was not Phil Kingsley Jones, comedian, not Phil Kingsley Jones, Lomu's mentor, but Phil Kingsley Jones, coach of the 1997 Tongan rugby tourists. Did I mention his roles were many?

We'd already developed a relationship that had gone beyond the professional. We'd become friends. When he brought Jonah Lomu back to visit his home and see the part of the world Alexander Cordell had made famous in his book, *Rape of the Fair Country*, Phil had arranged for me to do a broadcast with the biggest name in the sport from his daughter's front room. It was a surreal moment, sitting in a small Valleys house with the neighbourhood children banging on the windows, talking live to probably the only rugby player to merit the label 'superstar'. It was a perfect example of how forging friendships is essential to a journalist's work. No relationship, no 'exclusive' interview.

There was no Jonah Lomu to bolster the fiercely proud Tongan team, but that hadn't stopped them recording a famous win over Bridgend. I interviewed Phil live on *Grandstand* before his South Pacific Islanders took on Wales at a wet St Helen's ground in Swansea on a dank November afternoon. He was telling me of the emotions that his side had felt, coming out on top against one of the traditional powerhouses of Welsh club rugby.

'You know, Bob, when our hooker came off the field, he could celebrate not one great moment, but two, because there was a message in the dressing room from his wife to tell him that she had just given birth to the baby they were expecting. He had his first-born son, which for someone from Tonga – maybe even more so than for those in many other parts of the world – is a quite tremendous moment. He knew just how to mark both events. '"Phil," he said to me, "I know now what to call my son. To remember this day and our triumph on the rugby field, I am going to call my son . . . Bridgend!"'

Something clicked. It didn't often when I was doing a pre-match interview.

'Well, Phil,' I said, 'I suppose they can both count themselves lucky you weren't playing Nantyfyllon . . .'

To be fair, the BBC didn't seem to mind the sight of Tonga's coach creasing up. I felt rather proud of myself.

Sadly for Phil's Tonga and Bridgend's new dad, Kevin Bowring's Wales won that game 46–12.

After that, for Bowring it was mainly downhill, downhill and down the motorway. For the first time in its hundred-years-and-more history, the spiritual home of Welsh rugby went on the road. The Cardiff Arms Park that had become the National Stadium was now a building site. The bulldozers, the wreckers and General Norman Schwarzkopf, otherwise known as 'Stormin' Norman' from Operation Desert Storm, had moved in. He probably soon decided that the first invasion of Iraq was a mere gambol in the park compared with his new troubleshooting role in the construction of the new Millennium Stadium, but while the building went on, the new home to the Wales rugby team was the world-famous Wembley.

World-famous it might have been, but it was also tired and crumbling. Going there was like a first visit to a really elderly relative you'd only ever seen in pictures of in his middle age. The features were familiar but the reality was very different. Television had shown Wembley Way and the twin towers, but it hadn't shown what time had done to it since those grainy black-and-white pictures of the 1923 version of 'health and safety' – having the couple of thousand workmen who'd laboured on the new stadium jump up and down in unison in the new stands, to make sure they didn't fall down!

They'd survived the eighty-four intervening years, but only just. As we filmed our preview of the first Welsh rugby game there, against New Zealand, a big screen played pictures of the great Wembley moments of the past: the sound of the crowd celebrating the 1966 World Cup win, 'They think it's all over' and all that. It was meant to raise the hairs on the back of your neck. It served only to remind you that this was a mausoleum well beyond its sell-by date. The local Greyhound pub might have brought in Brains Beers to make the travelling fans feel at home, but this was an alien place.

It showed on the converted rugby field. A Wales team captained by Gwyn Jones, just weeks away from the catastrophic neck injury that would end his playing career for ever, was outplayed by the All Blacks. Christian Cullen scored tries for fun for New Zealand, Nigel Walker scored one for luck for Wales. Not that luck was much of a travelling companion when it came to trips to London that season. Twickenham saw a record 60–26 walloping by England to set the Five Nations Championship off to a dismal start, while it had an equally miserable conclusion when a France side, inspired by the mercurial Thomas Castagneide, again broke the half-century and kept Wales pointless in a 51–0 rout back at Wembley. I stood gloomily behind the Welsh posts, waiting for the referee to bring a merciful end to the trouncing and for the part of post-match interviewing I didn't like.

5.4.98 *Wales v France*

Wales hadn't finished bottom of the championship, there was no whitewash or wooden spoon to bemoan – wins over Scotland and Ireland made sure of that – but the manner of the Wales team's capitulation against France meant the 'r' word, 'resignation', would have to be brought out again. The role of the after-the-game interviewer is to ask the questions the fan would pose if he or she were in that position. Many are banal, some are incisive, others are intrusive. And it was strange how they went in cycles. A Welsh coach is appointed. Cue the obvious: 'How delighted are you?', 'What are you going to bring to the job?' The Welsh coach has some success. Time for the easy interrogation: 'Good start to your career in charge, but how are you going to build on it?' The Welsh coach has a result like a 51–0 beating, where they were lucky to get nil. No more Mr Nice Guy: 'So do you think you've taken the team as far as you can? Isn't it time for you to step down.'

It's what the fans are talking about in the pubs around Wembley and at home, so it's what you have to ask. You are those fans *in absentia* . . . but it doesn't mean you have to like it. Many of my colleagues seem to relish the confrontation, they gnaw away at their bone like a big cat that's finally brought down the antelope it was stalking. I'm never quite sure what they expect their prey to say . . . 'Gosh, you're absolutely right! I was amazed when they gave me the job, I was even more amazed when the team won a game doing what I told them to do, and I'm completely dumbfounded that anyone could think a failure like me deserves to stay in the job. Quick, hand me that sword so I can fall on it!'

They don't, of course. I had a grudging admiration for Mike Smith, the Wales football manager thrown into the deep end for a second spell in charge after John Toshack walked out of the job. They say never go back. It was advice Smith should have heeded. He was not an archetypal football manager. Rather than rant or rave, he cultivated a rather cerebral demeanour, giving his interviews in the manner of a well-spoken schoolmaster discussing a bright pupil's GCSE results. Until, that is, Bulgaria came to Cardiff in 1994, for a vital qualifying game during Wales's bid to reach Euro '96 which would be held just over the border in England. Extra incentive if ever it were needed. Bulgaria won 3–0, leaving me to ask the inevitable. I couched it as unprovocatively as possible: 'Mike, you've had a bad result here, do you really want to put up with all the pressure that comes with the job?'

He looked at me as if I were responsible for a bad smell that was coming from the sole of his shoe. 'I've just come straight from the touchline where my team's had a very disappointing result, and you've got the ill-grace to ask me that!' Or, at least, that was the gist of what he said. I didn't have the ill-grace to ask him anything else.

I didn't have the chance. He turned on his heel and left me, not to mention the camera now focused on a blank stadium wall. The director cut back to the studio where the presenter Alan Wilkins and the pundit didn't pick up with a 'Bob Humphrys with the tough questions there', but pondered on the manners of the reporter who'd driven a previously unemotional man to reveal his feelings in so spectacular a way. They weren't the only ones. The BBC's head of English language programmes had similar concerns the following day. So much for supporting your staff doing their job without fear or favour, I thought.

Nowadays, a question like that is so commonplace as to be completely unremarkable. I'd probably be rebuked for not running after the hapless Smith shouting, 'So I'll take it that's a "Yes" shall I, Mike? . . . you will be resigning in the morning?' But I rather admired the man for doing what he did. I always regretted being expected to ask a question that, no matter how hard-skinned the image the coach in question might portray, would inevitably hurt. It would hurt him because he would know he was on his way to a P45, it would hurt his family, it would hurt his friends. Also, and not to the same extent admittedly, it would hurt me because I recognised that I was interviewing a human being, not a job title.

Maybe I shouldn't have felt so guilty – not when Robert Howley, with his 'towel still wet in his bag', was being confronted by a member of the WRU committee and asked whether Kevin Bowring had a future as a national coach. The scrum half put two and two together, made four, and realised that Bowring's position had already been discussed and his time was up.

'Hindsight is a wonderful thing,' wrote Howley in his auto-biography, 'but if you had asked the players at that time whether a new face would change the fortunes of the side, the answer would have been "no". We were an average side who failed to perform on two separate occasions. It was as simple as that. Kevin was a top coach, a top person and he had principles. In the end he walked away and maintained his dignity. To Kevin, that mattered more than anything else.'

I can't remember what Kevin Bowring said when I asked him about his precarious future as Welsh rugby coach. Whatever it was, he maintained the dignity that Howley talked about and didn't leave me looking at a blank wall in the tunnel of Wembley Stadium. The coaches had probably got better at playing the game too. They knew they were giving us the story. They were also buying themselves time by inviting their employers to step in and give them their backing. Or not.

I do remember it was the last time I interviewed him. A month later he was gone. Given his current low-profile but highly-regarded role in the English rugby football union's coaching set-up, it was a wise move.

Wales, though, were in the market for a new coach, and one man emerged as favourite. He'd proved his credentials, not just in Welsh club rugby with Swansea, but over the Irish Sea in the province of Leinster, where he'd unearthed the precocious talent of Brian O'Driscoll. Mike Ruddock, it seemed, was about to be announced as Bowring's successor.

We had a bizarre conversation on the phone, where I knew that he knew that I knew, and he knew that I knew that he knew, but neither of us could come out and say what we knew.

'Hi Mike . . . I hear there could be some good news coming out soon.'

'What's that, Bob?'

'Oh, something like you might be coming back to Wales.'

'I often come back to Wales, Bob.'

'Yeah, but not for an ice cream in Mumbles, Mike, for something more . . . er permanent.'

'Lots of things more permanent than ice cream, Bob.'

'Well, let's say you did come back, how would you fancy a pint in the BBC Club?'

'Always fancy a pint, Bob.'

'And we could always do an interview first about why you'd come back . . . always assuming you had of course.'

'I suppose we could.'

'See you tomorrow then . . . if you're back.'

'Fine . . . if I'm back.'

I then had a pint with Vernon Pugh. He wasn't the most powerful man in world rugby for nothing. I mentioned the coach-in-waiting.

'I wouldn't be too sure about that, if I were you. It could be that we're going to be looking rather further afield.'

It was as good as saying, What you think is going to happen, ain't!

Mike Ruddock would be back . . . but it wouldn't be for a few years yet.

Chapter 23

The Sound of Sirens

While the Welsh Rugby Union was scouring the world off the pitch for a new coach, on it the Welsh rugby team was being scarred – for some of their players irrevocably – on a mid-winter South African afternoon in Pretoria. I wasn't there. I was in the *Wales Today* office in Cardiff, waiting to do a report on the game using the pictures going out live on Sky Sports. I can't say I minded being an absentee reporter. Three years earlier, the 1995 World Cup had given me as much insight into South Africa as I needed to last me for the time being.

It had not been the best of trips, with Wales's inglorious exit before the quarter-finals at least providing the opportunity to head home sooner rather than later. If a trip to Bradford, Sheffield and Leeds wouldn't provide the ultimate vision of ye olde picturesque England, or Wrexham, Mold and Kinmel Bay take lead billing in the essential guide to Wales, then Bloemfontain, Johannesburg and Pretoria would probably not top the list of must-go places for those visiting South Africa.

Bloemfontain, memorably described as a one-horse town without the horse, provided all the allure of an English new town with bluer skies, while Johannesburg was the cutting edge in cutting edges, mainly those in various switchblades. With uncommon BBC largesse, my Welsh-language colleague and I had been booked into a five-star hotel. At least, it had been a five-star hotel. The owners had spent millions of rands on whatever comprises the opposite of improvements. There was nothing wrong with the fabric of the building, everything wrong with a neighbourhood that had once been the height of chic but was now the pinnacle of crime.

We should have suspected something when we drove there for the first time. I was behind the wheel, my colleague was navigating from the street map.

'Next turning on the left,' he said.

'What? That left? The left with the security guard in a box on the corner?'

'That's the one.'

'Left it is then.'

'Now we should see the car park over on the right.'

'You mean the car park with the armed policeman sitting outside what looks like another guard box?'

'Must be . . . don't see another car park.'

We took our cases from the car and walked towards the hotel lobby, delayed only by another checkpoint with its armed guards patrolling the entrance. Check-in was straightforward, navigating the small arms of the final thick-set bruiser by the lifts less so.

'Think they're trying to tell us something?'

'Whatever it is, I don't think we want to know . . .'

Buying a newspaper posed a logistical problem, mainly in the wait for the gun-toting escort needed to take you over the road to the nearest shop. Still, when we eventually made our escape, with a degree of difficulty that would have had the inmates of Colditz sympathising, the security issue at least made an interesting film. The Johannesburg police chief happily pointed not to *Crimewatch* but to a crime clock that showed around 5,000 murders being committed in the Gauteng province of Jo'burg and Pretoria every year, while the hotel's head of security (which presumably left him in charge of something the size of a small army) took us on the roof to tell with disturbing relish how at least three people had been shot dead within a hundred yards of the building in the few days we'd been staying there. Somehow, I can't listen to a car's backfire with the same sangfroid as before.

We quickly learned the city's take on the Green Cross code – never stop the vehicle lest a crazed car-jacker leaps in with intentions other than describing the best way to the local super-market – while those who lived there, without exception, had a tale to tell of the crime visited either on them or those they knew. The BBC correspondent matter-of-factly spoke of the two fathers in his child's small school class who'd been shot dead, the girl from SABC recounted the break-in and kidnapping at her flat, and another BBC man never made our leaving drinks. His house had been robbed.

A trip to Soweto with the Welsh team was uplifting in the wide-eyed joy of the young kids playing uninhibitedly with a rugby ball, yet depressing in the motorcade of armed vehicles that sped us into the sprawling township. It was all done, I broadcast at the time, adapting that magnificent Simon and Garfunkel song, with the sound of sirens . . .

And the violence wasn't confined to the cities. It was there on the rugby field too. This time, though, it was legitimate.

27.6.98 *Wales v S. Africa*

The Welsh players could have been excused for saying, 'Told you so!' They reckoned that after the British Lions tour the year previously, a hectic domestic season, and with a World Cup looming on the horizon in 1999, it was a perfect opportunity for the WRU to say 'Thanks but no thanks' to the trip to the southern hemisphere. They could have blamed an injury list of unprecedented proportions. Skipper Rob Howley said as much in a controversial article in the *Wales on Sunday* only to be loudly lambasted for his temerity.

It didn't help that — not for the last time — they were close to refusing to get on the bus to go to the airport. Money had raised its head once again. Why should they put their bodies and reputations on the line for £4,000 (if they were lucky and an unlikely string of results went their way), while the English players were getting three times that for their trip to Australia?

Four thousand might as well have been forty thousand, anyway. The way they played in warm-up matches against the likes of the Emerging Springboks and Natal made sure that any prospect of picking up their maximum bonuses was about as likely as the local fans giving up biltong for Lent.

Pundit Jonathan Davies reckoned Wales would be lucky to keep the score down to about 70 when he bumped into the by-now injured Howley before kick-off, and for once in his life he was being conservative. Back in Cardiff, I tried to stave off the risk of writer's cramp as I attempted to keep up with listing the South African try scorers. It wasn't easy. That part of the world is not known for its egalitarian outlook. If it had been, it could have shared out the tries one apiece to each of the starting line-up and still have one left over for a replacement. Sixteen they scored in all, leaving a crowd of forty thousand predominantly Afrikaners baying for the one last score that could have them applauding the century and a possible declaration. They would have got it too, if the Springbok forward Naka Drotske had not revealed his humanitarian streak by dropping the ball as the hundred points mark beckoned. A final score of 96–13 made that 51–0 in Wembley look almost respectable.

There is an accord between the major broadcasters that allows the companies who don't own the rights to sporting events to use pictures on their news programmes once they have been shown by the rights-holder. In the southern hemisphere, coverage of rugby — the Tri-Nations, Super 14s, British Lions and the summer tours — is in the hands of Sky and its affiliates. The pounding in Pretoria, then, had been shown on Sky, live on Saturday afternoon, giving us the opportunity under the news access agreement to show highlights on the BBC. The timing was strict – we weren't meant to use more than a minute of action, and there was a limit to the number of times we could show it.

It's an agreement that passes most fans by. Fans of the likes of Cardiff City, Swansea City and presumably non-premiership teams from around the country, are forever contacting the BBC to complain about the paucity of coverage their favourite team is given on the news. 'It's not fair,' they wail. 'If that was a rugby match, it would have been given wall-to-wall coverage, and all we get is a couple of goals shoe-horned into a minute.'

The legend of BBC bias is thus given more and more credence. And why? Because BBC Wales has the rights to domestic and international rugby – with the exception of the Heineken Cup and World Cup – while the rights to show the Welsh teams in the football league lay, until last season, with the ITV companies. So the fans were right. We did shoe-horn a couple of goals into a minute because that was all we were allowed to show. It's a fact of broadcasting life that if you are allowed carte-blanche usage of the pictures of a particular competition, then you tend to concentrate on it, rather than on one where your access to pictures is limited in the extreme.

On that fine June day then, I had sixteen Springbok tries and the ultimate consolation score from Arwel Thomas to squeeze into a minute. As it turned out, that was the least of my problems. The relationship between BBC News and BBC Sport is often a fraught one. I covered sport as a correspondent employed by the news and current affairs arm of the Corporation, not as a commentator or pundit in the sports department. It's an important distinction that needs to be kept. Those responsible for negotiating the contracts with the various governing bodies – the WRU, the Football Association of Wales, the English FA, Wimbledon or whatever –

need to be close to those they are negotiating with. The all important rights to cover the Grand National or the Six Nations are in their giving.

The sports correspondent can keep his distance from those commercial interests. If, say, a senior figure in the WRU is caught in a scandal, the dealings with BBC Sport need not be compromised by the coverage the story is given on the BBC's news outlets. The two can be kept at arm's length to the benefit of both.

Unfortunately, the lack of communication that can be the result of two separate departments had its effect that day. There was I, somewhat deflatedly saying, 'RIP Welsh rugby' on an afternoon BBC news bulletin, unaware that immediately after we came off air, BBC Wales Sport would strike a subsidiary deal with Sky to show the match, and all 109 points, in its entirety. The score? Well, for the benefit of all those who did not have access to Sky and wanted to watch the drama of Loftus Versfeld unfold before their eyes, it was meant to be a secret. It was one of those *Likely Lads* moments where Bob and Terry booked a day trip to Antarctica or wherever to avoid hearing a football result before it was shown on their 17-inch black and white. Sadly, if I'd been around them that day, they'd have known not just the result but the inside leg measurement of the guy who scored the goal before they got on the bus to get to the train station.

In those days, you knew when a call came into the BBC newsroom because a light came up above an extension number. No sooner had I finished my report with something akin to 'So where does Welsh rugby go from here? One thing's for sure, it can't go any lower!' you could almost hear in your subconscious the countdown in Oxford Street to the Christmas lights going on. 'Three . . . two . . . one . . .' and there they were, every damn light above every damn extension in the entire damn newsroom blinking together. You felt like telling the fourteenth 'aggrieved from Abertridwr', spitting with the rage of one who had been thwarted, that they should be eternally grateful you'd saved them from the shock of having to watch such an avalanche of points unprepared. Who knows how many heart attacks we prevented that day? What price the number of anti-depressants that stayed on the chemists' shelves because of us. The National Health Service in Wales should have struck a medal for us.

For some reason, the BBC's head of sport in Wales at the time, a former rugby international by the name of Arthur Emyr, didn't see it like that. His was the light sandwiched between the aforesaid 'Aggrieved' and 'Furious from Felinfach'. He didn't say too much, but apparently what he did say contributed greatly to our producer's ever-growing grasp of what could be called 'industrial' language.

A drubbing 96–13 and a cock-up of seismic proportions, all in a couple of hours. Enter the 'Great Redeemer'.

Chapter 24

'I'm Off to Coach Wales'

Not far from the South Pole there is a cairn with a cross. On it is an inscription: 'Hereabouts died a very gallant gentleman, Captain L.E.G. Oates of the Inniskilling Dragoons. In March 1912, returning from the Pole, he walked willingly to his death in a blizzard, to try to save his comrades, beset by hardships.'

There is a certain Edwardian stiff-upper-lipness about the message left by the search party looking for Captain Scott and his group of ill-fated polar explorers, but that is as nothing to the words of 'Titus' Oates when, with his feet severely frostbitten and with a war wound re-opened by the side-effects of scurvy, he walked out of their tent in his socks into the teeth of a polar blizzard and temperatures of minus 40 degrees Fahrenheit . . . 'I am just going outside and I may be some time.'

'I am just going outside and I may be some time'. It's got all the drama of the guy in the pub having to leave his pint while he pops out onto the pavement for a smoke. But sometimes brevity is best, a lesson learned by one of New Zealand's finest rugby coaches, a serial trophy winner with an Auckland Blues team that would have given most international teams a run for their money, when he faced a well-attended press conference in the Central Hotel in Auckland. 'I'm off to coach Wales and I'm going tonight!' Captain Oates, in his icy grave not that far away in the great scheme of things, would have smiled at its terseness.

30.7.98 *Graham Henry, New Coach, Live*

Cardiff International Airport on a Friday morning in mid-summer is usually awash with people going about their own business: holidaymakers, with the tanned faces and resigned expressions of those who know their two weeks of sunshine is over for another year, decanted from the planes that had left Parma and Portugal a couple of hours before; others slamming the doors of their taxis or kissing their friends goodbye, wearing smiles that tell of the cares of home being swapped for the beach and the bar. Amid it all, a couple of television cameras and the reporters with them awaited the arrival of the man charged with not just picking up the pieces of Welsh rugby but putting them back together again too.

The airport press office was helpful. 9/11 was still more than four years away. The security noose had yet to be tightened, so, instead of waiting in Arrivals, craning to see who was next out of the baggage hall, we were at the side of the runway watching a small KLM jet make its final descent. The Welsh Rugby Union was looking after its expensive new employee well. Instead of an exhausting 24-hour flight from Auckland to London, they'd given him an overnight stay in Amsterdam to recover. The steps were lowered. Down them walked WRU chairman Glanmor Griffiths, secretary Denis Gethin and the main man at the party . . . Graham Henry.

A press conference had been arranged in the Sports Bar in Cardiff Bay. That would be standing room only, but here at the airport was an early chance to beat the crowd and look for the answer that would make the *Wales Today* producer's day.

'Hello Graham . . . Bob Humphrys, BBC Wales . . . welcome to Wales. I know you've had a tiring journey and you've got a press conference to go to . . . but any chance of you coming into the studio live tonight?'

I waited for the inevitable excuses about jet-lag, people to see, documents to sign, meals to eat, family to phone.

'Yeah . . . no problem. What time?'

'That's OK, Graham, fully understand . . . perhaps some time in the future then . . . Sorry?'

'What time do you want me there?'

'Oh, we'll send a taxi at six!'

A media-savvy coach. God was smiling down on us.

Henry remembers the press conference that followed. 'Fortunately, having had seven seasons with Auckland and three with the Blues, I was accustomed to talking into a proliferation of microphones, peering down the end of television cameras and answering questions that varied from the cute to the acute. I'd learnt to say the right things over the years, not to make boastful claims I couldn't fulfil.

'What did I hope to achieve? Well, obviously I wanted the Welsh team to play to its potential and with passion. At that stage of course, I had no concept of what I was getting myself into!'

He would soon learn.

30.6.99 *Take Graham to Heathrow*

This time the statement had changed subtly: 'I'm going to New Zealand and I'm going tonight!'

Henry-mania was at its height. In little under a year he'd gone from one-time Auckland headmaster to Great Redeemer. It hadn't been win after win. South Africa had repeated their victory of the summer when they travelled to Wembley in November. There was no repeat of that humiliation in Pretoria, though. Wales could even have come out on top until a streaker, Henry reckoned, interrupted his team's concentration. 'He wasn't even good looking,' he moaned.

He'd also been ambushed by the Five Nations. We met at the Balmoral Hotel on the Thursday evening before Wales played Scotland in the first game at Murrayfield.

'Jeez,' he said, looking out of the window at the fans in red thronging the pavements and the bars. 'You wouldn't have thought there were enough tickets for all those guys. There must be 20,000 down there.'

'There's not,' I said.

'How many haven't got one?'

'Oh, about 20,000!'

'Jeez!'

It was a steep learning curve, made steeper by the fact the Scots were 7–0 ahead after ten seconds.

'Shattering. But who would know? The face wouldn't have changed!' he wrote.

At Wembley Ireland made it two defeats out of two – another result that wasn't in the script – and with France and England to come, this honeymoon looked as if it might end with a visit from the marriage counsellors.

8.3.99 *Graham Henry; Max Live*

Then, the turn around. Paris in the spring, a France team that hadn't been beaten there by Wales since 1975, when a hirsute Graham Price forgot the responsibilities imbued by founder membership of the Pontypool front row to gambol up the field like an ersatz winger to round off the scoring. Twenty-four years on, the class of '99 played like the fabled perennial Grand Slammers of the seventies. Henry had told them, 'Guys be bold. Being bold wins rugby matches, being shy doesn't.'

They were and they did, thanks to a last-minute swing of Thomas Castagneide's boot that sent what would have been a match-winning kick wide. Henry reckoned it was the most satisfying moment of his career. 'The Quinnell boys would, tearfully, remind me later that their famous father Derek, who played a huge number of games for Wales, never once sampled the delights of a victory in Paris. There were lots of tears from grown men in the wake of the victory. It was a hell of an important success for Wales, giving us the confidence we needed to go forward. I think we were all a little stunned at what we had achieved.'

The same Cardiff International Airport that had seen the low-key arrival of Graham Henry eight months before, now had its

Arrival hall packed with fans wondering whether the Great Redeemer would be there in person to give them an autograph. Rumour had it that he had forgone the plane to walk back across the Channel.

He was there, bemused by the public reaction. In the great scheme of things, that success over the English Channel meant little. There was no Grand Slam, Triple Crown or even Five Nations Championship in their sights. The New Zealander remembered when his Auckland Blues team had picked up a major trophy back home. The limit of their adulation was clapping themselves off the bus. Here a large chunk of South Wales had given up their Sunday afternoon to join in the backslapping and the applause.

It didn't end there. By Monday night's programme, we had persuaded Max Boyce to join us at the team's Copthorne Hotel on the outskirts of Cardiff to celebrate the win. He didn't need much persuasion. Less easy to convince was the reporter we asked to dress in the style of the mid-1970s.

'Er, why?' he'd asked, I thought not unreasonably. Now, you could have argued it was a serious journalistic device to remind the viewers through the visual medium just how long ago our last success in France really was, a bit like telling them you could have bought a pint of beer for a groat or snapped up a six-bedroom mansion in Barry Island for what you pay now for a candy floss and Knickerbocker Glory in a sea-front café. You *could* tell him that, but it wouldn't have been entirely true. More to the point, we knew people liked to see the strait-laced figures who intoned serious words on murder and mayhem from outside Cardiff Crown Court dressed like a prat.

One trip to a theatrical costumier that left him looking like a refugee from the long-forgotten and hardly-lamented pop duo 'Pilot', and it was mission accomplished. Graham Henry had long suspected that anyone connected with Welsh rugby was a prop forward short of a front row. Now he had his confirmation.

If beating France had seen the release of the pressure cooker that had held in the longing for success, and mixed in the hope that this time it would not be a one-off celebration quickly followed by a return to mediocrity, a month later the unthinkable was happening and Wales were beating an England side that seemed to think it had only to get off the team bus at Wembley to win the Grand Slam and put the precocity shown in Paris back in its box. It didn't end there. Two wins in Buenos Aires meant a first-ever series win over Argentina.

And then, just a year after that ultimate humiliation by South Africa, who should be the guests invited to open the half-completed Millennium Stadium? You've got it . . . a Springbok side Wales had never beaten.

Twelve months on, Wales improved by 16 points, South Africa declined by 77. A 96–13 defeat became a 29–19 win, and Wales were six games into a record sequence of ten successive victories. It was a good time to join Mr and Mrs G. Redeemer on a return home to New Zealand.

3.7.99 *New Zealand*
I like to think I played my part in saving the world!

'In the year 1999 and seven months, from the sky will come the great King of Terror. He will bring back to life the great king of the Mongols. Before and after War reigns happily.' So said Nostradamus, way back in the sixteenth century. The French astrologer widely credited with predicting the assassination of the Kennedys and the rise of Hitler was, claimed those adept in interpreting these sort of things, telling us that the end of the world was due on July the 4th.

All I can say in a reasoned, philosophical response to the bearded one is, yah, boo, sucks, me old astrologer, because thanks to an International Date Line you never encountered – unless a) you'd heard the crew of the Portuguese explorer, Magellan, somehow mislaid a day during the first circumnavigation of the globe in the 1520s, or b) you'd predicted it – when the crew of the Air New

Zealand jumbo suggested we move our watches forward from July 3 to July 5, in my little existence July 4 became the day that never was. I never lived through it, ergo the world couldn't end on it. Or something like that.

Beyond my altruistic mission to save mankind, television producer Rob Finighan and I wanted to show a Welsh nation that couldn't get enough of their new coach what made him tick. It didn't take long to discover how the renegade himself was regarded. He may have left All Black rugby licking its wounds like an unrequited lover, but there were no hard feelings from the New Zealand media. 'The man himself is back . . . except now he's the Great Redeemer,' said Paul Holmes, a Wogan with an antipodean accent, on his primetime TVNZ chat show. It is eye-opening to visit different television stations. TVNZ was the country's main channel in the centre of downtown Auckland, but there was a homespun feel to it. There were none of the security checks we were used to at the BBC, or the small battalion of minions scurrying around looking as if they had something important to do but weren't quite sure what it was.

It was more a case of find you own way in, have a bit of powder slapped on for make-up and sit down and strut your stuff in the hot seat. It was symptomatic of a different culture, more laid-back, less intense, a bit like watching a re-run of the sitcom *Frasier* where he walks into a studio, hears 'five seconds to air' and sits down to present the perfect show. It was like that with Paul Holmes, then the country's highest-paid television performer. His stint with the Gorseinon-based Swansea Sound commercial radio station twenty years before had obviously come in handy on his CV.

Graham Henry was a regular on the show, an indication of the profile he enjoyed there. And it wasn't just his profile – the reflected glory meant Finighan and I were guests on the station's main breakfast-time programme too. They didn't just want to talk to the man himself, they wanted to talk to the men who were making a programme about the man himself. There was a pride in what they had exported to the only other part of the world that had made a strange sport of largely incomprehensible rules, suited to all shapes from the fat to the spindly, its first love.

'Got a Welsh grandmother?' Wales's new coach looked out of the half-light of an Auckland dawn at a Polynesian behemoth in training kit putting in a stint with the city's NPC rugby team before heading off for day in the office or on the building site. The ghost of Auckland rugby past is back, and when the face of Auckland rugby present is asked if his untimely departure had anything to do with the team's dramatic down-turn in fortunes, a laconic All Black legend in the shape of Grant Fox says, 'Didn't help!'

Fox was one of Henry's prodigies. They met when Henry was a teacher in Auckland Grammar and Fox was a skinny thirteen-year-old in blazer and grey trousers. Together they forged a school team that was pretty much invincible, but as we look at the fading class photos on the school wall with the smell of floor polish all around, there are other reminders of the pupils that went there: Russell Crowe who stepped back a couple of millennia to unleash hell as a Roman officer soon to be betrayed in *Gladiator*, Jeff Crowe the cricketer, and enough famous rugby players to start their own hall of fame. Come to think of it, they probably have.

Fox was the privileged head boy, and what are privileges if they can't be abused? He duly obliged and after umpteen years and umpteen honours, he was suspended by the disciplinarian teacher they came to know affectionately as 'Ted'. 'You know what . . . that was my last day at school! And you know what else . . . he enjoyed doing it!' said a reformed head boy, now reconciled with his old nemesis.

At Eden Park, the home of New Zealand rugby, Henry talked of the protracted contract negotiations before he went to Wales, over who owed what to whom, how Auckland wanted contract money repaid and how the NZRFU put pressure on him to stay.

They marked his card. According to the *New Zealand Herald*, 'Should Graham Henry be appointed the national coach of Wales, he will never be given the All Black job.'

> In a move which looks to be a direct result of the current Henry furore, the NZRFU yesterday announced a new policy which precludes any New Zealand coach who has been in charge of another national team from getting on All Black staff.
>
> The decision is immediate but not retrospective, so therefore it will not affect John Mitchell (assistant coach of England), Warren Gatland (national coach of Ireland) or Brad Johnstone (national coach of Fiji).
>
> 'We are simply protecting our investment in coaches,' said chief executive officer, David Moffett, 'in the same way we protect our investment in players.'

Bizarrely, it wouldn't be long before 'chief executive officer, David Moffett' would also be taking the WRU's shilling. Or Warren Gatland, come to that. The path would become a well-trodden one.

It soured Henry's going, however, and gave him plenty to think about on his solitary walks – solitary if you don't count the boisterous company of golden labrador Zac – up One Tree Hill in Cornwall Park near his home. It was fortunate it didn't have to be renamed No Tree Hill after a Maori had used an axe to protest against European settlement in New Zealand a few years before.

At the country's foremost wine expert's we tested Henry's liking for a good red. 'Are you a sipper or a spitter?' I was asked. Silly question! If you've been given a glass of something approaching liquefied velvet, you don't treat it like the aftermath of a visit to your dental hygienist! Still, in such company you should adopt some of the proprieties of the occasion, so I commented knowledgeably on the full-bodied flavour and delicate bouquet of one vintage. It doesn't pay to get above yourself.

'Bullshit, Bob!' Mr Henry was obviously a spitter at heart.

On the South Island in Akoroa, scene of his youthful holidays, we ate cod and chips and debated their merits. 'Best in the world,' he reckoned. I was forced to stand the corner for the Top Gun in Whitchurch. It's a sad fact of life how a ten per cent staff discount for loyal custom can influence your judgement. We visited Wainui where he and Raewyn had spent their honeymoon and flew even further south, over the countryside that filled in for Middle Earth in *Lord of the Rings*, to Dunedin, which is about as far as you can go without bumping into an Emperor Penguin or two million.

The city where the Henrys met at university had been taken over by an undertakers' convention. Either that or the All Blacks were in town. It turned out to be the latter. They might have beaten South Africa comfortably in a Tri-Nations match, but that didn't stop the fans hailing the one who'd left them behind. 'Hey, it's King Henry . . . when you coming back King Henry?'

And on an Auckland mid-winter morning doing its best to be midsummer, we ate crayfish and oysters with well-chilled New Zealand Chardonnay that was most definitely for sipping not spitting. I wrote at the time.

> It's easy to see why this is, and always will be, home. But 12,000 miles away there's a job to be done and he'll do it – as long as the Welsh Rugby Union doesn't boot him out – until his contract ends in 2003.
> 'No question?' I ask.
> 'No question.'

It was an exchange Nostradamus might have enjoyed. He might even have made a prediction: that Graham Henry, Great Redeemer or no, might make it through to 2003. For once, he'd have been right.

Chapter 25

He'll Never Work for *Grandstand* Again

11.4.99 *Wales v England; Max; Tom Jones*
Mention at Wembley, one spring day in April 1999, that the Great Redeemer might not have a job for life with the Welsh Rugby Union – or possibly longer, given his elevated status in the ecclesiastical stakes – and the men in white coats would have been on high alert for an early call-out. It was carnival time, with a cast and pre-match entertainment to match.

For once I wouldn't be interviewing just those who made their living burrowing in scrums, leaping in line-outs or alternatively teaching them how to do it. This was one of those events that deserved the title, 'Occasion'.

Max Boyce was there with a new version of 'Hymn and Arias', including a verse that spoke of the still-under construction Millennium Stadium's new roof sliding back 'so that God can see us play'. Max tends to polarise the Welsh public into those who characterise him as an anachronistic stereotype and those who laud him as one of Britain's best entertainers. I make no apologies for being firmly in the latter camp. We first met over lunch in his village pub in Glynneath in the early '70s, when the *Western Mail* asked me to write a piece on the guy with the leek and the red-and-white bobble hat starting to make a name for himself with his humour and songs. The slightly insecure, quietly spoken man, interested as much in talking about a reporter he'd never met before as about himself, surprised me.

I was there when he had a sell-out audience at the Palladium eating out of his hands, as he made a foray out of the comfort zone of smaller venues and familiar audiences on to a London scene not known for its tolerance to entertainment from over the Severn Bridge. We played in charity football matches together in the Valleys, where he'd happily stand in if a sweating MC in a tight-fitting suit tapped the top of a malfunctioning microphone to announce, 'Our very own siffleur can't make it this evening, because he can't get out of his night shift in Llanwernl.' We'd thrown a Frisbee to each other on a Majorcan beach, where it was best not to let it sail over your head, lest you find yourself having to retrieve it from a sun-bathing beauty wearing nothing but an annoyed grimace. We'd shared my surprise fiftieth birthday together, where, if my hazy memory serves me correctly, he picked up the bill for the small lake of red wine as well as keeping the other diners in stitches with a sit-down routine that will stay with them rather longer than their king prawn with spring onions and ginger.

I ran 'Bob's Bar' when the BBC commissioned a series of *Planet Max* to run through the 1999 World Cup, where I had the onerous role of playing the barman for the live audience of fans who'd listen in a mocked-up nightclub while he did the hard work of songs, jokes and interviews with special guests. In short, he was a friend, and even though I was still surprised that someone as seasoned as him got nervous before performing, there would be no problem with our interview. We'd done it all before. Many times.

Tom Jones was another matter. Unlike Max, he didn't travel alone. He walked out of the Wembley tunnel with a small army of managers and advisers. We must have spoken about how he was looking forward to belting out 'Delilah' in front of 80,000 people, and what he thought about Wales's chances at a sport which, unlike his fellow headline act, he presumably didn't watch up to his Gucci shoes in mud on a Glynneath touchline. We must have spoken about such things, but for the life of me I can't remember if we did. My attention was fully focused on a face perma-tanned by the Californian sun and drawn tighter than the skin on Ringo Starr's drum. I'd never seen such a statement for anti-ageing. It quite threw me.

And while there wasn't a pair of knickers thrown in anger it didn't stop a very Welsh pre-match knees-up battering at the door of the English dressing room, with the invitation: Do your worst.

They did – for a time. Hywel the floor manager and I sat in our seats just in front of Graham Henry, David Pickering the team manager and the rest of the Welsh coaching team, with the resigned expectation that as usual I'd be asking them about another defeat by our nearest neighbours – the BBC didn't like the term 'old enemy' – albeit a plucky one. Occasionally, I'd look up to see their expressions. I'd done that once, a few years earlier, when Wales were on their way to a nerve-jangling, against-the-odds win at home to a France team the bookies had made overwhelming favourites. The precise moment I looked up, with a face that was obviously seeking divine intervention in the matter of preserving our slender lead, Princess Diana happened to look down. She smiled and patted her heart in sympathy. She understood the tension. Nice lady, I thought.

When, towards the end of the match, we left our seats to go to the interview point at the top of the tunnel, Wales were trailing by six points. They were still behind when we got there. I picked up the microphone and plugged in my earpiece, mentally rehearsing the questions a nationwide audience on *Grandstand* would want asked. For England there'd be the Grand Slam, a twelfth in all, for Wales a disappointing place at the bottom of the Five Nations Championship along with Ireland and France. Who would I talk to?

Clive Woodward, obviously. The try scorers, probably. The man of the match.

There were three minutes to go. On the small television monitor we used to show the main protagonists their greatest moments from the game, in the hope that they could 'talk us through' them with an element of eloquence, I noticed Wales were in a promising position. There was a line-out on the English twenty-two. Wales were throwing in. The tunnel went suddenly quiet.

Garin Jenkins throws in, the three-man line-out lifts Chris Wyatt, he flips the ball down to Robert Howley, Scott Quinnell has a slight juggle with the ball before giving it to Scott Gibbs, who jinks past one, two, three. He raises his left arm to point to the sky, and all Wales is screaming, 'Put the bloody ball down, Scott!' Bill McLaren is saying, 'Scott Gibbs has scored . . . what an amazing try,' and I'm in a bear hug with the guy who drives the Wales team coach. Where the microphone has gone I'm not sure. The fact the tube from my earpiece is trying to strangle me is immaterial.

It could all be premature. Wales are still one point behind. Neil Jenkins takes the conversion. It's not premature, it's 32–31. Just a couple of minutes to go. Time to be professional, to reprogramme the questions. It's all changed. Wales, the Grand Slam destroyers, are the story now. The seconds drag by. There's a last England chance. Mike Catt tries a drop goal. He misses. The whistle blows and the cameras focus on the Wales coach. Graham Henry rubs his eye. 'Piece of grit, Bob,' he tells me later. Max Boyce prefers the version he puts in a song, '. . . and a tear fell from Graham Henry's eye'.

'We'd defied the odds, defied the critics, defied everything really,' said the Redeemer. 'It was time to go and celebrate.'

Not if you were England it wasn't. There are times to ask for interviews and there are times to realise you might be invited to stick your microphone where the sun don't shine if you do. This was one of them. The England team trudged past me, the sweat still on their brows and a look of total incomprehension on their faces.

This couldn't be. A few minutes before they were heading to the World Cup as Grand Slam winners. Now they were chokers. Or so tomorrow's headlines would tell them. Their eyes didn't move from the ground in front of them. If whoever said, 'It's only a game,' had been standing by the side of me then, he'd have revisited his original premiss and thrown it in the bin marked, 'I got it wrong!'

Scott Gibbs was the first one up for interview. I don't know if it helped to have a familiar face on the other side of the microphone, but I remembered 1991 when he'd been given his first cap against England as a nineteen-year-old. I interviewed him then, along with another nineteen-year-old making his debut that game, Neil Jenkins. There was a neat symmetry about it. They started the decade together in the news and they'd be ending it together in the news.

Not surprisingly, the Wales centre was bubbling. We talked about the try, what it meant to beat England. Towards the end, I reminded him that his score alone wouldn't have been enough to win the game. It needed the extra two points provided by the conversion. Did he ever have any doubts about Neil Jenkins kicking it? He looked at me as though I were slightly simple.

'It never crossed my mind,' he said. 'If there's one person in the world you'd rely on to make a kick like that, that person would be Neil Jenkins. I don't think I even looked. I just knew it would go over.'

Neil Jenkins, with his slight flush as ever accentuated by the red hair, surprised me at the end of his interview. I asked whether he had been nervous about the kick that had a nation holding its breath – three nations if you want to be precise: Wales and Scotland in the hope that it would sail over straight and true (the Scots would then be the Five Nations champions by default), and England in the vain wish that it would lurch from the ground like a drunk leaving his seat after an all-day bender.

'Not really, you don't think about that. You just get on with it.'

It was typical Neil Jenkins understatement. I told him that it hadn't entered Scott Gibbs's head that he might miss.

'Well, I don't know about that . . . but tell you what, Bob . . . I've got to go now . . . my gransha's not very well and I want to get back and see him.'

And with that he was gone.

It was one of those interviewing moments. How many other people who had become an overnight hero to his rugby mad country would have had the chutzpah to walk out of a slot on national TV because he wanted to head home to see his poorly grandad. My liking for him went up enormously. It was yet another example of the imprecise art of the live television interview.

18.2.95 Grandstand *(Wales v England)*

For Welsh rugby, 1995 was not a vintage year. Played four, lost four: not just the wooden spoon but the whitewash. As such, it's probably been expunged from many a memory bank, much like being dumped by your first girlfriend (wasn't it me that finished it?) or that expensive book you borrowed and always promised to return. February the 18th 1995 would probably only register vaguely as another defeat by England in those days, when such a thing was expected on the way to the greater humiliation of losing four out of four.

At that time it was still a championship with an odd number of teams – the Five Nations. It was England's third game, Wales's second, so as England cantered to a comfortable 23–9 win at the National Stadium they knew they were only one game away from a Grand Slam. Again! As for the team they'd be meeting in the decider for that, Scotland, they'd just won their second game of the championship thanks to a totally unexpected victory against France in Paris.

The *Grandstand* producers had hatched a cunning plot. They would show the Wales v England game, carry the reaction to it and

170

the post-match interviews, then go to the Parc des Princes and show the France v Scotland game as though it were live. No one would know the score, everyone would be gripped. At least that was the plan. And it all went swimmingly – for a while.

After the game, Victor Ubogu, the Bath prop, came into the interview room to talk about what turned out to be the only try he ever scored for England. It hadn't exactly been a lung-bursting length-of-the-field job, where he skilfully skipped past half a dozen flailing tackles. In fact, as befits a front row forward he'd lumbered over from a couple of yards out. Still, we made a joke about how the distance would increase in direct proportion to the number of drinks he had at the post-match dinner. It was all nice knockabout stuff. So far, so good.

Then came the England captain, Will Carling. He was always good value: articulate and informative. I would have much preferred to be standing there talking to a victorious Welsh captain, but he wasn't to know that. Just before the interview began, I heard the stadium announcer tell the crowd of Scotland's success. There was a loud cheer. It didn't matter them knowing, just so long as the *Grandstand* viewing public were kept in the dark. There was only one problem with that: no one had told me.

'Yes thanks, Steve,' I said as the *Grandstand* presenter handed over to me again, 'Will Carling's with me now . . . well Will, it looks like you could be set for a Grand Slam showdown against the Scots?'

The director was a good friend of mine, Gareth Mainwaring. He was not one to be easily fazed, yet he gave a curious sound, the sort you might imagine accompanying someone having their throat cut. Strange, I thought. Still, Carling had finished his answer. It was time for question number two. As I spoke, I heard another voice on my talk-back. I didn't recognise it. It didn't come in friendship.

'*Tell the stupid . . .*'

'Right, Will . . .' I carried on.

'*. . . twat we're getting phone calls from Land's End . . .*'

'. . . did you always . . .'
'. . . *to f*****g John O'Groats . . .*'
'. . . feel in command . . .'
'. . . *complaining about that . . .*'
'. . . of the game or . . .'
'. . . *bastard spoiling their . . .*'
'. . . did you reckon . . .'
'. . . *enjoyment of the . . .*'
'. . . Wales always had it . . .'
'. . . *game. If he thinks . . .*'
'. . . in them to come back . . .'
'. . . *he's ever going to work . . .*'
'. . . and maybe even . . .'
'. . . *for Grandstand again . . .*'
'. . . snatch it themselves?'
'. . . *he can kiss my arse!*'
'Good question, Bob,' said the England captain.

The following Monday's *Western Mail* had Steve Rider, who'd been fronting *Grandstand* that day, apologising for the overzealous reporter who'd given the game away to millions of viewers who were hoping to watch the France v Scotland game in blissful ignorance. Me . . . I took a week off. I thought it best. I never asked who it was on my talk-back either. I thought that best too. After all, ignorance is bliss. Ask the viewers.

11.11.95 *Wales v Fiji*

I did work for *Grandstand* again. Armistice Day seemed as good a time as any to make our peace. It was Humphrys to Humphreys in the National Stadium's interview room after a narrow win over an unfancied Fiji in 1995. I'd noticed the Welsh skipper, Jonathan, come off the field just before the end after a bang on the head, but had thought little of it.

'OK, Humph?' I said, when the director indicated they'd be coming to us in about a minute.

'Fine, Humph . . . what are you going to ask?'

'Just a couple of questions about the game.'

'And what game's that?'

The bang on the head had been harder than we thought.

'Cue Bob,' said the director. There followed the longest question since Garth Crooks swallowed a thesaurus.

'So, Jonathan . . . it was a pretty even first half, though you probably thought you should have been further ahead at the break, and yet you couldn't finish the Fijians off. And in the second half they proved they weren't going to be the easy touch that many of the pundits predicted. At the end you were hanging on a bit and they could even have snatched a win. But I suppose, after the disappointments of last season, it was important to get a win under your belts in front of your home crowd. Is that the way you saw it?'

He looked at me with gratitude . . .

'Well, Bob, the way I saw it, it was a pretty even first half though I think you can say we should have been further ahead at the break. We couldn't finish them off, though. And in the second half they showed they weren't going to be the easy touch that many of the pundits had predicted. In fact we were hanging on a bit at the end, and I suppose they could even have snatched a win. But the most important thing of all was to get a win under our belts in front of our home crowd after the disappointments of last season. And at least we did that!'

'Thanks, Jonathan, interesting stuff . . . now, back to you in the studio.'

Live television? Don't you just love it!

Chapter 26

'O'er the Hills and O'er the Main'

A make-up chair is not a very masculine place. Neither is it terribly butch to forget you're wearing foundation and powder when you head off for a post-programme pint, though it does help to have a local where such peccadilloes are understood and forgiven. 'Oh that's Bob . . . it's OK . . . he's on the telly!' someone will say with the slightly condescending air of a nurse with a backward patient.

It can be relaxing. A soft brush feathering its way down your cheek is the upside; an infuriating tickling as the lines under your eyes are painted away, the down. But, despite Tony Blair doing all he could to boost its popularity by going nowhere without a thick layer of orange on his face, just in case a TV camera leapt in front of him on his way to the toilet, for most men, make-up is a strange concept and the chair in which it's done an alien environment. Which perhaps is why it can take on the attributes of a confessional. Sit there with a cape around your shoulders, your glasses off and your defences down, as the make-up artist obliterates a recurrence of middle-aged acne, and you say things you would not have said in the more normal surrounds of everyday life.

'The problem with Terry,' said the senior man from the Football Association of Wales as he sat in the make-up chair and the shine was taken off his bald patch, 'is that the managers send us down Premier League footballers and we send them back hardened drinkers. It couldn't go on.'

Alun Evans, the FAW's chief executive, was talking about the end of Terry Yorath's time as Wales's football manager. Yorath had come within a crossbar's width of taking Wales to the finals of the 1994 World Cup, only for Paul Bodin's penalty kick to crash back to the National Stadium's turf. With it crashed Welsh hopes of beating Romania and getting on the plane for the United States for a first major finals since 1958.

It had been a night of high expectation and desperate disappointment. At the end of the game when we should have been talking about there still being no end to the decades of hurt for Welsh football, came news that eclipsed the game. A distress rocket had been fired from one stand to the one opposite. Television pictures showed the missile's trail as it passed high above the pitch at a speed of 240 miles an hour. The ground had been packed. Had it hit someone? It seemed inconceivable that it hadn't. The initial report from the police was that a man had been injured.

I was now in the stadium's tea room, waiting for Yorath's reaction to the defeat out on the field. Injured? If it had been a distress rocket travelling at that speed, he'd be lucky to escape with just an injury. Years of hearing initial police statements rapidly turned into news of a much more serious outcome made me fear the worst. I said as much to Yorath when he arrived.

'Tel . . . I think this is going to be one of those occasions when a result is put into perspective by a much greater tragedy.' It made for a surreal conversation on air. The viewers had obviously been told something had happened, but didn't have the inside information we'd been given. We spoke about missed penalties and lost opportunities, while elsewhere in the ground a son was grieving the death of his father who'd been killed instantly when the rocket had hit him.

It was to be the last time I interviewed Yorath as the Wales manager. The missed penalty cost him his job.

Ostensibly, it was about money. Before the game against Romania, the FAW had made it clear they wanted him to carry on. Contract talks were scheduled for Caersws in Mid Wales at the beginning of December. Yorath wrote that he was on £45,000 a year, around half as much as his Scottish counterpart Craig Brown. He was offered another two-year deal on the same terms. Not enough, he said. How about £60,000.

The legacy of the Romania result was in the room like an uninvited guest.

'You do realise that if we'd beaten Romania, you could have come in here and asked for anything?' he was told by the then FAW president, Elfed Evans. 'If that penalty had gone in, you would be a God in Wales now.'

Yorath began to hear rumours that the pay demands he made had been 'non-negotiable'. He begs to differ, saying he'd have accepted a £5,000 rise rather than the £15,000 he'd initially wanted. On Christmas Eve, he had a letter in which seasonal joy and goodwill to all men were noticeably absent. His contract would not be renewed.

It was a very public dispute. Neither side was averse to playing it out in the full glare of a Welsh media which by and large rounded on the FAW for their treatment of a decent man who'd done a decent job. Who'd take his place? John Toshack was managing Real Sociedad in Spain, Terry Venables, whose mother came from the Rhondda and who spent much of the Second World War as an evacuee there, was soon to take on the England coach's role, while others supposedly in the frame included the Norwich manager Mike Walker and Brian Flynn.

At least this time there was no mention of Brian Clough. In 1987 it had been proposed that he manage Wales on a part-time basis with Nottingham Forest. It would have been his last opportunity to prove that he could have been as big a character on the international stage as he had been on the club scene, but he never had the chance to take it up. The directors of Forest refused to allow him to combine the roles. But they couldn't stop what must have been an entertaining afternoon for the recruitment panel from the FAW when they turned up to interview him.

'I can't promise to give the team talk in Welsh,' Clough told them, 'but from now on I'm taking my holidays in Porthcawl and I've bought a complete set of Harry Secombe albums.'

John Toshack promised neither when the FAW's chief executive paid a clandestine visit to San Sebastian in the north of Spain to sound him out as Wales's new part-time manager. Evans refused to admit to going to Spain, only for the hotel to fax a copy of his bill to a Fleet Street newspaper.

Yorath then had a phone call from his former teammate to confirm that he'd be taking the job, with former Wales manager Mike Smith as his right-hand man.

'Don't think you can ride in like a knight in shining armour,' Yorath warned him. 'If you don't get it right, the public will have you.'

'If there's any trouble,' said Toshack, 'I'll walk out.'

They were prophetic words.

29.1.94 *Bilbao v Zaragoza*

There was something oddly familiar about the road our hire car was taking from Bilbao to Zaragoza. The names of the towns hidden away in the hills called up vague memories difficult to place until a reedy voice and a plaintive song came to mind:

O'er the hills and o'er the main
Through Flanders, Portugal and Spain

King George commands and we obey
Over the hills and far away.

This was *Sharpe* country, and in the recesses of my brain Rifleman Hagman was singing the ditty that saw our eponymous hero, Richard Sharpe, the faithful Harper and their troops fighting their way from battle to victorious battle as they put the French to the sword in the Peninsular War.

The only battle that Sunday was in the La Romerada stadium, where John Toshack's Real Sociedad were playing Real Zaragoza in La Liga. It was his first match since the announcement that he would now be in charge of a country as well as a club. My colleague from *Newyddion* and I had flown to Spain in the footsteps of the FAW to find out whether the man I'd watched as a teenager playing for Cardiff City, followed to a nightclub in Formby to chart his time as top striker with Liverpool, and met occasionally as he forged one of the brightest managerial CVs in European football, including a Spanish title with Real Madrid, really did have the appetite for the politics that so often beset a Welsh footballing world where personal ambition was often the overweaning motivation of those who purported to run it.

The short answer to that was . . . No he didn't. There were indications a-plenty that this might not be the marriage made in heaven that the FAW spin was selling us. The president of Real Sociedad was clear. Yes, El Tosh could go to manage Wales in his spare time if he wanted, but it *would* be his spare time. There was no doubt about his number-one priority . . . that was bringing back success to a Real Sociedad club he'd rejoined with the aim of applying his Midas touch again. They were the people paying the bulk of his wages. They were a proud club in a proud Basque country. If club suffered, country would be the fall guy.

It was not the ringing endorsement the Welsh public, used to the relative success brought by a full-time manager in the shape of

Yorath, wanted. The qualifying campaign for the 1994 World Cup
had seen an exhilarating win over Belgium, as well as comfortable
victories over countries like Cyprus and the Faroe Islands. There
had been draws against the Czech and Slovak Republics, while Ian
Rush's goal that had beaten Germany in the 1992 European
Championship qualifying group was still burnt on fans' psyches as
one of the defining images of Welsh success on the football field.
For them it was Wales that came first, not a club in a city they'd
have difficulty pointing to if you offered them a map of Europe.

For John Toshack, my familiar face offered the chance of a
sounding board. His understanding was that there had been a backlash against Terry Yorath after the failure to make it to the World
Cup. The picture that had been painted for him was that the time
for change had been enthusiastically backed by a public who wanted
someone to take them to the next stage. Yorath had had his go and
ultimately his team had blown it.

'Is that right?' he asked. My answer – that there was still a huge
groundswell of sympathy for the former coach was not what he
wanted to hear. Nor was my opinion that he had been shabbily
treated. But there was a codicil to that . . .

'Tosh, you know better than me that all it needs is for a couple
of results to go your way and everything changes,' I said. 'You
qualify for the next European Championships and all that's
happened now becomes irrelevant.'

It was trite and it was obvious, but it was also true. He would
become that knight in shining armour if he added to the success
Yorath had brought. If he didn't, the armour could still come in
handy.

The omens weren't good that weekend. The cold winter sun of
Aragon set on a disappointing result for Wales's new part-time
manager, Real Zaragoza 3, Real Sociedad 0. El Presidente would
not be pleased. Tosh hadn't even taken the job properly and already
the club had lost badly.

The ghosts of Sharpe and his men could be imagined stalking the dark Spanish countryside even more vividly as we retraced our route along the deserted road back to Bilbao. The manager's day wasn't over yet. There was an appointment with a late-night television show and its Basque host to talk over the day's game. I've no idea what was said. My Spanish doesn't extend much past 'dos cervesas, por favor!' and I don't think there was much talk about drinks that night. But there was probably a question about combining two jobs and doing both well. It's what I would have asked. In fact, it's what I did ask.

We'd beaten the crowd to Toshack's Spanish backdoor. There was no beating the crowd to the press conference that welcomed him back to Wales a couple of days later. Around a hundred journalists turned up at Cardiff's Marriott Hotel. The FAW had booked a room with nineteen chairs. The man who prided himself on professionalism above everything was not amused to see the circus decamp to the bar, with the overspill in the foyer. It was a shambles, and manna from heaven for a media that had used just that word to describe the whole sorry affair. The knives were out for Alun Evans, calls were being made for his head.

According to Yorath, Evans has since admitted that not renewing his contract was one of the biggest mistakes ever made by the Welsh FA – an example of the faults in Welsh football politics. 'I believe I was sacked purely because I was too popular,' he wrote in his autobiography, *Hard Man Hard Knocks*. 'I was the people's choice but the Welsh FA – guided by their chief executive – were so jealous that they refused to choose me. The men who ran Welsh football refused to make room for the man running the team. They lost sight of the really important issue: the future of the game in Wales . . . I don't go in for professional or personal insults but it saddens me to think that petty jealousy rather than poor results ended my career as manager of Wales.'

Would they really have dumped their manager and brought all

the opprobrium heaped on them simply because of 'petty jealousy'? I doubt it. It might have played a part, but in the confessional of the make-up chair Alun Evans had mentioned another reason why Yorath had gone. He was close to his players – some of them indisputably world class and playing in the country's biggest clubs under the tutelage of harsh disciplinarians. When they came away from those clubs, they were in a totally different environment. They still wanted to win, they still wanted their country to do well when they were playing for it, but this was not their day job.

Yorath aimed for a happy camp. He treated these players like adults, and expected them to behave like adults. If they wanted to have a drink or go to a nightclub they would. I remember a training session where none of the journalists could recognise a blond-haired character going through his paces alongside some of the household names of nineties football. What we could recognise was that he wasn't very good. Nor should he have been. He wasn't a lower-division footballer called in to make up the numbers because of an injury epidemic that had hit the squad, but a mate of one of the players. The story went that he was a bookmaker, handy to have on the scene for any bets they might want to place.

This was the drink culture Alun Evans alluded to when he mentioned the metamorphosis that occurred between the time a player came from and the time a player went back to his club. Was the FAW naive to believe they could change what was probably commonplace nigh on twenty years ago? Were they simply rationalising a response to an unpopular decision? The answer to that came a few weeks later.

9.3.94 *Wales v Norway*

John Toshack was in matador mode on the cover of the match programme. Instead of a red cape diverting a couple of tons of bull from skewering his vitals, that job was left to the Welsh flag. Whether it was up to it wasn't tested. There tends to be a shortage of large bovines angered by a picador's darts in a Cardiff hotel car park in early March.

Inside the programme, the smiling new manager was optimistic about the future: 'When I first entered Ninian Park as a youngster joining Cardiff City's playing staff, I never dared to dream that some thirty years onward I would return to take charge of the Welsh National Team.

'But my life in football has taken many surprising turns and I firmly believe that I can help Wales to put the recent disappointments behind us and to make a confident challenge for the next European Championship Finals in two years' time.'

Most of the names that had been synonymous with Welsh football for the past few seasons were there for the Norway game, though it was a friendly so there was no Ryan Giggs in the programme line-up: new manager there might be for Wales, but Manchester United's Alex Ferguson was not to one forgo the protective instincts that had served his club so well. There was, though, one new face among the Southalls and Hornes and Rushes: Cardiff City's Jason Perry, affectionately known as 'Psycho'. He didn't know it, but this was to be his one and only appearance for his country. He'd be in good company. For a decade and more it seemed as if this would be Toshack's one and only appearance as manager for his country.

'Psycho' had every reason to be miffed at his own abandonment after a promising debut in what was a pretty dismal 3–1 defeat, but he also recognised what Wales missed in the loss of Toshack.

'He knew the continental game and how football needed to be played at international level,' he said. 'Not only did he have to contend with trying to educate the Welsh fans and the Welsh players, he also had the backdrop of the Terry Yorath saga. At our first meeting, John told us he didn't know what he was walking into. He thought he'd been brought in as a positive move, but things were whipped up in the press. Terry was rightly upset about it and it didn't help that John didn't come into the game smoothly. He should have been given the overall running of Welsh football after managing some of the biggest games in Europe. The fans should have put their trust in him. The new formation, which was alien to the British public, wasn't given a fair chance because of all the problems off the field.'

Jason Perry was one casualty of the night and for a long time he didn't understand why. The phone call explaining to him why he wouldn't be in the next squad, or the one after, or the one after that, never came. It was an oversight. Bigger forces were afoot than the international future of a player named Psycho.

18.3.94 *John Toshack resignation*

I was pretty pleased with myself. I had gone up to Brecon High School to discover how a model pupil with impeccable Welsh credentials, like appearing in the school eisteddfod, should have crossed the great divide and gone on to play rugby not for the land of his fathers but for – whisper it quietly – England. Even worse, how could he have connived in the blatant mispronunciation that saw the perfectly acceptable 'Dewi' become a weird 'Dowey'. My own satisfaction was down to the fact that his former sports teacher was a naturally humorous character who could transform humdrum television into a treat. There was no malice in what he said, just a rueful resignation that Dewi Morris, Brecon old-boy from Crickhowell, should have succumbed to the dark side – and it was all said with the deadpan, dry delivery of a natural successor to Les Dawson. An unlikely star was about to be born on *Wales Today*.

Then the phone rang.

'Bob, we're getting unconfirmed reports that John Toshack's quitting Wales. Think you'd better get back here pronto,' said the office.

I did, and those unconfirmed reports were right. A quick call to a Basque journalist close to Real Sociedad, whom I'd met when I was in Spain a couple of months earlier, confirmed them.

But for the next few days it was Toshack himself who forced the agenda.

He may have spent the bulk of his time away from Wales, but he'd never given up his home near Swansea. He was absent in body, but in spirit he was still here. He needed to know how the Welsh public was reacting to what he had done – and I was one of the conduits he used for that. It was useful for both of us. He knew what was going on, and I could abandon speculation for fact. Programmes I didn't normally appear on, such as Radio Four's *World at One*, would ring up for reports on what was going on in the shambolic world of Welsh football that had just seen another manager fall by the wayside.

What did I say? That it was an appointment that had never had a chance of succeeding? That was what I believed. Even though his interviews at the end of the defeat by Norway spoke of the future and how he could turn the fortunes of the Wales team around, the inevitable was only postponed. Jason Perry talked about him 'educating the Welsh players'. He didn't need to teach them to kick a ball or clear a corner. He did have to educate them in a new playing system – and he did have to teach them a new lifestyle. The laissez-faire days of Terry Yorath were numbered under him. When he had walked into the team hotel to meet the players, some were heading off on a night out.

It was not a situation Toshack could tolerate. Nor could he accept the post-Yorath picture painted by the FAW, one that existed in their own minds only. He was shocked by the public reaction to his appointment. He might not have expected to be the knight in shining armour, but he didn't expect to be the black knight either. The pro-Yorath chants at Ninian Park for the Norway game shocked him deeply. In short, he'd been sold a pup.

He became Wales's 'Forty-day Manager' . . . and it stayed that way until the winter of 2004 when Wales came knocking again. There was still a legacy to overcome – that of the popular Mark

Hughes – but it was Hughes's choice to go; this time there was none of the bad taste of a botched sacking. It had taken a decade, but Toshack now had the chance to turn what he'd written in a programme that cost a pound back in 1994 into reality. Welsh football finally had the manager it needed.

Chapter 27

'What's a Pervert, Dad?'

It was a lesson I should have learned. Work and holidays don't mix. If you're on one, you shouldn't be doing the other. But on a sunny August afternoon in 2000 I decided to ignore the little voice that was telling me: Stay away, stay a long way away.

For weeks there had been speculation about Cardiff City getting a new owner. No one could argue they didn't need one. When fans had to have a whip round to buy a new striker, in the hope that he could score the odd goal or two – and I suppose the household name that wasn't Kurt Nogan did exactly what it said on the box: he did score the odd goal or two, no more, no less – you sort of knew you weren't in the presence of a boardroom run by Roman Abramovich or even his not-very-well-off next-door neighbour back home in Chukotka. When Cardiff went out to shop they did so in the football equivalent of Poundstretchers . . . 'four defenders and a goalkeeper for a fiver? You've got a deal, providing you throw in a midfield general.'

Every so often there was talk of the businessman who would ride into town and spend, spend, spend until the club was back up where it belonged – except that after twenty-eight years or so of traipsing around the lower reaches of the Football League, no one was terribly sure where that was. The Premiership? Well, if possession is nine points of the law, Cardiff City could hardly claim rightful ownership of a spot among the Arsenals and the Manchester Uniteds, or even the Aston Villas and the Middlesbroughs.

There had been an occasion when they were one game away from the Football League Championship, only for the football fates to put in an appearance and, with gob-smacking relish, bite them on the backside. They went into the last game of season 1923–24 one point ahead of second-placed Huddersfield, needing just a win over Birmingham City to make sure of the title. Huddersfield did their bit for the Yorkshire cause by beating opponents Nottingham Forest 3–0. Not to be outdone, Cardiff top scorer Len Davies also did his bit for the Yorkshire cause by missing the penalty that allowed them to spend their 24-hour journey back to Ninian Park bemoaning picking up no more than a point. It's amazing how quickly you could travel back then, without the congestion at Spaghetti Junction.

Whoever had to work out the final league positions probably rued the fact that Sir Clive Sinclair was still sixteen years away from being born. He could most definitely have done with one of those new-fangled pocket calculators to confirm that, although Cardiff had scored one more goal than Huddersfield throughout the season, they had also conceded one more. 'Aha,' said the official statistician, 'that means that Cardiff have a scoring to conceding ratio of 1.794, compared to Huddersfield's 1.818. Therefore, Huddersfield are the First Division champions of season 1923–24!'

And before the fans could take off their cloth caps, scratch their heads and say, 'Yer what?', Cardiff City's chance of their only championship ever had disappeared quicker than you could say 'scoring to conceding ratio'.

It had, though, left the impression that the club was something of a sleeping giant. 'You know,' I'd say to manager Frank Burrows/ Eddie May/Terry Yorath/Kenny Hibbert/Russell Osmond/Phil Neil/Billy Ayre/Bobby Gould/Alan Cork/Lennie Lawrence/Dave Jones – or whoever was the latest free transfer arriving to transform

Cardiff's fortunes – as we stood on the side of the pitch, looking out over Ninian Park before the dark shadow of reality had eclipsed the bright light of optimism, 'This place is a sleeping giant.'

They'd normally give me the jaundiced look of the old pro who's been there, seen it, done it, got the P45s in the drawer to prove it. They were usually too polite to ask, 'Should you be drinking this time in the morning?' but you knew that's what they were thinking. 'Sleeping giant? Now if you'd said "comatose", we might be getting somewhere near it . . .'

The trouble was, I was a fan. I'd tell the transients who'd come to take up temporary occupation of the chair in the room with 'Manager' on the door, or who'd borrowed the blue shirt with 5 or 9 or, in the inflationary era of the twenty-first century, 66 on the back, how I'd been crammed onto the bob bank when it only cost two bob to get in, watching a drab goalless draw against Arsenal in the third round of the FA Cup in the mid-sixties. Fifty-five thousand people had been watching, the biggest crowd in Britain bar none. Old Trafford? Parkhead? Ibrox? Forget them. Ninian Park was the place to be that wet Saturday afternoon.

I was probably wrong. Maybe the crowd wasn't 55,000 and maybe Old Trafford or some such place had a bigger attendance, but it was good to think my version was the correct one. Selective amnesia, after all, is the major prerequisite of being a football fan. If you can't forget the pain and hurt your team has caused in serving up the sort of dross that should be put on a charge of causing grievous bodily harm to the nerves, then you'd never go back.

You forget the 5–0 defeats at home to Maidstone, and remember what your memory wants you to remember: your first match, a 3–2 win over Spurs in 1961 that made the City one of a handful of teams to beat them in their double-winning season; a Cup Winners Cup semi-final against SV Hamburg, where the ghost of Len Davies winced as those football fates returned to arrange a last-minute goal that knocked them out of Europe; Brian Clark's winner against

Real Madrid; a play-off final against Queens Park Rangers, where I said 'Pass' on a press-box ticket to join my family among the Millennium Stadium fans – not a wise move for my street credibility in Swansea as the Sky Sports cameras caught me celebrating in my blue-and-white scarf at the end; and, bizarrely, a 3–0 win over Aston Villa one Christmastime, when Cardiff finished with eight men, and for some reason a little fellow called Les Lea remained captured as an image in my mind for ever more.

Supporting a football team back then was about walking the four miles from your home to the ground, no matter the weather; feeling slightly ashamed as a twelve-year-old at joining in with a chant of 'We all piss in a green-and-white pot' against Shamrock Rovers, a sentiment that would nowadays get you thrown out of the Grange End for the inoffensiveness likely to cause offence; the smart-arsiness of my A-level English days, when I turned around to a foul-mouthed man on the terrace behind and asked him to 'temper his obscenity with a modicum of common sense'.

It was the trip to Bolton when your mum went with you and your friend, on the pretext of an afternoon's shopping in Manchester – but really because she didn't want her little boy exposed to the football loutishness she'd read about in the *Sunday People*; the nights when insomnia was staved off by reciting the team of your imagination: 'Wilson . . . Coldrick . . . Ferguson . . . Williams . . . Murray . . . Harris . . . Jones . . . Brown . . . Dean . . . King . . . Bird'; and getting your membership card back from *Soccer Star* magazine, with the name of Bobby Brown on it as your favourite player.

It was making sure Alan Warboys, who scored four goals on his debut, got a vote in the election of a new Chancellor for Exeter University. Unaccountably, Princess Anne won it. And it was having your first hangover, the day after Cardiff had gone to Sheffield United in 1971 needing a win for promotion to the old First Division. They lost 5–1, and I discovered the meaning of 'drowning your sorrows'. I also discovered that I can never again hear Neil Diamond singing, 'I am, I said', without recalling the nausea and cold sweats that went along with me listening to it time after time as I lay next to my tinny transistor radio, regretting those eight pints of the Jolly Porter's finest.

Cardiff City's search for a new owner, then, resonated with me. I wanted them to find someone who could restore even the semblance of respectability we had had playing in a European semi-final and tilting for the First Division. David Sullivan had been mentioned as a possibility. He had the money – half a billion pounds or so was not to be sniffed at. He also had the inclination.

I'd been to London a couple of times to see him in his incarnation as 'Dai Top Shelf', the man from a council house in Penarth who'd made his fortune out of soft-porn magazines and newspapers that owed more to breasts than breaking news. His enormous home in Chigwell was testimony to the sort of taste that would reach its apotheosis when *Footballers' Wives* hit the TV screens of Britain. It was a strange experience to sit in his office as he opened his mail.

'Look at that, willya?' he said in an accent more Del-boy than Dai-boy. For all I knew he was passing over a letter telling him that all he had to do was send a cheque for £36.50 to a post office box in Luxembourg and the deeds to a villa on the Algarve would be his by return of post. Or the Chigwell Conservatives could be asking for his vote in the forthcoming local council elections. It was neither. It was a picture showing more of a young lady than anyone but her gynaecologist would normally see.

'Get 'em all the time,' he said. 'After a shoot in a magazine, i'n't she?'

'Not *Horse and Hound*, I take it.'

Quizzical is the word you'd probably use to describe the look he gave me.

'No.'

Our morning post didn't have a lot in common, but at least a mutual birthplace – give or take a few miles – a similar upbringing and a shared love of football provided something of a link. So did our fondness for Cardiff's football team.

'Always thought I'd like to put a few bob into them . . . take 'em over, know what I mean?'

'Why don't you? You could afford it!' I looked at a sofa the size of Stansted's proposed new runway. 'Sell that and you'd have enough to buy the club and still get change . . .'

'Mmmmm . . . maybe I will . . . one day.'

So far, the closest he's been to doing that is an abortive bid by his brother Clive to buy into the club. But at least David Sullivan is a football man. Others, even richer, have the wherewithal, but not that inclination.

15.5.99 *Celtic Manor; Terry Matthews; BBQ*

There is something disquieting about Terry Matthews: probably the fact that you could have a drink with him and by the end of it know that he had earned more in interest on one of his minor accounts than you'd earn in a year. It was a bit like sharing a pint with the Queen: with a billion pounds or so sloshing around, who's going to notice if he had to borrow a tenner from one of his acolytes to stand his round?

But if pretensions are meant to come with wealth, it was a part of his education that had passed him by. Meet up with him after the monarch's sword has tapped him on the shoulder to signify the arising of Sir Terry and you ask him if you should give him the full works when you address him in the future. Only if I can call you 'Baron Humphrys,' he said in his mid-Atlantic drawl, '. . . yeah I like that, Baron Humphrys . . . it has a ring to it!'

He was born in the grand old house you could see from the M4 as you made your way into Wales. It didn't mean his was a silver-spoon-in-the-mouth arrival . . . a lot of youngsters from around Newport had squealed their first cries there. After all, it was the local maternity home. But he was the only one who'd go away to Canada to make his fortune and come back and buy it lock stock and barrel as the first part of the extraordinary development that will house the 2010 Ryder Cup.

It was difficult to miss the old house as it hunkered down alongside the motorway. It is now completely impossible to avoid an involuntary 'Good grief' as you come across the new Celtic Manor for the first time. Even the Red Dragon flying outside it is so big it can reputedly be seen from near Birmingham. Back when he was plain Terry, he put on an early summer barbeque to show off the progress on his £100m project. It was one of those do's where you didn't have to dwell too long on whether to pop into Threshers on the way for a cut-price bottle of red, or bring along the packet of beefburgers that had been in the back of the fridge since you'd shut your gas-fired grill down at the end of last summer. Bugger it, let him think we're mean, we're not taking anything. If a billionaire can't put on a drop of free booze who can?

So we unashamedly ate his food and drank his wine, and at the end of the evening took him up on his offer of a tour to the enormous building taking shape at the top of the hill. It wasn't quite finished. The huge reception area, which would so impress in years to come with its artwork and opulence, was now just bare concrete with electric wires protruding every now and again.

'I suppose this is your way of telling us our rooms aren't ready?' I said testily. 'A billion quid and you can't get the builders to finish on time. Jeez!'

It was earlier that evening that the question of money had come up again. Terry Matthews has always been clear that for him, the Celtic Manor Resort is a business project. Bringing one of the world's biggest sports events to his own backyard will mean huge benefits for the local economy and the image of Wales, but it is not being done out of altruism. You don't become as successful as he had become by being anything other than focused on what is the bottom line for you.

'So, Terry,' I said, 'you're spending a not so small fortune developing this resort. You've admitted you're not doing it because of any great love of golf. So why don't you spend a fraction of that amount investing in, say, Cardiff City. Buying the club would be small change and you could get the players needed to climb the divisions. You'd build a new ground, success would come . . . and how would you feel about a packed stadium with sixty thousand or whatever Welsh football fans all chanting, "There's only one Terry Matthews . . ."? Surely that would be worth what you'd spend?'

'You know, Bob,' he said, 'I'd hate it!' Sadly, he meant it.

8.8.00 *Sam Hammam Takeover*

So, a little over a year later, I was breaking my holiday to go to meet the man who had finally decided to put his money where many people's mouths had been. Sam Hammam, the man who'd taken Wimbledon to the First Division and a Cup Final win over Liverpool before jumping ship in controversial circumstances, was back in football. Cardiff City had its new owner.

After so many abortive takeover bids that I thought 'false dawn' was a woman of dodgy repute who lived in the Grangetown area of Cardiff, I thought I'd go along to the press conference, where the Lebanese millionaire was being introduced to a curious media pack, to make sure it wasn't just another mirage.

There was one problem. We were due to fly away on holiday first thing the following day, and I was looking after my eight-year-old son while my wife was sorting out the packing. No problem, I thought . . . he can come with me. He did, and he acted impeccably. He probably didn't understand the ramifications of how much Hammam was paying for the club, what would be available for new players, or that the former Wales and Wimbledon manager Bobby Gould was being brought in as some sort of football supremo – but to be fair, there were many other judges in the audience much older than eight who didn't understand the last bit either.

At the end of the usual bravura performance from the larger-than-life Hammam, I thought it best to explain why I had a small boy in tow: 'Mr Hammam . . . Bob Humphrys, BBC Wales. We're likely to have a lot of dealings with each other in the future, so, although I'm not actually working today, I thought I'd come along to say hello.' I explained we were just about to go abroad.

'So, young man,' said Hammam to my son, 'where's your father taking you on holiday?'

'Ibiza,' I said in the sort of stage whisper that had Jamie dutifully picking up the answer.

'Ibiza . . .' he said.

'Ibiza,' boomed Hammam. 'Only perverts go to Ibiza . . . your father's a pervert!'

Ah, I thought . . . not what I expected there! But he was on a roll.

'And him,' he looked around at someone in the crowd, 'he's a cross dresser.'

I suppose we should have been thankful sheep's testicles hadn't taken the place of the digestive biscuits to be served with the coffee. Still, I reasoned, looking at the blank expression on Jamie's face, no harm done. I'd got away with it.

And I had. Until we got in the car.

'Da-a-ad?' he said, in the elongated version of the word that usually prefaced a request for money or the sort of question you weren't going to want to answer.

'Yes, son?'

'What's a pervert?'

Chapter 28

'THE DREAM'

It cannot be happening. But it is. I am in a trance, dazed, swept off my feet, gobsmacked, or perhaps hypnotised. In short, I am in love with Cardiff City Football Club.

Having recently come out of a 22-year love affair with another club (which will always be my baby) I have never thought that I would fall in love again. But I have!

How did it happen? You, the fans of Cardiff City – the Bluebirds – have cast a spell on me.

The surprising thing in all this is that I have yet to meet a fan, young or old, wise or wild, who does not think that Cardiff City is bigger than Liverpool, Manchester United, Arsenal and even Barcelona, and we will have a 70,000 lock out gate if we are doing well in the Premier League. Is everyone insane around here?

Difficult question, Mr Hammam! But there's no doubt a certain collective madness gripped Ninian Park as its new owner imported the Crazy Gang philosophy that – for good or bad – had propelled Wimbledon and its bunch of footballing misfits to success that would have been unimaginable just a few years before. Admittedly it had later had catastrophic effects, with Wimbledon ending up playing non-league football while a franchised version of the club ended up in Milton Keynes, but Hammam was nothing if not loyal. 'I'm still a foot-soldier, whether I'm here or in China. Wherever I am, Wimbledon can always count on me,' he said on the day he sold his final share in Wimbledon FC.

So now Cardiff City, the club, remember, that had relied on its supporters for a whip round to buy a player, was acting like a lottery winner who'd torn up his advice on financial prudence and embarked on a policy of 'spend, spend, spend'. Cheques with the number of noughts that had previously only been seen on demands from the Inland Revenue were now being written for new signings Peter Thorne and Graham Kavanagh. The million-pound barrier was being breached more regularly than flood defences on the River Severn. Other clubs began to realise that when they picked up the phone to hear, 'Hey Baby . . . it's Sam' . . . and that their letter to Santa Claus had been answered in full without it even being Christmas.

I particularly liked the tale of a small club who had received a bid from Hammam for a strapping young centre half who might or might not have a bright future ahead of him.

The club's manager looked at the fax his secretary had brought into the office.

'They've got that arse about face,' he said. 'Look, the comma's in the wrong place. They've only gone and bid £400,000, not £40,000. Give 'em a ring and tell them they've made a mistake. That'll be a pretty good deal for us.'

It would have been. But Cardiff City were having none of it.

'Do you think we're made of money, or what? Four hundred thousand pounds and that's it. Not a penny more. Take it or leave it!'

They took it.

Cardiff City was going places. Sam Hammam said so. He had a dream!

The response I have received from you guys and girls, has been overwhelming. I am very flattered, but I also believe that flattery is great as long as you do not inhale. In other words – thank you very much, but I will not get carried away. The game is played on grass and the only thing that matters is success on the pitch. All the hype is nice and all the gimmicks will make the journey more fun, but 'talking the talk gets you nowhere, walking the walk does'!

So please allow me now to set down the reality behind THE DREAM, the facts as they stand today, the way issues will be handled and some of my ideas for the future.

THE DREAM

Cardiff City Football Club has no business to be playing the 3rd Division of the Football League. If what the fans tell me is true, then this club has no business to be playing in the Football League either – THE DREAM is to be challenging in the top reaches of the Premier League and beyond to the elite of Europe and doing that in a top quality stadium.

Let us pledge here and now to try together to achieve that dream. Personally I do not believe we will come anywhere near making it a reality, but like hell we will all give it our best shot.

It is my considered opinion that we have no more than a 1 in 10,000 chance of achieving this impossible dream and even then we would require about 20 years or more to achieve it and only then if we are very lucky, we are willing to put in a lot of hard work, we are very focused, we are willing to stick together when things go wrong and we are prepared to make sacrifices and make brave decisions when necessary.

THE PRESENT

The Club is in the lowest division of the League, it has debts of over £1.5 million, it is losing between £0.5 million and £1 million a year, it does not have enough good players, it does not own the training ground, Ninian Park leaves a lot to be desired, and the youth system can be greatly improved and the Club has not achieved what many fans and key officials tell me it can achieve.

But we're not running scared. Far from it. The Club has an excellent fan base both in terms of quality and quantity. I have been in football for over 22 years and have never seen such fanaticism of support for such a team as much as I have seen in Cardiff. The only fans that seem to compare are possibly those of Newcastle. They are the Toon Army. I dream of the WELSH ARMY. They are a middle sized city. We are a whole nation.

That is the only key thing going for the Club. But believe me that is the only thing that matters. Everything else we can work on. It has a great foundation upon which we can build.

This is what attracted me to Cardiff. You! That is all I need – you!

When things go bad as they surely will – when I am down – please put your arms around me and lift me up so that I can stand and fight another day and I will do the same for you.

STADIUM

It is vital that the stadium should be progressing at the same pace as the team, or even a bit ahead.

The main problem here is I do not like to spend Club money on improving stands or building stadiums. My style is that I would like to spend everything we have on football.

The way I propose to improve Ninian Park and eventually have a brand new stadium, is to make any improvement self-financing. For example if we are to erect a stand at the Grange End we will see how much money it is earning the Club now, and then we will try to arrange separate finance in such a way as to give the Club the same money it would have earned and use the extra profits to repay the loan. In a few years it would have paid for itself and all the income would then become the Club's.

What this effectively means is that there is no point in improving the stadium if we are not being near capacity at least a few times a year, and it goes without saying that we are not going to fill the stadium if we are not doing well on the pitch.

The bottom line sequence therefore is:

The team does well and therefore the fans are happy
The stadium gets full

We improve the stadium
This brings more money
More money means we can improve the team
A better team will then fill the bigger stadium
This will generate more and more money

In short, the money always goes to football and the stadium takes care of itself without jeopardising what's needed on the pitch.

The economics were more Janet and John than John Maynard Keynes, but a mass-hypnosis had settled over the club and its fans. They wanted it to be so, therefore it would be so.

I used to share the occasional drink with an acquaintance of mine who was a financial consultant at the club. On the face of it all was going swimmingly. Crowds were up, results were good.

'So what's the break-even figure when it comes to attendances?' I asked one evening. 'Thirteen thousand? Fourteen thousand? Bit more?'

'Oh, about thirty-four thousand,' he said airily.

'But it only holds twenty thousand.'

'Quite.'

25.5.03 *City 1 QPR 0; Tore Stromoy*

We joked about results, how a perfect score would be 2–1 to the City, thanks to two own goals, so that there would only be the win bonus to pay out and no punitive bonuses to those who got more for scoring or to the defence for keeping a clean sheet. Oh how we laughed! And how we partied when Cardiff City won their play-off final in front of a full house at the Millennium Stadium. Sam Hammam had spoken of riding an elephant, like some modern-day Hannibal, from Ninian Park to the Stadium at the front of an army of Cardiff fans. For once wiser counsel prevailed, but I'd been seduced by the atmosphere, filming the carnival that unfolded at the dilapidated old ground before the mass exodus towards the city centre.

One of Norway's top entertainers had flown in wearing his Cardiff City top. Tore Stromoy was a Scandinavian Jonathan Ross. Where his brothers had followed the usual path of supporting the top English teams of the seventies, he'd taken another route, adopting, for reasons even he didn't quite understand, the unfashionable, lower-division side playing out of the Welsh capital. His journey was being recorded by a glossy Norwegian magazine, its staff presumably wondering how the hell they'd ended up in Cardiff rather than Liverpool or Manchester or Newcastle, the usual destinations for fans flying out of Oslo.

For this day we were a band of brothers. Whether they'd flown in from Australia or America, or just got the bus from Llanrumney or Ely, or came by train from Treorchy or Tonyrefail, the fans made up a city united as seldom before in the quest for the footballing recognition it had been starved of for so long. An unlikely saviour called Andy Campbell – not the pint-sized local hero Robert Earnshaw who'd broken all sorts of scoring records – grabbed the only goal in the half hour of extra time that had my wife fearing I'd be heading for intensive care rather than the bar at the end of the match. That's what tension does to you. But all was well. Sam Hammam was on the pitch, hugging and kissing the players and staff who seemed to be making that dream come true. 'Sam Hammam, my lord, Sam Hammam . . . oh lord, Sam Hammam,' sang the fans. I have to say I preferred 'Men of Harlech'.

'By then the wage bill, £8.3m, exceeded the club's entire earnings,' wrote the investigative football journalist David Conn in November 2006. 'The debts, £1.5m when Hammam arrived, had ballooned to almost £23m. His plan for the Bluebirds turned out not to be a blueprint at all; Cardiff had risen by borrowing excessively.'

The fans finally woke up from Hammam's dream in August 2004, when Earnshaw, by then a Wales international, was sold. The following month Cardiff City borrowed £24m in loan notes from sources that Hammam was reluctant to identify, to pay off Citibank. The crisis came seven months later when Kavanagh was abruptly sold to Wigan to pay the previous month's wage bill. Defender Danny Gabbidon soon departed, staff were laid off and the Welsh dragon had to simper to the Professional Footballers' Association for a loan.

4.3.05 *Cardiff City Meltdown*

The clue had come the previous day. I'd been sitting in my car waiting for my daughter to feed her horse at the farm just outside Cardiff where we kept it. The Radio Wales sports news carried a story about unpaid wages at Cardiff City. The manager, Lennie Lawrence, blamed a technical hitch. A large pig took to the air and flew above the horses in the field. By the following day, Jamie Owen was telling Wales, 'They owe £30 million, they haven't paid their staff, they've called in the auditors and today Cardiff City sold their captain to help balance their books. That's the extent of the financial crisis at Ninian Park, where skipper Graham Kavanagh became the first casualty of the club's problems when he was sold to championship rivals, Wigan. More from Bob Humphrys . . .'

It was 'Black Friday' and we filmed two of Hammam's chief disciples outside Ninian Park. With commendable speed they'd had T-shirts printed. One was wearing the slogan, 'Mug', the other 'Bigger Mug'.

Chapter 29

'Over the Severn and Down to the Taff'

'Good morning . . . and it is a VERY good morning,' said a beaming Ron Davies.

'Bloody hell!' I thought. 'What's a secretary of state doing in my bedroom, wishing me a good morning. Doesn't he have anything better to do?'

Fortunately for my – and probably his – peace of mind, I realised it was just the state of limbo that exists between sleep and wakefulness that had transported the Welsh secretary from Cardiff City Hall to a Taunton Travelodge. I had fallen asleep with the television on while watching the results of the voting in the day's referendum on whether there should be a Welsh Assembly. When I'd slipped into unconsciousness, Huw Edwards was looking a little grim.

Good enough for him! I still haven't forgiven him for a dinner where I'd been shortlisted for a sports reporter of the year award at the Dorchester in London. Huw was the compere for the evening.

'And before we begin,' he said, standing at his carefully lit podium in front of the glitterati of British journalism sitting in their dinner jackets at their no-expenses-spared tables of ten. 'Can I just say . . . bad luck, Bob, you haven't won, so if I were you I'd pop over the pub now!'

It wasn't bad advice. Knowing you're an also-ran does mean you can get stuck into the Chilean Merlot without the fear that somebody's going to say, 'and the winner is . . . Bob Humphrys' . . . only for you to perform an ungainly triple forward roll into the table housing the BBC's senior hierarchy on the way to picking up your gong from some clearly embarrassed middle manager from the awards' sponsors. My brother had filled Huw's role at the same prize-giving another year. Maybe it was me and the insouciant air I gave out at these back-slapping events – the indifference that masked the unspoken thought, 'Gotcha, you bastards, that's another year you won't be able to sack me' – but John adopted the same approach.

'You do know no one from Wales has won a bean, don't you, dear boy?' he asked as we grabbed a pre-dinner glass of something fizzy from the circulating tray.

I didn't, but thanks a bunch. He'd left me with a dilemma. Did I keep the news to myself or tell the other shortlisted nominees in the various categories who'd made their way up from Broadcasting House in Cardiff that they were about to join me in being cast on the scrap heap of thwarted ambition? Not to mention miss out on a cheque for a couple of hundred quid. After five seconds of deliberation, I came to a decision. I told. It turned out to be the right one. With the pressure off, we made bets on who'd be carrying off the various awards. All very childish, I suppose, but if anyone from the *Wootton Bassett Bugle* or wherever is reading this, it explains why a table of hollering hacks from Wales should be so interested in the destination of the 'local newspaper (weeklies) feature writer of the year award'. If it was you, my apologies – and congratulations.

By now, on the television, Ron Davies and his political partners were holding their arms aloft as those who'd voted 'Yes' for the creation of a Welsh Assembly celebrated a win that had looked ever more unlikely until the voters of Carmarthen had snatched the proverbial victory from the jaws of defeat. I'd nipped in to my children's primary school in Cardiff to do my bit for the democratic process before driving down the M5 to Somerset. Wales might have had devolution on its mind, but the cricketers of Glamorgan had the County Championship on theirs.

9.7.97 *Southampton; MM/WY interview*

It had been a turnaround season for Glamorgan. Rock bottom of the County Championship as recently as 1994, they'd brought in a new coach in the shape of Zimbabwean Duncan Fletcher from Western Province in South Africa, plus one of the world's great fast bowlers, Waqar Younis, the man dubbed 'the Burewala Express' – though probably only in Burewala. Most people probably thought it was a newspaper.

Far from the taciturn figure painted by the Fleet Street media in 2006 as a beleaguered man railing against the world as he sought to retain the Ashes in the embers of his career in charge of England, the Fletcher of 1997 was an urbane, articulate character, happy to talk at length about the game and his new charges. Waqar Younis was a westernised son of Pakistan, very much part of the 'team' and all that the 'team' was about. It was BBC Wales's good fortune that both arrived on the scene in a season when the channel had decided to devote vast swathes of air time to cricket. And it was my good fortune to be in the dressing room or on the boundary as one of the most memorable periods in Glamorgan's history unfolded.

It wasn't without its drawbacks. The old County Ground in Southampton was the venue for an attractive looking NatWest Trophy tie against Hampshire. For once in a British summer, the sun shone and the runs flowed, even though Matthew Hayden, the Australian opening batsman known for bludgeoning bowling attacks from South Africa to Sri Lanka, had yet to reach the imperious form that has made him one of the most feared players in the world. He was out for 20, lbw to Darren Thomas, but

England's Robin Smith made light of his dismissal by flaying the Glamorgan bowlers for 120. By the time he was caught by the Glamorgan captain Matthew Maynard, Hampshire were well on the way to amassing 302 for six in their sixty overs.

Five an over? For 60 overs? There were few takers in the ground for a Glamorgan win, particularly when Robert Croft was caught for a duck. Nought for one. Hardly an auspicious start. But after that the batsmen all began to chip in with runs. Hugh Morris made 53, Adrian Dale 71, Matthew Maynard 30, and even though Tony Cottey went for 5, Steve James, the eventual man of the match, picked up the pace with 69. Even then there was still work to be done. Wicketkeeper Adrian Shaw got a quickfire 34 and he was still in the middle when Waqar Younis walked out to join him. Eight wickets down for 292 runs, 11 still to win, anybody's game, but Shaw was doing well, and Waqar, as the Hampshire bowlers and the crowd knew, could live up to his name with the bat.

They reached the 300 mark. Whack . . . four. Six hundred and six runs had been scored in a couple of balls shy of 120 overs and Glamorgan had won by two wickets. By any standards it had been a breathless game of cricket, with most of it going out live to an increasingly enthralled audience of viewers in Wales. The crowd spilled onto the pitch at the end and Matthew Maynard, a good friend who, when he wasn't touring with England (and he didn't tour with England often, given the shameful record of selectors who seemed unable to afford the Severn Bridge toll when it came to assessing the Welsh county's players for a spot in the test team) played for the BBC's football team in the winter, came over for a live interview.

It was breathless stuff: an ecstatic captain, a delighted interviewer and a special game of cricket to talk about. Then, one of the floor managers managed to extricate the unlikely batting hero from the small boys desperate for his autograph, and manoeuvre him next to Matthew in front of the camera.

'Right Matthew, we're joined now by the man who hit the winning runs, Waqar Younis. Well Waqar, it didn't go so well with the ball today [he'd taken one for 62 in his 12 overs] but you certainly made up for it with the bat!'

It was a half volley of a question – well, a statement if you want to be pedantic – which he duly belted back for four with a few well-chosen platitudes, all you can really expect in such circumstances. *In the Psychiatrist's Chair* with Professor Anthony Clare, it was not!

'One final question, Waqar . . . it's your first season with Glamorgan, how good would it be to round it off with an appearance at Lords?'

He was hardly going to say he'd prefer eight-inch long needles heated on a Bunsen burner then inserted in his eyeballs, but if he had, he couldn't have created much more of a stir.

'It would be f*****g lovely!'

Nowadays, when a gauche England outside half can use the 'f' word at the end of a Six Nations match with only the mildest of admonitions, and Gordon Ramsey's show wouldn't be Gordon Ramsey's show without expletives sprinkled more liberally than the salt and pepper, it would hardly be noticed. However, Alan Wilkins, the studio presenter, hadn't handed to me by saying, 'Now over to Bob Humphrys who's got some reaction to the game . . . viewers are warned it might contain some strong language.' That sort of thing just didn't happen then. There was no real protocol for when it did.

As Waqar spoke, there was a sharp intake of breath in my earpiece. That and a few words that would have put the Burewala Express to shame if they'd actually gone out on air. No one told me to wrap up.

'Er, thanks, Waqar, so, Matthew, to sum up . . .'

Matthew did.

'Back to Alan, Bob,' said the director in my ear.

'Thanks, Matt . . . well, let's hope for more of the same in the next round, but now back to Alan Wilkins in the studio.'

Matt looked at me as I handed the microphone to the sound man.

'Did he . . . er . . . did he actually say what I thought he said?' he asked. 'He did say "f*****g lovely", didn't he?'

There was one possible saving grace: Waqar's thick sub-continent accent. Maybe no one had noticed.

They had. *Wales on Sunday* had a field day.

18.9.97 *Taunton: Glam v Somerset*

It didn't turn out 'f*****g lovely' for Glamorgan in the NatWest Trophy. In the semi-final against Essex in Chelmsford, marred by the ill-feeling between the teams, they lost another nail-biter by just one wicket when Essex overtook the Glamorgan total of 301 for eight in their sixty overs by scoring 303 for nine in 55. It was as close as they'd come to a Lords final since 1977.

In the Championship, it was another matter. Despite what Jamie Owen might have said in the banter we used to indulge in when he introduced his antediluvian sidekick on *Wales Today*, I was not around when Glamorgan won the title for the first time in 1948. I did know that the penultimate game of that season, against Hampshire in Bournemouth, the one that sealed the title, contained one of the more memorable quotes from an umpire. The scorecard doesn't give anything away: 'Hampshire Second Innings (following on) . . . C.J. Knott lbw b Clay 4'. It doesn't for instance say that, after J.C. Clay's successful 'howzat' that had Charlie Knott out and left Glamorgan winners by an innings and 115 runs, the umpire said, 'That's out . . . and we've won the Championship!'

The fact that the umpire happened to be called Dai Davies, who happened to have been born in Carmarthenshire, and who happened to be the first-home bred professional to make an impact for Glamorgan in first class cricket prior to the Second World War is, of course, entirely coincidental.

I was around, though, in 1969 when, after a gap of twenty-one years, Glamorgan won the title again. It was a good summer for me. I was seventeen, slap in the middle of sixth-form life, at the end of the first-year sixth at Cardiff High School and before the second-year sixth when little things like A levels got in the way of enjoying yourself. I realise that, in terms of education in the twenty-first century, I might be talking a language about as comprehensible as Sanskrit but, put in the vernacular, it meant I had little to do but walk along to Sophia Gardens and sit with the Taff at my back, watching the likes of Alan Jones and his brother Eifion, the ungainly but effective Ossie Wheatley, Tony Lewis and the rest manage not to lose a game on their way to outpacing Gloucestershire and Surrey to the County Championship.

It all culminated with admirable timing in the last week of the holidays, in early September, when Majid Khan (another overseas player from Pakistan blazing the trail for the Waqar Younises of years to come) obviously realised the time constraints that would have me facing double-French and an essay on why Henry VIII had to chop off Anne Boleyn's head by the time the final – and possibly deciding – match came along in ten days' time. On a tricky pitch he belted a hundred before lunch on the first morning of the game against Worcestershire and, with his ten teammates contributing the sum total of 109, went on to score 156 out of 265.

His display of virtuosity was all too much for the county from up the M5. Their first innings saw them score 183, then Glamorgan rattled up another 173 before declaring with five wickets down. When commentator Wilfred Wooller, the man who'd led the 1948 team to the Championship, was fittingly at the microphone to yell 'He's done it!' over the BBC's black-and-white pictures of Don Shepherd having last man Brian Brain caught for 9, Glamorgan had won by 147 runs.

They are images I've seen many times over the years, in fact just about every time I did a story about Glamorgan's past. There was something quaintly antique about the way the players went about celebrating just the second title in their history. Don Shepherd – who'd taken his 2,000th first-class wicket in the Worcestershire first innings, to make a mockery of an England team that never picked him – didn't leap in the air with his index fingers pointing skyward, kiss the daffodil logo on his chest and ring his agent on his mobile to negotiate a new contract with the highest bidder. It wouldn't have been seemly. After all he had celebrated his forty-second birthday just a few weeks before.

Instead, he collected his sweater from the umpire and strode away with the air of a man who had an urgent appointment to take his car for a service. It was left to the crowd to inject some drama into the proceedings as they flooded the field to gather in front of the pavilion. I must have been one of them, but, try as I might when I looked at the flickering images a few decades on, I could see neither hide nor hair of me. Memo to self: next time they win the title, don't make yourself invisible.

I didn't. I did the opposite. Twenty-eight years on I made sure I was as visible as possible. I've found it helps if you're working in front of a television camera.

Day one was excellent for Glamorgan. They won the toss and decided to field. Good decision, Mr Maynard. It was all very straightforward for me, with the trickiest part entailing finding the unattended studio in the centre of Taunton to send a voice track that told how Waqar Younis, with his haul of four for 41, and Steve Watkins, with his three for 61, had put Glamorgan in poll position for their third County Championship. With Somerset bowled out for 252, Hugh Morris and Matthew Maynard made hay in the evening sunshine, after the loss of a couple of quick wickets, by running up 159 for two at the close of play. You could tell Maynard was serious about things: not by the 76 runs he'd hammered in double-quick time, but because he went straight to his room when he got back to the hotel. The last time he'd done that he'd been twelve.

Sadly, Ron Davies's 'very good morning' didn't take any account of the weather. Wales might have bathed in the figurative sunshine

(*Above*) With Graham Henry

(*Left*) St David's Day in London: pictured with Bob after a splendid lunch are BBC Wales's Jamie Owen, HTV's Hywel James and BBC sports commentator Rob Phillips

(*Clockwise from top left*)
Celebrating Glamorgan's
County Championship;
in the studio with Matthew
Maynard; with Colin Jackson;
with Nicole Cooke;
pitchside with Rob Howley,
then Wales rugby captain

Dressing up at the BBC…

Abseiling off the
Millennium Stadium

John (Harris)
and Shades
(Chris Hallam),
World Champions!

With his wife Julie
on their wedding day

With his son Jamie

Nicole Cooke wins
Olympic gold

Joe Calzaghe
celebrates with
his dad Enzo after
defeating Jeff Lacy

Peter Rogers
celebrates with
Scott Gibbs –
scorer of *that* try –
after Wales beat
England,
11 April 1999

Cardiff City win
promotion!

In his element…

that came with having its own Assembly, but down in Taunton it rained. And it rained. And it rained. Outside broadcast cameramen watched the drops slide down their lenses, the crowd did their crosswords and read their latest John Grishams, the players bid solo in their games of cards, and whenever BBC Wales went on air I found someone to talk to. There was a lot of time to fill, so if you'd spent a holiday in Rhyl and read an article on Glamorgan winning the snappily named Axa Equity and Law League in '93, we probably grabbed you for an in-depth ten-minute grilling.

By mid-afternoon, the rain relented and the M and Ms, Morris and Maynard, continued their ritual dismemberment of Somerset's bowlers. Maynard's early night helped him to 142 before he was caught by Bowler – as opposed to being bowled by Catcher – and at the end of a rain-shortened day Glamorgan were 353 for four, with Hugh Morris still there on 136.

I faced a dilemma. Thanks to the rain, it was odds-on the game would go into the scheduled fourth day. I had an appointment back in Wales. It seemed I could keep it and still be back for the climax to the season. I was wrong.

On Saturday morning, Robert Croft and Adrian Shaw kept up the assault and battery on the boundary ropes with a couple of half centuries, before Glamorgan were all out for 527, two hundred and seventy-five runs ahead. No problem, I reasoned back in Cardiff: Somerset will make a bit of a fist of their second innings and leave Glamorgan a highly gettable target on Sunday when I'll be back in Taunton. The timing couldn't be better. Their opening batsmen proceeded to put on 60 for the first wicket.

But hang on! Sixty for one became 67 for two, became 88 for three, became 133 for four. I thought about all the days I'd covered that season, and all the interviews I'd done. It wasn't 'f*****g lovely' at all: I was going to miss the end. It was a bit like reading a best-selling whodunnit, only to find someone's pinched the last page. I got in the car and started driving.

Chris Stuart was presenting *Sportstime* on Radio Wales: 'There's been another wicket in Taunton . . . let's go straight over and join Edward Bevan.' One hundred and forty-five for five. Bugger. 'He's gone!' One hundred and fifty-three for six. Where was I? Only the Severn Bridge. Shit! Never mind, Bowler was batting. A captain's innings, that's what they needed!

'What are you doing, you pusillanimous pile of poop?' I screamed at the car radio as Eddie Bevan exulted in Bowler being lbw for three. One hundred and sixty-six for seven and I wasn't even at Gordano services yet. My goose was not just cooked but cremated. They'd be all out by the time I made Bridgwater.

Enter two characters who deserve to be a couple of *Wisden*'s cricketers of the year for ever more: Graham Rose and Andy Caddick. Run by run, mile by mile I got closer to Taunton. Chris Stuart wasn't handing over to the County Ground quite so often. When he did, Eddie Bevan was beginning to sound ever so slightly downbeat. 'These two Somerset players really are making it difficult for Glamorgan's bowlers at the moment,' he said sadly. 'It's getting a bit difficult to see where the next wicket is coming from.'

'You bloody beauties,' I shouted. Taunton 20 miles, said the motorway sign. My old Mondeo stretched itself to another couple of miles per hour. I banked on any patrolling policeman being either sympathetic to my plight or a Somerset supporter. Either way, he might let me off a ticket. Taunton 5 miles. I was going to make it. There was the ground. And the car park.

'Let's head back to Taunton now,' said the radio. 'You've got it right, Chris,' I said. 'And Glamorgan have got the breakthrough they need,' said Eddie. 'Somerset are now 261 for eight, with just a couple of tail-enders between Glamorgan and their third County Championship.'

'Never in doubt,' I muttered, walking into the ground.

Gareth Mainwaring the director, otherwise known as 'Captain' for reasons that were always beyond me, was in the television scanner as wickets nine and ten fell for the addition of another 24 runs.

'Thought you might be here,' he said.

Openers Steve James and Hugh Morris knocked off the handful of runs needed and the players' balcony became not organised chaos, just chaos. Down below, the Glamorgan fans sang their songs and I interviewed whoever there was to interview. Adrian Dale faced the camera, Robert Croft (I think) opened the bottle and the viewers were treated to the sight of a champagne shower soaking interviewer and interviewee. Croft led the crowd in a croaking version of 'Alouette' and then from the dressing room came the Glamorgan song . . .

Over the Severn and down to the Taff,
Like lambs to the slaughter, they take on the Daff!
Now they will know how hard the Welsh fight,
As they travel back to England, beaten out of sight!

We are Glamorgan, Dragons you and me.
Together we play for the pride of Cymru!
We play to conquer, we play to thrill.
We play for the glory of the mighty!

I now faced a more sedate return journey back to Cardiff. I couldn't even have a drink to celebrate because I was driving. Actually, I lie. Somewhere along the M5 I had a lick of my tie. It still tasted of champagne.

Chapter 30

No Ordinary Joe and the Cinderella Man

10.10.97 *Joe Calzaghe*

You couldn't exactly say these were the environs of a glamorous lifestyle: a small housing estate at Oakdale in the Gwent Valley, the properties functional but hardly eye-popping for anyone with their eye on becoming upwardly mobile. Millionaires' Row it was not. A red Ford Mondeo, which has long since seen any better days it might have had pretensions to, pulls up to the house at the top of the cul-de-sac. A young man carrying a kit bag comes out, pausing to kiss his wife goodbye. He could have been nipping out for a game of football, so casual is the departure. His father is with him: a short energetic man never content with using one word when a hundred will do.

They get in the Mondeo for the short drive down the Valley to the nearest big town, Newport, and its railway station. 'Two returns to Sheffield please,' says the father, his idiosyncratic accent not exactly Welsh, not exactly Italian, not exactly anything. It's uniquely his. The tickets are second class. They get on the train, sitting opposite each other with a table between them. A tabloid newspaper is taken from the bag. So far, so ordinary. It's only when the paper is opened that the mundane becomes something unusual.

On one of the back pages, before the stories on football and the Premier League, is a picture of the young man.

And outside on the platform, a camera is filming. He's on his way to become a world champion.

12.10.07 *Wasps/Swansea*

Two days later, a mobile phone rings on the touchline at Loftus Road. It's the ground of Queens Park Rangers, but this Sunday afternoon is being rented out by the football club's tenants, the London Wasps for a Heineken Cup game against Swansea. The driver of the red Mondeo answers the call.

'Hello?'

'Hi . . . did you ring this number?'

'I might have done, who's that?'

'Mandy . . . Mandy Calzaghe . . . we've just got back in. Sorry we missed you!'

The normality continued. She could have just got back from the weekly shop at Asda, not from cheering on her husband to beat a monocled boxing legend by the name of Chris Eubank on a night that would change both their lives irrevocably. Her husband would later write an autobiography called *No Ordinary Joe*. This was the opposite to that. He was still an 'ordinary Joe'.

We'd met for the first time the day before he left for Sheffield. His father Enzo had described how to find the Newbridge Boxing Club where he trained his son. I arrived early. 'He's having a laugh,' I thought, staring at the blue-painted hut in the car park of the local rugby club. I'd been to enough boxing gyms to know they might not rival the Hilton or even Basil Fawlty's finest room with a view for opulence, but there was no shabby chic about this place. It was just plain shabby. I was trying to remember if there were any other buildings hidden around the Welfare Ground that might better fit the bill for 'gym of an aspiring world champion' when Enzo arrived to open up. 'Ah . . . you found it!' I had. It was a relief to discover the inside matched the exterior. I hated people with pretensions.

It would be the first of many visits. Each week before a fight, usually on a Thursday, we'd head to Newbridge to film boxing's best-kept secret. Joe would shadow box, beat the hell out of the punchbag, show his lightning speed on the floor-to-ceiling ball, smash into the pads worn by his dad and, if I was feeling in particularly sadistic mood, dance around the cameraman standing in the middle of the ring, each jab and hook ending just millimetres away from the lens. On the Saturday he would fight and on the Monday I would drive to Gwent to interview him about his win. Occasionally, we might have to favour one side of his face if he'd picked up a bruise. It wasn't often.

I didn't have to act as a taxi again after he'd beaten Eubank, but, as he quietly went about accumulating successful defences of his WBO world super-middleweight title, the boxing fraternity at large seemed largely dismissive of the phenomenon that was hidden away in a nondescript Welsh town. There were other boxers only too willing to hog the limelight. Naseem Hamed or Audley Harrison might grab the headlines. Calzaghe didn't mind. Sure, he would play to the gallery with his pre-fight predictions of what he was going to do to an opponent, but you always had the impression it wasn't him that was speaking, it was the image. It was what was expected of the fighter, not the father of young sons.

He accepts as much. 'I started watching interviews of myself and it was like I was trying to mimic Eubank or Naz mouthing off,' he said. 'It wasn't me.'

Only once did he get irritated about our filming.

Since his childhood in Sardinia, dad Enzo has played the guitar. When he arrived by chance to settle in Wales, the guitar came with him. He worked as a bus conductor, he sold windows and he played in a band with his brother. The story came out about how they'd supported The Barron Knights in concert. It was a fact that intrigued my programme producer.

'You know Enzo well?'

'Yeah . . .'

'See if he'll play his guitar for us!'

'Your wish is my command,' I said, I hope facetiously.

One wet Thursday afternoon, after a press conference in Cardiff to promote one of his son's fights, we drove back to Enzo's house in Newbridge for an impromptu rendition. It was all very ad hoc and the amp wasn't working, but we filmed what we could, with plenty of shots of fingers strumming strings and feet tapping out the beat.

'How could you do that?' said Joe the next time we met.

'Do what?' I asked.

'Let the old man play his guitar . . .'

'Why?' I asked. 'I thought he was pretty good . . .'

'That's got nothing to do with it . . . why the hell didn't you ask him to change out of his carpet slippers? He looked a right idiot!'

He had a point. Carpet slippers? It wouldn't do for a Barron Knights support band.

Inevitably, the secret that was Joe Calzaghe got out. Just before he went to Las Vegas for his fight with Bernard Hopkins in the spring of 2008, more than ten years and 22 title defences after I'd given him that lift to Newport station (the Ford Mondeo has long since ended its association with me – dispatched on the back of an AA recovery vehicle), the *Sunday Times* and its star interviewer Paul Kimmage recounted a conversation between Joe and his father dating back to September 2006, just before he fought Sakio Bika.

> 'ITV have been in touch. They're talking about a documentary,' said Enzo.
>
> 'Yeah I heard you,' Joe snaps. 'What sort of documentary?'
>
> 'I don't know,' his father says. 'They just want to come down and film you.'

217

'Film me? Where? Doing what? What's it about?'

'Just speak to them, Joe.'

'No, I'm not interested.'

'What do you mean you're not interested? That's crazy! How the f*** can you not be interested?'

'Look, dad, we've had this conversation before. I've told you not to bother me with any celebrity bullshit!'

'That's crazy. You've got to think about things like this . . . you've got to project yourself more.'

'No, dad. I've got to keep winning . . . that's my only priority.'

'I've told them to pop down tomorrow.'

'What?'

'I said you'd talk to them after training.'

'No, dad, I'm not talking to anyone – you speak to them. You're the guy who wants to be a pop star.'

It wasn't a conversation I'd have remembered from those early days in Newbridge Boxing Club. Much had happened since then. Father and son had survived a period when it looked as if they'd split, after promoter Frank Warren reckoned they were getting stale. The old gym had been swapped for a newer, shinier version. And Joe wasn't the only kid on the block. Other Welsh fighters had joined the Calzaghe stable. Enzo Maccarinelli was a world cruiserweight champion. Gavin Rees won a world super-lightweight title. Enzo Calzaghe became coach of the year. His son added to three BBC Wales Sports Personality of the Year awards by becoming the first Welshman to win the overall Sports Personality of the Year title. His win over Hopkins in Las Vegas in 2008 cemented the reputation an earlier victory over another American, Jeff Lacey, had given him as arguably the best boxer ever to come out of Wales.

With all that came a new professionalism in their approach to the ever growing numbers of those who wanted a piece of the Calzaghe empire. The homespun attitude to the press was a thing of the past. The public sparring sessions weren't carried out with a laugh and a joke and a 'What d'you want to do next, Bobby?' under the watchful eye of old fighters on fading posters advertising fights long gone peeling from the yellowing walls of the old gym. They were staged in the sparkling and impersonal surrounds of a modern city centre shopping complex or a Las Vegas casino. They were planned, orchestrated, synchronised: reminders of the slick campaign that had rolled into town when Lennox Lewis and Frank Bruno fought for the world heavyweight title at the old National Stadium in October, 1993. That was also the night when a young unbeaten hopeful by the name of Joe Calzaghe made his debut on a professional bill.

The interviews with Lewis in the build-up to the Bruno fight were a thing of military timing and precision. 'BBC Wales Television News? Is that you?' asked an aide, just so there could be no mistake and some interloper from BBC Wales *Radio* News wasn't sneaking in uninvited. 'You've got three minutes with the world champion.'

'You're most kind!' The irony went unnoticed. Or maybe it didn't.

'Starting from now!'

Strangely, after one of the most impersonal encounters since Gordon Brown and David Cameron bumped into each other in the House of Commons gents, a couple of months later I opened a Christmas card sent to my home. There was a picture of a smiling Lennox Lewis doing something Christmassy and inside was a handwritten seasonal message: 'To Bob' from 'Lennox and Frank'. (Frank Maloney was Lewis's small-in-stature but larger-than-life manager.) Three minutes and we'd become best of mates. If they'd given me five I might have got a present as well.

It was media management at its most cynical, though personally I've always had a sneaking regard for the way the Dutch PR people organised matters for the superstars of the Holland football team when Wales went to Eindhoven in one of their forlorn attempts to reach the finals of a major championship. This one was more forlorn than usual. They lost 7–1 after soon-to-become Hollywood hardman Vinnie Jones had won a team ballot to decide who'd be captain for the night. It was another of those innovative pieces of management Bobby Gould became renowned for, like turning up at a press conference in a Max Wall mask. The score might make it seem Wales had Max Wall in goal that night. They didn't, they had Neville Southall . . . and he was man of the match!

The Dutch weren't just good on the pitch, they were good off it. If they could help the press without affecting the players' preparations, then nothing was too much trouble. So when it came to individual pre-match interviews they put their entire 16-man squad behind desks in a large room at the plush Philips training ground – well, they owned everything else in the town so why not the training ground? – that was home to PSV Eindhoven.

The queue to talk to Arsenal's Dennis Bergkamp reminded me of the New Year's Day sales at a department store where a 60-inch plasma TV is on sale for a fiver. But no matter. Show patience and Holland's favourite son would grant you an audience. Somehow, my eyes kept being drawn to the back-up goalkeeper brought in from some less than fashionable team like Twente Enshede or Heerenveen. If he'd worn a sign around his neck saying, 'I'm carrying the Ebola virus', he couldn't have been more isolated. Such is the price of fame and the cost of mediocrity.

The public image of the Calzaghes was now in the controlling hands of the Warren organisation. They were big business, it was how it had to be . . . but how strange it was to hear that most affable of Welsh Italians, Enzo, in a radio interview where he not only got on his high horse but whipped it into a lather and rode off at full pelt at a perceived slight to his coaching abilities, after both Maccarinelli and Rees had lost their titles in close succession.

Is this a criticism? It's not meant to be – simply a realisation that even the most unassuming of characters become the victims of their own success. Meet them individually and they are still the products of their upbringings, considerably wealthier but essentially unchanged, the poor boy from Sardinia and the lad from the Welsh valleys who was bullied at school. But it is no longer Joe and Enzo, it's Team Calzaghe. They might even have started referring to themselves in the third person. I hope not.

19.4.93 *Steve Robinson and Ronnie Rush*
There was another double act in Welsh boxing that rivalled the Calzaghes: not father and son, but mentor and fighter, the man they called the 'Cinderella Man' and his Ugly Sister.

It was one of those stories that, if it had been penned by a Hollywood scriptwriter, would most probably have been binned for not being believable. A storeman from the tough Cardiff suburb of Ely was earning a bit of pocket money from a career as a journeyman boxer. His record was nothing special: thirteen wins, nine defeats, one draw, respectable, nothing more. However, thousands of miles away across the Atlantic strange things were afoot. The world featherweight champion, a Colombian by the name of Ruben Palacios, was failing an Aids test. The ramifications went further than just him and his family. He was immediately stripped of his title and pulled out of a defence that had been arranged in the UK against the British boxer, John Davison.

What to do? Find a replacement. But who? The organisers tried to get hold of the Welsh journeyman . . . what was his name again? . . . Steve Robertson . . . something like that! It wasn't easy; he was usually in work. Two days before the fight, their frantic calls finally got some reward. They got through. You can imagine the conversation.

'Steve Robertson?'

'No.'

'That's not Steve Robertson, the featherweight boxer?'

'No it's Steve Robinson, the featherweight boxer.'

'Whatever. We've got a little proposition for you. How do you fancy a fight?'

'Sounds OK.'

'It's better than OK, Steel, it's a fight for the world championship.'

'Ah. When?'

'Well, it's Thursday now. How about we say . . . Saturday?'

'Saturday? That's two days away!'

'Yep, a whole forty-eight hours, Mr Robertson . . . sorry, make that forty-seven. Plenty of time!'

'But I was going to the cinema.'

'Oh, you can do that any Saturday, Sid.'

'OK, then.'

'Good man, Stan! See you in forty-seven . . . What's that? – make that, see you in forty-six hours. Oh, and, Simon . . .'

'*Steve!*'

'Sure . . . one more thing, Steve . . . don't worry, no one expects you to win!'

Except he did. Steve Robinson had the north-east promoters choking into their Newcastle Brown as he beat Davison, the local favourite, to become the WBO world featherweight champion. I first heard of it when an incredulous presenter stifled his disbelief to announce it on the radio. On Monday morning I was interviewing the new champion at the home of his trainer in Ely. If I was expecting the trappings of success, I would have been disappointed. It's the only thing that would have disappointed me though. The Cinderella Man and Ronnie Rush were as down to earth as the council house we met in.

Fairy tales are meant to have happy endings, and for a time this one did. The man who should never have been champion decided he quite liked it. Seven times he put his title on the line, and seven times he came out with it intact. For me it was much the same as the early days of the Calzaghes. Before the fight I'd go to the run-down gym in Fleur-de-Lys, where his manager Dai Gardner was based, I'd watch the fight with the sort of roused emotions boxing seldom raised in me and on the Monday I'd head off to Ely so see what would be the next unlikely chapter in the story of the storeman made good.

Murphy and McMillan, Hodkinson and Cruz, McKenzie, Damigella and Farradas were all beaten as the national press largely ignored the modest man who just went about his job. That all changed, of course, when a self-styled prince by the name of Naseem Hamed strutted into town. For Robinson it was the fight of his life – forget the Wales National Ice Rink or the Cardiff International Arena, this one would be in the National Stadium – for Hamed it was an irritation, a fly to be swatted and a belt collected on his way to taking to the ring with the big names at the small weights.

It was as if we'd wound the clock back two and a half years to the Davison fight – nobody gave the champion a chance. This time, however, they were right. Hamed may have an ego the size of his bulging bank balance, but he was also a rare talent. Cinderella Man had found his prince, and the prince was nothing like charming. Robinson lost in eight.

The following Monday, *Wales Today* was having a re-launch. It's a thing television programmes like to go through, a rite of passage usually experienced when a new editor comes on the scene. It doesn't mean there was anything wrong with the product before, but, hey, why not spend a wedge of cash changing something that doesn't really need changing. It shows we're doing something – usually doing something to irritate viewers who would prefer things were left precisely as they were before.

But then we wouldn't be seen to be pro-active, and we wouldn't be able to justify handing over a small fortune of licence-payers' cash to some firm of consultants – usually with American accents – whose *raison d'être* lies in going around revamping various news outlets. 'My . . .' the man from Miami would say about the programme that had got by with just one much-trusted anchorman for the last twenty years or so, '. . . one presenter, eh . . . that went out with dinner suits and Lord Reith. What we need is two! Two means inter-reaction . . . and inter-reaction, my friend, is the name of the news game now.'

Then, a few years later, when his female colleague from Santa Fe encountered a programme with two presenters she'd purse her lips, shake her head and sorrowfully announce that having two voices on a programme is 'so yesterday! What we need is one authoritative presence we can all trust. More than one and we dilute the authority. More authority good, less authority bad. That'll be £200,000 plus VAT.'

I can't remember whether we were adding a presenter to *Wales Today* or subtracting one. Maybe we were just having the title music re-recorded by the Welsh National Opera, or having the map of Wales redrawn so it was more viewer friendly, even if it did end up looking more like Mongolia. But I do remember they wanted Steve Robinson, win or lose, live on the 're-launched' programme to talk about his fight with Hamed.

It goes without saying that I've never been in a boxing match, let alone in one involving a world title. I don't know what it's like to punch or be punched, how it feels to win or to lose. I can, however, imagine that losing the sort of high-profile fight Steve Robinson was in would be a mortifying experience. You're not just being hurt outside and inside, you're doing it in the full glare of a chanting crowd of thousands, as well as millions on the television. It's your job and your vocation, your life and, when all was going well, probably your love as well. You've sweated and strained to be there, to prove your worth. And it turns out to be all for nothing.

I sort of understood that. So I phoned Ronnie Rush and Steve

Robinson, to make sure Steve would still come on the programme, despite the physical and mental beating he'd taken. Steve asked if we'd understand if he cried off. Of course, I'd understand . . . but this was a 're-launch', the population of Wales would be waiting with bated breath for all we could throw at them. It was probably the television event of the year. Or not.

'Steve, mate . . . you've *got* to come in!'

He did. Two and a half years ago he hadn't ducked a challenge at forty-eight hours' notice – sorry, forty-six – and he wasn't going to duck one now with four hours' notice. We did our piece, the editor who's long since left to re-launch another programme or six took the congratulatory calls, and we cut a cake and sipped a glass of wine to toast the success of the good ship, *Wales Today*.

It was the mark of a nice man and a fine sportsman.

Ronnie Rush went off to convert an old building into a gym that would keep some of the tearaways of Ely off the streets. There's no time for drugs or knives when you're worn out from legitimate warring inside a ring.

That too is the mark of a nice man and a fine sportsman.

I hope the Calzaghes' epitaph is the same.

Chapter 31

'*You* Woke Me Up'

3.8.02 *Nicole Cooke, Gold*
'*You* woke me up!'

I've heard some odd opening gambits when it comes to interviews with those who've just either a) achieved their lifetime ambition and surpassed the dreams they've had since they outgrew their last pack of disposable nappies, or b) discovered their hopes for fame and fortune had been flushed down the chute marked, 'Tough, you've been wasting your life . . . do something you're good at!', but this was one of the strangest.

Even the mistress of the banal that was Sally Gunnel, positioned behind her barrier at what seems like every major athletics championships since Queen Alexandra wanted an extra 385 yards added to the course of the 1908 Olympic marathon in London, so she and hubby could watch it finish directly outside their royal viewing box, had never had such a response.

The first Olympic marathons had mirrored the 24.8 miles of the original news-bearing run from Marathon to Athens that accounted for poor old Pheidippedes. But Edward VII and Alexandra had already put paid to that by having the race start outside Windsor Castle which made it 26 miles into the White City Stadium, before those extra few hundred yards were then added for the royal convenience. You can imagine what the 1908 version of Sal would have made of the little Italian, Dorando Pietri, who did a fair impression of the late, lamented Athenian by collapsing and damn near croaking just before the finish! Being the good sports we Brits are, the crowd helped him across the line, only for the judges to disqualify him in favour of a young Irish-American by the name of John Hayes who'd run the whole way without a helping hand being laid on him.

'So, Dorando,' the Edwardian Sally would probably have said, 'feeling better?'

'Si, amore mio . . . mucho improved, grazie mille for asking!'

'Now I don't know if you realise this, Dori, but if it hadn't been for the king and queen altering the course, far from having a near-death experience you'd have been standing here as the Olympic champion. How d'you feel about that?'

'Scusi?'

'What I'm saying, Dor, is that we're all going to remember you as a little fellow with a funny moustache who couldn't run another twenty yards without looking like a Pelham puppet after someone's cut the string, because a couple of meddling monarchs couldn't get off their royal backsides and move to where the start and finish should really have been. What have you got to say?'

'Merda!'

'Ah, well, see you in Stockholm in 1912 . . . and remember . . . keep on running next time! Now John Hayes, if I can just bring you in . . . it was tough on little what's-his-name, but what we all want to know, of course, is: just how does it feel to win a gold medal?'

And normal service would have been resumed! Don't get me wrong: standing in a line of broadcasters, each armed with his or her own microphone, while a group of athletes breathing as if they've just come from the set of a particularly energetic German porn movie, passes by, is not the most rewarding of experiences. The winners – normally American – stop, gasp for a while like a goldfish flipped from his bowl by the family cat, and eventually rasp out how this is the greatest day in their lives apart from the birth of any children they might have had in the past or plan to have in the future. The minor placings – usually the British – pull a wry face and say how much they've learned from the experience. The losers – quite often earnest-looking types from Switzerland – brush past at a pace greater than anything they've shown in their race without so much as a 'Sod off, you bunch of parasites!'

It is not the place for profound questioning or articulate answering. Which is not to say you have to descend to the level of inanity so often shown by those delegated to the job by the BBC. So, given the standard of such things, 'You woke me up!' wasn't a bad start.

The scene was the 2002 Commonwealth Games. It was my third. The other two had been at Victoria on Vancouver Island in '94 and in Kuala Lumpur four years later. 'And you call that a job,' I can hear the cynical spluttering as they check just how much they paid for their latest television licence. I say two things in my defence: the first is that the 2002 Games were in Manchester; the second is that covering a Commonwealth Games for regional television is a little like having root canal work without the anaesthetic. The pain of undergoing it is eased considerably by the pleasure of it finishing.

A major championships like the Commonwealth Games should be all about sitting in some state-of-the-art stadium in an exotic locale, watching and reporting on world-class performances from some of the finest athletes on the planet. I say should. It's not. It's about sitting in some converted warehouse, usually in some down-at-heel district of the city where it's best not to roam abroad at night, watching events unfold on a slightly smaller television than you'd have in your front room back home. The converted warehouse will have been given a posh name – something like the Host Broadcast Centre – but temporary toilets and a dicky air-conditioning system do not a palace make.

In this temporary world of partition walling and hired-in

machinery, the nations and regions – BBC-speak for the broadcasters from Wales, Scotland, Northern Ireland and all points north, south, east and west – go about their work, bringing the folk back home the tales of the bronze medallist from Melton Mowbray or unlucky loser of Leith. A dapper figure bounced in one lunchtime to inquire chirpily, 'And who's running Wales?' We've got one here, I thought. 'Last time I looked it was Rhodri Morgan,' I said with the jaundiced resignation of one who'd fielded enough stupid questions for one morning. Only then did I look up. 'Aah . . . Mr Dyke.' The director-general probably wasn't listening anyway.

The warehouse is your home from home for the best part of a fortnight, as a short distance away the 'Friendly Games' live up to their name without you personally experiencing much of the friendliness. Instead, you're the prey of the omnivorous beast that is the modern-day news schedule with, to the sound of violins playing in the background, a day going something like . . . Check into the warehouse – sorry, the Host Broadcast Centre – first thing in the morning, and before you can say, 'Cup of coffee, please,' the first request comes in for a round-up of everything from bowls to bad behaviour (if there's been any) for the lunchtime bulletin. Get that out of the way and there's the main evening programme to get your teeth into. Once that's been chewed up and digested, there's the 10.25 p.m. to update. Oh . . . and did the producer happen to mention they'd like something for the breakfast programme bulletins? No? Well, that won't be a problem will it? 'Course it won't . . . and did you say you'd like the floors swept on the way out? Splendid! I'll just place a broom up my posterior . . .

Sating the programmes' ever present hunger means there's time for little but watching a race, fight or whatever on the telly, recording a bit of commentary and, if you're lucky, popping out to see if life is still going on in the outside world as you do a quick interview or record a piece to camera to show you're actually in Kuala Lumpur and not Kenfig Hill. After a week of it, you're not entirely sure yourself. Palm trees and 90 per cent humidity indicate you're in the Malaysian capital. Bootlegged DVDs on sale in the local market make it an each-way bet.

Still, at least the BBC put you up in a decent hotel, somewhere you can unwind at the end of the day. At least, they do if you happen to be part of the team that provides the coverage on network TV and radio. If your profile ends at the Severn Bridge or Hadrian's Wall, then the caste system kicks in. Victoria is a delightful city in a spectacular part of the world where eagles soar over boat trips to watch the whales – it says as much in the copious tourist literature about the place – but that doesn't preclude it having the Canadian equivalent of what used to be called DSS accommodation. Picking that as our base showed a certain lack of knowledge of local topography, if not meanness of spirit. Still, the number cruncher in London probably imagined snow-capped peaks and caribou grazing peacefully on the front lawn. The 15-dollars-a-night room rate should have been a clue that the nearest any caribou got to the place was in the burgers at the fast-food outlet on the intersection down the road.

And Manchester? What saving graces were there for the cream of the Commonwealth press heading to this rather unprepossessing patch of northern England? Well, there was always the pub. The Farmer's Arms in Northenden might conjure up a bucolic image of meadows and milk churns, but if that ever did exist, it does so no more. For farmers read flight paths, as the jets roar in to the nearby airport. But it was an oasis away from Stalag Luft Host Broadcasting Centre and the depressing streets and industrial wasteland surrounding the City of Manchester Stadium which would soon be reincarnated into a new home for the light-blue half of the area's football supporters. The red half, as everyone knows, lives in Essex.

A couple of pints with my new best mates and their strange accents set me thinking about one of the Welsh team's best hopes for a gold medal. Nicole Cooke was racing the following day. Bingo! The bulb they like to show lighting up in a cartoon character's head when he/she/it comes up with a bright idea was switched on. Give her a ring to tell her we're thinking of her and wish her good luck! Great thought! Except it's a quarter past eleven. At night. People who have to ride a bike full pelt for ninety-three and a half kilometres up and down the hills around a village called Horwich tend not to be living it up in a local boozer less than twelve hours before they have to appear on the starting line. They tend to have gone to bed with an isotonic drink or three to dream of things golden.

No problem. I won't ring her, I'll ring her dad, Tony. When he wasn't sorting out equations as a physics teacher back in South Wales, he was also the inspiration and coach to the daughter he'd introduced to a bike. We'd always got on well, probably because he was always grateful for someone in the media showing interest in what his daughter was quietly achieving from their base in the little Vale of Glamorgan village of Wick. I'd become a pretty regular visitor there, ostensibly to catch up with the latest achievement of the young sportswoman who, if she'd lived in France or Germany or Italy, would have been a household name, but actually to see if he'd ever done any work on the dilapidated Triumph Herald (or some such make) he kept in the front garden as a restoration project. He never had.

I dialled his number. It rang. 'Another bitter, please,' I ordered. And it rang. For a long time.

'Hello . . .'

'Tony,' I said . . . before wondering why he'd had a sex change. 'Er . . . that's not Tony is it?'

'No . . .' There was an entire Antarctic ice floe in the answer. 'It's Nicole . . .'

How was I to know they'd switched phones earlier in the day?

'Just wanted to say good luck for tomorrow. Night!'

231

'Great,' I thought, as I took a large draught of the beer I'd been handed. 'Four years of hard work and I've given her the sort of build-up the England football team would get if they booked a pre-match hotel on the main square of Bratislava when there's a convention of oompah bands in town!'

The Games' organisers had generously arranged the women's road race for a Saturday when the production line of news bulletins slowed to just one in the late afternoon: Cinders could go to the ball! Not that covering a ninety-kilometre-plus battle between some of the world's finest cyclists is one of the easiest assignments you can have. I have never been one for watching Formula One Grand Prix races in person. A blur of colour, a roar of noise, then wait for the next blur of colour and roar of noise. A women's road race in the world of cycling is not dissimilar. Instead of engines committing grievous bodily harm on the eardrums, there's the slightly eerie swish of tyres, but once the riders have pedalled by there's a whole lot of nothingness, with only a loudspeaker to keep you in touch with what's going on.

And what was going on was a sleep-deprived young woman from Wick apparently sliding out of contention on the final lap.

'Oh dear,' I might have said – or was it another four-letter word? Then the excitable man on the tannoy announced: 'But what's going on here? She's recovered! The girl from Wales can still win the gold! Nicole Cooke is going for it . . .'

The BBC's on-line report was less emotional.

> Nicole Cooke of Wales took gold in the women's road race with a superb sprint, despite having looked out of contention moments earlier.
>
> The 19-year-old overshot a bend and dropped off the group on the final lap.
>
> But Cooke fought her way back and overtook Scotland's Caroline Alexander in the race for the line.

Canada's Susan Palmer-Kolmar came through to claim silver, with England's Rachel Heal in third.

Cooke, a multiple junior world champion, completed the 93.5km course in two hours, 35 minutes and 17 seconds to claim her first senior title.

Asked if she had gone into the race thinking she could win, Cooke said: 'Sincerely, yes.'

It wasn't what she said to me as I lined up to interview her . . .

'*You* woke me up!'

Good to know she wasn't bearing grudges.

Not that the world's – or even the Commonwealth's – press had turned up to witness her remarkable feat in winning the gold. The spartan report on the BBC was about as good as it got.

The paucity of publicity given to Nicole Cooke and her achievements is truly gob-smacking, something that struck me when my mobile phone rang one morning as I was walking through Cardiff market. It was a reporter from the *Western Mail*, telling me the newspaper was doing a series of articles on who various 'celebrities' reckoned was the greatest Welsh sports person of all time. 'Wrong number,' I said, 'I thought you wanted celebrities.' The self-effacing side to me was coming out.

Apparently there had been advocates for the likes of Gareth Edwards, and I couldn't argue too much with anyone putting forward the case for the man generally regarded as the greatest rugby player of them all. I did, though, have doubts over whether someone involved in a team game could claim the inner strength needed to push the body on when it's all down to you and you are alone in an individual event. Ryan Giggs, for all his achievements with Manchester United (where he won a tenth championship title in 2008) and Wales, falls into the same category. He had another ten people to help him.

He should, though, get a special award as the Welsh sportsman most coveted by England. Never am I happier than when one of my colleagues from over the borders, sighs, shakes his head, and mutters wistfully, 'I bet Giggsy wishes he'd thrown in his lot with England.'

'Nope,' I say.

'But all those major championships he could have gone to!'

'No he couldn't.'

'He lives in England, though.'

Cue my much-used peroration on how Ryan Giggs's parents are Welsh, how his four grandparents are Welsh, and how he's been happily playing for Wales since his days with the youth team.

'But he played for England schools!'

'Sharp that . . . because he went to school in England. Gareth Edwards competed for England at athletics when he went to Millfield.'

'Ryan's lived in England since he was a nipper though.'

'And there's an agreement between the four home football associations not to poach a player from another home country who might technically qualify on residency!'

'Aah!'

'*Precisely* . . . aah!'

Apart from all that, I asked Giggs about it while we were waiting to do an interview at a sunny Vale of Glamorgan resort when he was on Wales duty. It was the day David Beckham was hosting a huge party that celebrities were gagging to get into.

'Sad you're missing it?' I asked.

'You've got to be joking!'

My phone rang when we were in the middle of the interview. It was Jo on the *Wales Today* desk. 'I'm actually interviewing Ryan Giggs . . . say hello to Jo, Ryan.' I handed over the phone. 'Hi Jo . . . Ryan here . . . how's it going?' This was not your normal superstar. This was a nice guy.

And as to that question . . . do you miss playing for England?

'Why should I . . . I'm Welsh. I can't change who I am or where I'm from. And I wouldn't want to!'

I couldn't have put it better myself.

Another contender for greatest Welsh sports person was Lynn Davies. He did meet the criterion of doing it all on his lonesome, by becoming an Olympic long jump gold medallist, and was someone whose achievements on a rainy night in Tokyo in 1964 went far beyond what he or anyone else could have expected. I did have one grievance when it came to Lynn . . . sheer unadulterated jealousy. His level of personal preservation was such that somewhere in the Davies household attic I was convinced there was a portrait of him ageing horribly while the real thing lost years like a snake sheds his skin.

There was a reason for that. We'd shared a holiday in Cyprus a couple of years before. When I was stuffed after eating too much tzatziki and suckling pig, not to mention a couple of jugs of finest red wines, Lynn would shrug off his food to organise a midnight triple jump for the village kids. Or, instead of doing the sensible thing at lunchtime and staying cool with a large cold beer, like the very best of mad dogs and Welshmen he'd persuade my children to join him on a scaled-down version of the Paphos marathon. In Lynn's case, nothing succeeds like excess. When we did a live outside broadcast to mark the thirtieth − yep, thirtieth! − anniversary of the British record of 8.23 metres he set for the long jump back in 1968 − and which even then would stand for another four years − we had to go to the pub and celebrate with a pint for every one of those metres. It struck me the morning afterwards how grateful I was that he wasn't called Jonathan Edwards and hadn't made the triple jump his speciality!

Colin Jackson? Another more than deserving possibility. Joe Calzaghe? Maybe . . . though in his early days he was fighting the likes of the splendidly named Tocker Pudwill from Deadwood, South Dakota rather than Kessler, Lacey and Hopkins.

What about Jonathan Jones, the flying bank clerk from Cardigan, who'd combined his job counting out notes in Fishguard with going from nought to sixty in two seconds in his 400-horsepower catamaran, on his way to no less than four Formula One World Powerboat Championships? I once went on a test drive with him in a two-seater boat in Cardiff Bay, where he had almost single-handedly arranged for a round the world title to come to Wales in 1993. It was not a mistake I'd make again. You could always go onto a tennis court and hit a ball with Roger Federer and, apart from looking a complete idiot, you would walk off court with your health, if not your street cred, intact. But try to do what Jonathan Jones did as his form of sporting relaxation most weekends during the summer and you would be dead within moments. There would be no margin for error.

There hardly was for him. In 1991 I'd watched the pictures coming in from the Hungarian Grand Prix. His boat decided to defy the laws of gravity and take off from the water like a rather ungainly goose. When it got into the air, it wondered what it was doing there and decided it was time to head back to the surface again, though not before performing a less than elegant head over heels. The re-entry to the water was spectacular . . . provided you weren't the one in the cockpit. Jonathan suffered a compound fracture of the leg which would need an operation to install a metal plate, held in with eighteen pins, running from his knee to his ankle. Even for a bank clerk the credit crunch would have been preferable.

Taking on the sort of G forces you'd normally experience in a jet fighter wasn't the best of idea with your leg enclosed in plaster of Paris. Not surprisingly, he missed several rounds of the world championship – but three months later, with a Long John Silver limp to remind him of his day out in Hungary, he was back racing in Singapore: not just racing but taking the world title from the German Michael Werner by a single point.

So, Jonathan Jones? The affable, unaffected and necessarily

slightly eccentric speed merchant from the west? I'd happily have proposed him for the title of Wales's greatest unsung hero, but for the purposes of the *Western Mail*, I went with the cyclist whose bid for Commonwealth gold I'd done my best to derail.

Why? She was now in her early twenties, with hopefully her best still before her. She should have gone to the 2000 Olympics in Sydney, only for the cycling authorities to decide she was too young. Maybe they were concerned it would interfere with her exams at school in Bridgend. They needn't have bothered. She rather enjoyed setting out to prove them wrong. If anything, the serving of humble pie she gave those who'd made the decision was rather too large. So what had she achieved? Well, how about four world junior titles, becoming the first Briton and the youngest rider to win the women's road world cup, something she'd repeated in 2006 with a race in hand. Or there was becoming the youngest person to win the Giro d'Italia in 2004, though fifth place in that year's Olympic road race wasn't what the competitor in her wanted.

The lanes of the Vale of Glamorgan had to be swapped for the roads of Italy and Switzerland as she followed a professional path. On August the 1st 2006 she was named as the world number one women's road cyclist. That same year she won the 2006 Grande Boucle, the women's equivalent of the Tour de France, and, not wishing to be labelled a flash in the pan, she followed it up by winning it again the following year.

On the Continent she was a superstar. In Britain, apart from the odd eulogy in one of the quality broadsheets, she was the best-kept secret since Lord Lucan. The Welsh sporting authorities knew how good she was – she was part of their Elite Cymru scheme for years – but the budget hardly mirrored the achievements. Her dad did his best to keep her profile high – getting on the wrong side of the law by painting a Welsh flag along the route of one of her races was not one of his best moves – but it was an uphill battle. Becoming the first British woman to make number one in the world merited a brief mention on page 14 of *Cycling News*.

Winning a world cup race or the Grande Boucle swelled her bank balance by the princely sum of a thousand euros, less than £700. The winner of the men's Tour de France would get around half a million. Yet, despite being drug tested maybe fifteen times a year, there is never a suggestion her success has been based on anything other than perspiration and passion.

Unquestionably, she is the greatest cyclist Wales has produced. What she might produce in the future is the stuff of dreams.[*]

Just think what she could do on a full night's sleep!

---

[*]At the 2008 Beijing Olympics, Nicole Cooke won the gold medal in the road race. Following on from her victory at the 2008 World Championships, this made her the first woman ever to hold the Olympic and World Championship road race titles in the same year.

Chapter 32

A Little Refreshment

'Refresh.' It has always sounded such a nice word. As have its variations. 'Refreshment': a cold beer to slake your thirst in a pub garden on a hot summer's afternoon. 'Refreshing': the needles of cool water sluicing over you in the apartment shower after a day broiling on a Balearic beach. The connotations had always been good. There seemed no reason for that to change.

8.3.07 *M.O'C*
Dilys wandered over to the desk in the corner of the corres-pondents' room. where I was preparing a piece for the lunchtime bulletin on the Welsh rugby team heading off to Rome for the following Saturday's match against Italy.

'Bob . . . can Mark see you after lunch, about two thirty?'

'Mark' was Mark O'Callaghan, BBC Wales's head of news and current affairs. Dilys was his secretary.

'Sure.' I was preoccupied with the script. 'What's it about?'

'Oh, he doesn't tell me that!'

I thought it strange. Mark and I had worked together on *Wales Today* for as long as I could remember. He had been a producer on the programme, then its editor. I'd used my contacts at Chepstow Racecourse to help arrange his stag party. I'd been to his wedding. When he wanted tickets to watch his favourite team Arsenal play in the FA Cup final at the Millennium Stadium, an old mate of mine in the Football Association had supplied them. He was a friend. If he wanted to talk to me, it was done informally, not with his secretary arranging a meeting. Yep! Strange.

The two-thirty meeting never took place. I bumped into him in the corridor before that. 'You want to see me later?' I asked.

'Or we could do it now,' he said.

'Why not.'

It was the same office that had been used by successive heads of the news department over the years. The same one where I had toasted my first week in the job, with a different incumbent, nearly two decades before.

'There's no point in beating about the bush, although I always imagined I might be saying this over a lunch . . .' Actually, I thought, that *is* beating about the bush, but I didn't want to be pedantic.

'We . . . we want to refresh the programme.'

There was that nice, pleasant word again. Somehow, I didn't imagine he meant having a jug of Pimms on the studio desk, or persuading the floor managers to waft cool breezes over the programme presenters with palm fronds.

'Refresh?'

'Refresh!'

It's odd, the difference a question mark and an exclamation mark make.

'And, by "refresh", you mean . . . ?'

'You wouldn't be presenting the sport in the studio any more.'

Well, I had to admit that was pretty refreshing . . . more of a cold douche than a soothing shower, but refreshing nonetheless.

'Aah . . . so who will?'

'Jason.'

Jason was Jason Mohammad. I liked to think I'd taken him under my wing in his rise and rise up the BBC pecking order. I now felt like a sparrow who'd hatched a cuckoo egg.

'And that will leave me . . . ?'

I thought he was going to say, 'refreshed'.

'Well, you can still work on *Wales Today* . . . '

Which, I thought, is a bit like telling Michael Schumacher: You can still drive for Ferrari, but we'll only give you a go-kart.

'Or we've a new programme on Welsh sport coming out of the sports department . . . you could work for that. Geoff who's running it has always sung your praises.'

Nice of him.

'What's that called?'

'*Sport Wales.*'

Wow! I marvelled at the countless hours of focus group deliberations that had gone into the title. And to think Hollywood turned down 'Nut House' in favour of *One Flew Over the Cuckoo's Nest*.

'And who's presenting that?'

'Jason.'

I was beginning to discern a trend.

'There is a third alternative,' I said.

'And that is?'

'I could always leave.'

I felt rather refreshed.

23.3.04 *Lifetime Achievement*

Three years before I was refreshed, there was one of those very BBC shindigs, a night when all those who had ignored the yellow-brick road that led to London, and settled for local broadcasting in Bristol or Belfast, Leeds or Leicester, gathered together to have their backs patted for the loyalty they'd shown to life in the not-quite-so-fast lane. Many of those who gathered in one of the posher suites of the Millennium Stadium might have been tempted by the higher profile and bigger salaries of Television Centre, but been knocked back. Others, like me, had never bothered with the ascent up the greasy pole in the first place. As far as I was concerned, if, some-where along my career path, a door marked 'London' had opened, I might have looked inside. I sure as hell wasn't going to batter it down and demand entry.

I liked Cardiff. I saw no reason why I should swap a comfortable suburban existence in a city plenty big enough for me for a life sentence of sitting on tubes or fuming in traffic jams. Besides, I had what I considered a healthy distaste for the metropolitan ethos. Some of those I worked with would sell their grandmothers to Colombian crack dealers for a chance to appear at four thirty a.m. on News 24 from the middle of snow-swept Snowdonia. It may have been enormously gratifying to say, 'This is Hugely Ambitious [with the emphasis on "Remember this name – you're going to hear plenty more of it!"], BBC News, North Wales' for an audience of six insomniacs and a guy getting up to go to work, but somehow I never grasped its appeal.

So those of us who had yet to be seduced by the opportunity of getting into the White City lift alongside Terry Wogan or Jonathan Ross, sat down to find out who'd pick up the Ruby Award – don't ask, I think it might be something to do with the colour – for best running story, best camera work, best news journalist, best diversity issue (this was the BBC remember) and the rest. Someone who picked up a prize for best use of video journalist material explained how, when her piece on an anorexic had been shown to a local authority benefits committee, it had reduced them to tears. 'That bad, eh?' I thought ungraciously. But then I could. I wasn't up for anything.

The Millennium Stadium was my home turf, but there's no such thing as a free meal. The organisers had asked me to swap a few pre-dinner yarns down by the side of the pitch with Welsh rugby's record points scorer, Neil Jenkins, about his memories of playing there, for those guests who might have a passing interest in rugby or former internationals. And at the end of it all, I was to give a short speech congratulating the prizewinners, commiserating with the losers and wishing both a safe journey home or back to the hotel bar. Knowing the audience, it was a safe bet on the latter.

No problem. I'd fillet a couple of lines out of my usual after-dinner spiel about John and my early days in Splott. 'You know John . . . he's the guy who does all the programmes on the BBC that Huw Edwards doesn't [the ubiquitous son of Llanelli was the host for the dinner] . . . well, as the crow flies we were born a couple of miles over there' – I'd point out of the Millennium Stadium window – 'and as we've achieved a certain notoriety in the world of broadcasting, there's now a blue plaque on the house . . . it says: "Ted Jones, Tattooist and Body Piercer"!' As a self-deprecating knock at where we were brought up, it might not be Ricky Gervais, but it usually got a laugh.

The Chicken Liver and Wild Mushroom Parfait, Guinea Fowl Stuffed with Apricots and Bara Brith and Butter Pudding came and went, and I suddenly noticed a line at the bottom of the programme saying, Announcement of Lifetime Achievement Award.

'Hang on a second, that sounds familiar . . .' I thought when the director of nations and regions – a title which makes Prime Minister sound underpowered – started talking about the recipient.

The familiar voice of Jamie Owen came onto the big screen, making derogatory remarks about a young-looking guy talking to Anthony Hopkins. Nothing new there then. Then the familiar music and famous black chair of the quiz show *Mastermind* dissolved into my brother talking.

'Hi Rob, who'd have thought that fifty years ago I tried to drown you in that pushchair in a stream in a Cardiff park. Someone pulled you out . . . happily, I suppose, on balance. I'm quite pleased they did and I didn't succeed in drowning you because you've done all right! And you've probably done all right because you've rejected every piece of advice I've given you. I seem to remember telling you that you were such a good writer you absolutely had to stay in newspapers, not mess about with broadcasting. So, of course, you became a broadcaster. And when you did, I said you absolutely must come to London. And you rejected that advice as well and of course you were absolutely right. The boy done good.'

For a moment I thought he might have been telling the truth, until he said, 'Have a pint of Brains on me!' John buy me a pint? It was obviously an imposter.

Graham Henry, Jonathan Davies and Max Boyce were also on tape saying nice things – I now understood why one of the *Wales Today* producers, Alistair McGhie, had been running around in such a surreptitious way for the previous week or so putting it together.

My speech had to undergo a quick revision. According to the BBC staff magazine, *Ariel* – which was guilty of a large slice of hyperbole when it reported, 'The biggest ovation of the night was for local hero, Bob Humphrys . . .' – I said, 'The whole thing about nations and regions is friendship. There's no envy, no great rivalry. We're ambitious, but it's to do well for the programme. In the towns and villages they regard you as their friend – and then you know you're doing your job well!'

I don't remember using the words, but if I did, I deserved a lifetime achievement award for naivety. Personally, I remember paraphrasing a line I'd heard on Radio Wales, when the presenter asked the old man who'd phoned into the programme whether he'd lived in his home village all his life. 'Not yet,' he'd said in a flash of the blindingly obvious.

I hadn't worked in the BBC all my life, it just seemed like it sometimes. There was still plenty more to come. Or so I thought. Another three years as it turned out, before the BBC Wales hierarchy who had cracked the celebration champagne, and the man who'd been telling me what an 'example' I was to my colleagues deemed the 'example' needed refreshing.

*

5.9.07

There is no entry in my diary alongside the date.

I was meant to go back to work that day after a family holiday in Ibiza. (Sam Hammam had been right. I must have been a pervert. I'd obviously got a taste for the island's party scene along with beer at a tenner a bottle.)

I leaned over to switch on the bedside radio for that morning's 7.25 sports news on *Good Morning, Wales*. It was the way I touched base with what I might be doing during the day, an indication of any stories that might have broken during the night. It was just a couple of days before the Rugby World Cup kicked off in Paris. Wales were based in Normandy. 'So,' the bulletin's presenter was saying, 'let's go over and join our man in Paris . . . Gareth Lewis.'

Suddenly it struck me. People describe that sort of moment as an 'epiphany', but I never quite understood what they meant. I did now. I was meant to be the sports correspondent for *Wales Today*, I was supposed to be the reporter who brought the stories to an audience that was ever loyal to the people they'd got to know well – and the closest I'd get to anything French during the world's biggest rugby tournament was driving down the Boulevard de Nantes outside Cardiff City Hall. Welcome to the world of refreshment.

I'd realised much earlier that summer that I wouldn't be going to France. The editors and producers held their meetings to discuss how they planned to cover it. I wasn't invited. My dislike for BBC meetings was well known, but somehow I had the impression this wasn't their way of indulging my eccentricities before handing over a first-class ticket on Air France and a suite reservation for the Hotel George V. Call me a suspicious old devil, but I figured they had other plans. They did. Gareth Lewis would be providing *Wales Today*'s coverage.

There had been other big events I hadn't been to, the 2003 World Cup in Australia for instance. There was a reason for that. It was an expensive venture and *Newyddion*'s Welsh-speaking

245

reporter could provide material in both languages. I couldn't. I saw a census in the early seventies which showed there was apparently one monoglot Welsh speaker living in our Cardiff suburb of Splott, but I wasn't he (or she). He (or she) wasn't in the next census, a fact that didn't surprise me greatly because whoever it was had inevitably starved to death because of his (or her) inability to communicate with another human being in the neighbourhood. Ordering the Sunday joint and two veg would have been a nightmare.

So *Newyddion*'s Aled ap Dafydd would send back material and provide the occasional two-way, with me in the studio and him in Australia, and I would piece the packages together back in Cardiff. It wasn't ideal, but in straitened economic times it was understandable.

This wasn't the case with a World Cup in France. For a start I would have settled for a downgrade to business class on Air France and slummed it with a mere room at the George V. And, more importantly, Gareth Lewis was no more of a broadcaster in Welsh than I was. It was down to who the powers-that-be wanted covering the tournament. It wasn't me.

All this of course is surmise. They might have been told by the BBC's medical staff that I had a potentially fatal allergic reaction to snails, garlic and the smell of Gauloises. (Actually they could have had a point with the last one.) I wouldn't know. Nobody ever bothered telling me.

'Let's go over and join our man in Paris, Gareth Lewis'. An epiphany, or if you want it the dictionary's way: 'a comprehension or perception of reality by means of a sudden intuitive realisation'. My time with the BBC was over. I did what any man of principle and deep conviction would do after a life-changing moment such as that. I phoned in sick.

Chapter 33

Plus Ça Change

It's strange how, when you come back from holiday, nothing has changed. Two weeks of not being there, and your little local world has the temerity to stay exactly as it was. Something in your psyche tells you it shouldn't be like that. Step out of the familiar and you expect the familiar to be out of step when you return. But, maybe it's not strange at all. Look at a day two weeks back from now, then look at today, and ask yourself what of significance has altered in those fourteen days. Probably not very much. You're still alive; your house is still standing; reality television is as annoying now as it was then. Divide our lives up into fortnightly chunks, and very few of them would have us saying on closer inspection, 'Bloody hell, did that really happen?'

So, after two late-August weeks of life where a major decision was working out whether to read your historical drama by Bernard Cornwall or James Patterson's forty-third crime book of the year, opening up the *Western Mail* after a couple of hours' sleep to recover from the early morning flight was not expected to send the post-holiday blues into overdrive. After all, nothing ever happened when you were away . . .

Except this time it had. I read the headline and skipped over it. Hang on a moment, it didn't say what I thought it said, did it? I read it again. It did. When I'd left work for my break, there were the usual 'goodbyes' to the workmates you expected to see once you'd topped up your tan and expanded your waistline: nothing special, nothing terribly emotional, just the usual niceties; 'Have a good time'; 'See you when you get back'; 'Don't do anything I wouldn't do!'

'We're looking to the future, not being ageist, insists BBC Wales'; 'The end of the news from Sara'. I was astonished. The *Western Mail* was telling me that one of those workmates, a friend I'd worked closely with for nearly twenty years, wouldn't be there when I went back. Sara Edwards, said the *Mail*, would tonight be presenting her final edition of *Wales Today* before being replaced by Lucy Owen from the *Wales Tonight* programme on ITV. If the newspaper had revealed that a dinosaur eating a beefburger had been found wandering down Westgate Street before a Wales Six Nations game shouting, 'Any spare tickets?', I would have found it rather more believable.

It was laughable. This was BBC Wales committing hara kiri on the pages of Wales's national newspaper, publicly disembowelling what had been by far the country's most successful news magazine. Sara wasn't the perfect television anchor. If I was following her in the programme I would occasionally inwardly groan as she turned a two-minute interview into an epic with a 'Briefly . . . one last question, Mr Evans . . .' And after Mr Evans had answered it with all the brevity of a Methodist minister given an exclusive on the second coming, a couple of sports stories would be sent spinning into the waste-bin marked 'never to be broadcast'.

Annoying? A tad. But at the end of the programme, after she'd unplugged the microphone, smiled and said, 'Well, I think that went rather well, don't you?', you'd figure that your couple of stories weren't that important anyway. You could always find some other way of telling the nation Graham Henry had quit.

Sara had a master's degree in being nice. Filmed reports might be late or not appear, scripts might have to be rewritten just seconds before she was due to read them, guests might fail to turn up, but while others in her position would berate the floor manager, the producer, the person who cleaned the studio floor and all the fates that had conspired to put him/her in such a god-awful embarrassing position, she would purse her lips, frown slightly and mutter, 'Oh dear.' It was a character that came through the screen and into the living rooms of an audience that had taken to her like a favourite member of the family.

Appalling cliché it might be, but – 'one last question' apart – she was a consummate professional. And this was what BBC Wales was tossing aside, to be replaced by the presenter of a programme that for years had been not so much beaten in the audience ratings as soundly thrashed. It made no sense. Sara and Jamie Owen epitomised the style that *Wales Today* had evolved over the years: unfussy, authoritative, down to earth. It was one – given the evidence of the ratings – the viewers liked. Also, the standards Jamie and Sara brought to the programme had been passed on. Younger presenters like Claire Summers and Sian Lloyd could slip seamlessly into their chairs when they were away.

But now one of the main faces of the programme was being replaced, not by someone imbued in the ethos of *Wales Today*, but by a younger presenter whose style was alien to everything that had made the programme the success it was. Don't get me wrong. Lucy Owen was an accomplished television performer, but in a completely different genre from that previously offered by BBC Wales news. The chit-chat of ITV's *Wales Tonight* had never had a place on its BBC rival. Now it would. Why? Because BBC Wales had decided it was time for more 'refreshment'.

I watched Sara's dignified exit from the programme on the Friday night. If you hadn't read the morning's headlines you wouldn't have known anything was different from the countless *Wales Today*s she had presented over the last couple of decades. Not until right at the end, when, with a touching reference to her little daughter

Hannah, the experience that most news programmes would have sold their eye teeth for was allowed to walk out of Studio C2 of Broadcasting House for the last time. I wasn't there, those who were, those who had worked on *Wales Today* with her for so long, were stunned. Few, if any, could understand why replacing such a well-loved figure with someone whose main attribute seemed to be that she was ten years younger could possibly benefit a programme that was more than an employer. It was part of everyone's lives, and now an integral part of it had been cast adrift on the whim of fixing something that wasn't broken.

I spoke to her the following morning. She still hadn't come to terms with what had happened.

'I didn't have a clue, Bob,' she said. 'I got a message saying that Mark wanted to see me, and that was it. He told me he wanted the programme to go in a different direction. I was out and Lucy was in.'

It sounded familiar.

By the end of the weekend the Welsh media still had its teeth in the story. 'Was Sara Edwards pushed or did she jump?' asked the *Western Mail*. The paper quoted an interview Sara had given to the *Wales on Sunday*, saying she had 'effectively been sacked'.

> I was given the impression that things had already been decided and that the editor of BBC Wales had made the decision.
>
> I don't think it was about age. I was told by the editors of *Wales Today* that they wanted a different approach, a different look to the programme. It [the media] is supposed to be a hard, competitive world, but I am thin-skinned. I was taken aback. I was bewildered.
>
> It's an abrupt end to an era. It has been very bewildering as I have been doing this job for so long. But the main thing is that as long as I know I have done my best and behaved properly then that's the most important thing.

The BBC did their best to behave properly too. They issued a press release which said nothing and everything: 'Tremendous ambassador for BBC Wales . . . ultimate professional . . . been a superb anchor' . . . all phrases probably taken from the latest hugely expensive think-tank they'd attended on 'How to get rid of high-profile staff'. For the folk at Thomson House it was their chance to resurrect the furore that had accompanied the dropping of 55-year-old Moira Stuart from her news-reading slot on the Sunday morning political show and Nick Ross from *Crimewatch*, for no discernible reason other than they were older than those who replaced them. PR guru Max Clifford – as ever – said his bit, damning the BBC's thinking, while former Conservative AM Glyn Davies on his blog described it as 'the most heinous act in the Welsh media since S4C pulled the plug on *Garddio*'. I wouldn't know about that. 'Heinous' though was a pretty apt word.

So, the Welsh hacks now had a Welsh equivalent to Moira and Nick. They would soon have another.

20.4.07 *Last Studio*
The BBC showed its sentimental side for the last night I would present the sport from the studio . . . they asked Jamie Owen to anchor the programme.

As he would tell anyone who had an afternoon to spare and the boredom threshold of a £1,000-an-hour psychiatrist, he used to watch me on the telly when he was a boy in short trousers back in Pembroke Dock. Sadly the difference in age had not instilled a sense of respect. Jamie – or Lord Owen as I preferred to call him – liked nothing better than a little repartee in his handovers to me. One night I'd arranged for the FA Cup to come into the studio as part of our build-up to the final being held at the Millennium Stadium. 'Right, time for sport now . . . and I'm delighted to say we've got one of the great old relics of the football world here with us tonight . . . and the FA Cup is in the studio too . . . Bob.'

The banter seemed to go down well, given the number of old dears in Asda who would come up and say, 'Ooh . . . wasn't that Jamie rude to you last night?'

I used to tell them that, far from being bothered, I had actually written the script of what he'd said, on the grounds he wasn't capable of such wit and originality. Ours was a relationship based on the mutual extraction of urine.

That day I had marked the eightieth anniversary of Cardiff City's FA Cup win by taking a splendid character called David Morgan – who'd been at the game to see Hughie Ferguson score the goal that beat Arsenal 1–0 – back to Ninian Park, where we relived his memories with some modern-day fans who were still at school. It made for a nice piece, the young and the old, though none of us could have forecast then how in-demand the nonagenarian from Penarth would be in twelve months' time, when the club he supported all those years ago made it back to Wembley. I can't recall whether Lord Owen introduced me by remarking unfavourably on my state of preservation compared with David Morgan's, but it seems highly likely.

Now, after a preview of the Scarlets' Heineken Cup semi-final against Leicester the following day, Jamie was looking into camera explaining how, after nigh-on twenty years, this would be the last time I'd be joining him on the *Wales Today* sofa. I made a crack about it being the only way I could get a long weekend off, and that was it, finito, the end, the last waltz in studio. All those years of having your facial blemishes disguised by the long-suffering mother confessors that go by the name of make-up ladies had come to an end. If I hadn't been in such a hurry for Jamie Owen to break the habit of a lifetime and buy me a drink across the road in the BBC Club, I could have got quite emotional.

*

24.4.07 *UWIC*

'Plus ça change, plus c'est la même chose' is a phrase I've always liked, partly because it's one of the few lines of French I can remember from my A level days, partly because it's in common enough usage not to make you sound a smart-arse, and partly because it does sum up so many facets of life. At least it did for me after my final Friday evening on the sofa. There was still work to be done. On Tuesday I was at the Cyncoed campus of the University of Wales Institute Cardiff, filming a piece on both their men's and women's rugby teams reaching the finals of the British Universities Cups. Direct the shots, think of the questions, conduct the interview: it was as I'd done it thousands of times before. 'The more things change, the more they stay the same' . . . except that, almost subliminally, something was different.

A slightly embarrassed cameraman muttered, 'Sorry to hear what's happened, Bob.' I had to think what he was on about. As far as I was aware both my cats were hale and hearty – or they had been when I left home; my kids were still bleeding me dry, but nothing unusual in that; my health, as far as I knew, hadn't taken a sudden downturn over the weekend. And then I twigged why he was commiserating with me: I'd reacted to being 'refreshed' with my usual introversion. Jamie Owen and I had spoken about what I should do next, my wife had discussed it, but I preferred to toss the various permutations around inside my own brain.

'You can continue being *Wales Today*'s sports correspondent . . .'

'There's a new programme over in the sports department you can work on . . .'

Mark O'Callaghan's phrases came back to me. I'd decided to stick with the status quo. After years of fighting off the sports department's attempts to take over the production and presentation of sports news from *Wales Today*, I had no real wish to sleep with the enemy. No big deal, I rationalised. It just means I'll be in the pub a bit earlier, rather than talking to a few hundred thousand people from the studio. I can live with that. 'Plus ça change . . .'

But a broadcasting organisation is not a place for still tongues. When someone who had worked there since many of the people in the newsroom were debating whether to clear off early from double maths is relieved of a key part of his role, it didn't pass unnoticed. What was said, I've no idea. But sympathy was not a sentiment I'd encountered often before in my career. 'Sorry to hear what happened, Bob.' 'Er . . . thanks . . . now what about that shot of the team getting on the bus?' It wasn't 'la même chose'.

30.5.07 *Ryan Giggs Goes*
I was in limbo land, a bit like an American president as he watches the contenders scrabbling their way through the primaries in pursuit of his job. Ryan Giggs took us by surprise in calling time on his international career with Wales. It was a big story. The Football Association of Wales had arranged a lunchtime press conference to react to the news. I prepared a package looking back on his fifteen years with Wales, and went to the Vale of Glamorgan to present a live insert into the programme at one thirty. Roy Evans, John Toshack's assistant and the former manager of Liverpool, agreed to a live interview. We did it. News 24 wanted a live hit shortly after two. Roy agreed to do that too. We did another interview. I went back to the office to prepare an updated piece using clips of Giggs from the news conference. The main evening programme wanted another live interview at six thirty. Dean Saunders, a one-time teammate of Giggs for Wales, was doing a coaching course at the Vale. I spoke to him. He agreed to do it. Two months, two years, two decades ago I would have presented it. Now I was sent to the location to make sure Dean turned up and had his microphone attached properly. Claire Summers in the studio did the interview.

It was the blow to the solar plexus, the reminder that you aren't what you were. The title is still the same, an outgoing president is called 'Mr President' right up until his successor's inauguration, but most people are too polite to put 'lame duck' before it. Just as they were too polite to put it before 'sports correspondent'.

Oddly, I did do other live *Wales Today* broadcasts, maybe they slipped under the radar, but there are only so many times you can have a colleague come up and say, 'I thought you were treated like shit, Bob.' There's not much of an answer you can give.

At least my new-found penchant for questioning what was, is and will be, led to an examination of what modern-day television sports reporting is about. I wasn't enthused by what I saw. The cult of personality was alive and well and living in studios around the country. Style had triumphed over substance. For some reason it has become more important to insert yourself in an item than it is to let your subjects speak for themselves.

Now it's not enough, when you interview a rugby player, to go armed with a few well-researched questions aimed at cajoling interesting responses. You have to don tracksuit bottoms and boots, join in, and then make yourself look bloody stupid by saying, 'Ooh, don't you pass the ball hard!' What did you expect? A puffball from a dandelion wafting on a light summer breeze? This guy is a professional scrum half, for God's sake, passing the ball hard is his living. 'Oof, does everyone tackle like that?' Of course they don't. Nineteen-stone forwards with the chiselled features of a statue from Easter Island normally pirouette across the pitch like a prima ballerina from *Swan Lake*. 'Oh . . . what a long way up in the air that kick went! Silly me, why didn't I catch it?'

Why didn't you catch it? You didn't catch it because you're a sports reporter, a professional who's there because you're meant to educate and explain, not someone panting like a dog after a biscuit who thinks he is going to be pitched into the next Wales versus England match at the Millennium Stadium. Sports reporting is not about having your mum ring up to say how much she enjoyed you playing with those big rugby players this morning, it's about eliminating the ego in the interests of the people who really count – the audience.

There is still room for the professional, for the expert at script writing or the inquisitor-general of interviewing – the BBC's Kevin Gearey comes to mind – but if you're to be the face of the broadcast you're now expected to be a *pretty* face, a cheeky chappie who can bounce a few cheesy platitudes off the equally photogenic presenter. Or maybe you should do a weekly series where you can try out any unusual sport you can find as long as it offers you plenty of opportunities to mess it up, smile ruefully and say, 'Fancy not being able to play cricket on an ice floe, what sort of an idiot am I?' One of the great things about television is that all such questions are rhetorical.

I had a good run and got too old for it. My theory – that the self is less important than the sport – was rapidly going out of fashion. Why bother putting the effort into crafting a script and marrying it carefully with the pictures that tell the story, when you can get away with an offering everyone recognises as sub-standard but can't be bothered to criticise? Even better, get someone else to do it for you! Being in front of the camera is *much* more important. After all, this piece is about – you! Until it's time to refresh the programme.

2.10.07 *J.J. Live: Whither New Coach; GH Vale of Glam; Last Day!*
There was one last day for me at the BBC. My sick-note had run out – though not as dramatically as Gareth Jenkins's luck. His Wales team had lost their World Cup qualifying match with Fiji that weekend and the Welsh Rugby Union had obviously forgotten how to spell 'pusillanimous'. They showed a startling new taste for decisive action by sacking Jenkins before he could even leave France.

There was still an appetite for the story when I went in the following Tuesday. The news hierarchy were away somewhere in Cardiff Bay – debating some vitally important issue that couldn't be discussed in one of the small-hotel's-worth of meeting rooms that existed in Broadcasting House. The stand-in producer asked me for a live broadcast to talk about who could be the new coach. I suggested a guest, J.J. Williams, the former Wales and Lions wing, who, before fashions changed, used to be one of BBC Wales's foremost pundits. It rounded the circle. One of my first live broadcasts had been with J.J. in the days of the eighties when the buzzwords were 'up and coming' rather than 'fading fast'. I was ending where I had begun.

Stranger still, Graham Henry, the guy I'd got on best with during my time in the job, was giving a press conference with his New Zealand team who'd arrived in Cardiff for their ill-fated quarter-final against France. They asked me if I could cover that as well.

Before I went, I looked at the previous night's scripts. Jason Mohammad had covered the coach's sacking with a broadcast from the Millennium Stadium: 'I was here when Graham Henry went . . . I was here when Mike Ruddock went . . . ' And so he was – as studio presenter on those days. He'd done a live interview from the studio on both occasions.

An image of a May Day parade in Moscow came to mind: a year later, a Red Army general would find himself airbrushed from the general salute on Red Square. I knew how he felt.

It was time to go.

'Thanks, J.J. . . . fascinating stuff,' I said as we finished our slot outside the Millennium Stadium, 'now back to you in the studio, Jamie . . . '

I went.

Chapter 34

'I Don't Follow the Cricket!'

'You'll be busy today!' smiled the old lady as she paid for her mushrooms in our local greengrocer's.

She wasn't the only one.

'What you going to say about that on Monday then?' asked the man I bumped into occasionally in the local.

'Not a lot,' I said.

It was the truth, but he looked at me as if I had claimed the sun wasn't going to come up tomorrow.

I hadn't been on television for months, not unless you count that Sky Channel which shows repeats of rugby games where the players look as if they are little boys from the under-14s squad who should be sent home to grow. Every so often someone would say, 'Saw you on the telly tonight.' This was a slight embellishment on the actual truth – usually it was just my voice asking a couple of questions of the guy with the long sideburns who'd scored the winning try.

It wasn't easy to wean yourself off the screen. To most people I was still that comfy old chair in the corner, part of the furniture, an expected presence at half past six. Even when I wasn't there.

It was the day Wales could clinch their second Grand Slam in three years. Back in 2005, the weather had been sunny and spring-like, mirroring the optimism of the thousands with and without tickets who flooded into the city; but this Saturday, the rain sluiced

258

down from a sky that was slate grey. Was the gloom preparing us for the misery of defeat?

For me, however, there was none of the gnawing tension that was normally my bosom buddy in the build-up to a vital match. I could eat. The thought of the kick-off didn't sneak into my mind and whisper mischievous words every couple of minutes. There was none of the feeling of sympathy for the consequences that defeat would bring for a coach you'd come to call friend. There was . . . nothing.

It was bizarre. Ever since the first game in the Six Nations six weeks before I had been a husk of what I usually was. I'd watched England's domination of the first half at Twickenham as I sat at home with an air of resignation as my companion. I put this lassitude down to the fact that I thought it was going to be one of those tournaments I'd seen so often before, where pre-match bravado was followed by the cold douche of reality. I consoled myself with the thought that it would only take a Welsh try or two to ignite the spark that would lead to my usual explosion of passion.

Sure enough, those tries came: Lee Byrne and Mike Phillips scored . . . no spark. Wales won, a win I'd been waiting to see for twenty years . . . still no spark.

I thought back to 1988. My brother had been invited into a box with the BBC's hierarchy. Not knowing his props from his penalties, he asked me for the information that would make him sound at least marginally knowledgeable about what was unfolding in front of his eyes.

'Mention the backline,' I said. Backline? 'The backs – they're the people who play behind the scrum.' Scrum? It promised to be a long conversation. 'Look, I'll put it in words you'll understand . . . Wales have gone for a high-risk strategy' – this was his sort of jargon – 'and picked all their most talented players: Jonathan Davies, Mark Ring, Bleddyn Bowen, Tony Clement. That's four outside halves – no don't ask, just take my word for it – so they're going all out to win the game through skill and running the England backs (see above) off their feet. Oh, and if all that fails, tell them that Spike Milligan has sent the Welsh team a telegram saying, "Kick shit out of the English bastards." That should go down well with the director-general.'

That then was his contribution, and when all four of those Welsh players combined to create the two tries for wing Adrian Hadley that gave Wales their 11–3 win, he was slack-jawed with amazement and his audience incredulous at the level of sophisticated analysis coming from a self-acknowledged sporting novice. They preferred the Spike Milligan story though!

If John had had his moment of glory in the analyst's chair, then I had had the self-satisfaction of seeing Wales win. They could have rumbled in a try from two feet or kicked one penalty to nil and I'd still have smiled manically for the next week. It had been ever thus. In the early eighties when a Welsh win at Twickers was an assumption rather than a mirage, Paul Ringer had been sent off – controversially – early in the game. Still, Wales led 8–6 late on – but I could take no more. Such was the suffocating tension, I left the BBC Club where I was watching it to wander the deserted streets of Llandaff. I'd stop and listen outside a house, hoping to hear a cheer. Nothing. By now I figured the final whistle must have gone. A walk back into the club and one look at the despair and disappointment as I opened the door told me what I didn't want to know. England had won 9–8!

I had been devastated. Yet all those years on, here was Wales doing what I'd wanted them to do for so long and there was scarcely a flicker of emotion.

Was there a doctor for this sort of thing, a Frasier Crane I could call for a consultation on the radio?

'We've got Bob from Whitchurch on the line . . . I'm listening Bob!'

'Well, it's like this Dr Crane, it seems as if I'm going to be given something I have craved for for twenty years and now I'm not sure I really want it. It doesn't seem to matter any more . . .'

'Can I ask you, Bob . . . how did you get on with your mother?'

Sadly there was no Frasier Crane show on Radio Wales. I tried self-analysis. At first, watching Wales had been fun, drinking lakes of beer and singing songs. Then it had become a profession, but, as a professional working in Wales for BBC Wales, partiality was expected rather than frowned on. If John Motson is commentating on a game between England and Croatia in the European Championship and he refers to England as 'we', that to me is unacceptable. He is speaking not just to the BBC viewers in England but to the BBC viewers in Wales, Northern Ireland and Scotland. A fair proportion of those in Leith or Londonderry or Llanelli would not be backing England – far from it, many would be honorary Croats for the night – and any overt English patriotism would be an irritant they could do without.

However, when you are BBC Wales's sports correspondent, broadcasting in Wales to a Welsh audience, you have carte blanche to wear your heart on your sleeve. Parochial? Yes, but parochial on behalf of your country and your countrymen. You would not make that mistake on behalf of a club or a region – unless of course you happen to be Leighton James, who astonishingly admitted to wanting a team from Yorkshire to beat a team from his capital city in the semi-final of the FA Cup.

James might have believed he was speaking as the honest broker of Welsh football, but he succeeded in making himself seem little more than an embittered rival. What should have been a bit of tub thumping for one of the country's three – then – football league clubs on the brink of an historic achievement, instead provided, for many of us, the unpleasant reek of sour grapes. The BBC recognised that by suspending him from the pundit's chair – before cravenly reinstating him. Now, every time a Cardiff fan listens to him opine on the club on their national station, he or she can legitimately question why they should take what he says seriously. They believe they know his bottom line . . . he does not want their team to win, he does not want their team to gain success. It should be an untenable position – unless, it seems, you work for BBC Wales.

In a sense I was a professional fan for Wales and all teams Welsh – not one slavishly toeing the party line when things were patently going wrong, but one who'd much prefer success to shambles. But now the professional had been removed from me, and so, it seemed, had the fan. I had become just an interested observer.

Wales had beaten England, and I was feeling not elation nor relief but a disappointment at the standard and the style with which Wales had seen out their win. For five minutes at the end they had been camped under the English posts, but it was a case of what we have, we hold. No ambition and flair but discipline and determination. If a Martian spaceship had landed on the West Stand with a brief to find a new sport to take back to the Red Planet's equivalent of the Millennium Stadium, they'd have quickly set the afterburners in the direction of the nearest netball court in the search for something more exciting.

But surely the feeling of ennui would pass? By the time we played Scotland in Cardiff, the sea of red, the crowds spilling out of the doors of the pubs, the tuneless singing that could smash glasses all by itself, would restore the good humour. It didn't. I watched it at home again. The temptation to be part of the international day experience wasn't being resisted; it wasn't there!

What *was* there was a jaundiced insight that I wouldn't have recognised before. I reckoned that if one of the worst Scottish teams it had been my misfortune to see had been labelled Penarth, and Wales had been Pontyclun, we'd have been throwing up our hands in horror at what rugby had come to.

Italy did little to stir the soul either, but surely redemption would come in Ireland where Wales were looking for a Triple Crown. My mind went back to 1978 when Wales had achieved a Grand Slam there. I thought of the drive up through Wales to Holyhead for the ferry . . . 'I remember this when it was all houses,' said one of the party, looking out on the unspoiled tracts of Mid Wales and the sparkling water of Llyn Clywedog. There were the interminable games of Switch on the trip to Dun Laoghaire; the four-bedded room in the North Star which was to opulence what a bed and breakfast in Aberavon is to Windsor Castle; the loudspeaker announcement at a dilapidated Lansdowne Road, beseeching all those who'd come in through the exits to go out through the entrances. Moments of magic like those would be the restorative potion I needed now. They weren't.

So, little old lady in the greengrocer's, I wasn't busy when Wales won their 2008 Grand Slam. And no, man in the bar, I wouldn't be saying anything about it on Monday. I'd have had nothing to say. While those around me danced their jigs of delight and my phone beeped with texts of congratulation – though what I'd done to achieve it escaped me – I felt empty.

But why? Was it because I hadn't met Warren Gatland or Sean Edwards? Was it the fact that, for the first time, there was no personal investment in a relationship with the men driving the Welsh team that was sapping the spirit of feeling part of it? Perhaps, but many of the players were still people I called friends, I wished for them the success they wished for themselves. And I still wanted the bragging rights, I wanted to read the words of praise penned through gritted teeth in the English media.

And then I realised. There was no end product. When I was a fan there was the celebration to act as the full stop. When I was a professional, the final whistle didn't sound the end – the full stop came after the description and dissemination of all that had happened for those who liked to hear what you had to say. Now there was neither. There could not be the celebration as a fan because I was missing the fulfilment of the professional.

I hope that will change. Two trips to Wembley for an FA Cup semi-final and final resurrected old habits: try and park your car in the same place as you did when they won, buy the same number of mushrooms, wear the same clothes – all the ridiculous superstitions that your conscious knows cannot have the slightest bearing on their chances of winning, while your sub-conscious tells you only *your* actions can control the fates. My sub-conscious was wrong of course – although I'm not entirely sure about the number of mushrooms I bought before heading to Wembley for the final. It could have been five rather than six, in which case, Cardiff City, I humbly apologise for personally being responsible for scuppering your chances of bringing the cup back to Wales for the first time in eighty-one years.

At least I felt elation at the win over Barnsley, and the familiar sick disappointment of those last few minutes against Portsmouth when the spectre of defeat sidled up to sit alongside me. Maybe I'm on the road to recovery, maybe I'll come to terms with the fact that my thoughts are mine now and mine alone. They're not to be shared with a few hundred thousand. And maybe I'll be able to talk about things other than sport in the future. At least I've made a start.

'Bad business in Pakistan today,' I observed to the man standing next to me at the bar, the day Benazir Bhutto was assassinated.

'Dunno . . .' he said. 'I don't follow the cricket.'

There's a long way to go.

Afterword

There is, I'm afraid, no happy ending to this wonderful book. While he was writing it, Rob had been getting some pain in the side of his chest and shoulder. He thought it was the usual aches and strains that come when you sit at a computer keyboard for hours at end, but his wife, Julie, made him go to the doctor just in case. She was right to be worried.

Rob phoned me a few days later to tell me he had a malignant tumour on his lung. He might have been calling to warn me that he was coming up to London next week and I'd be buying the first round. There wasn't an ounce of self-pity. Not once did he say: 'Why me?' Instead, there was the usual gallows humour and irreverent banter that we'd shared for half a century. But he was worried. Desperately worried.

Not that he let on. In fact, he shared his terrible news with only a tiny handful of people including, of course, Julie. That was partly because it was the wedding of our niece, Nicola, the following week and he did not want to cast a shadow over such a happy occasion. That was typical of Rob. But it wasn't easy for him, nursing his own dark secret while everyone around him celebrated.

I suspect he knew right from the beginning that he was not going to get well. We had many long conversations over the weeks that followed, during which we mostly pretended to each other that the chemotherapy would do its work and kill off the loathsome intruder, but I doubt that Rob was ever fooled. A few weeks later, while I was out of the country at my home in Greece, I believe he decided that he was going to die and he turned his face to the wall.

Julie was magnificent and showed him all the love and care any human being could have wished for, but she knew she was fighting a losing battle. What Rob feared – almost more than the cancer itself – was losing control over his own life and becoming an object of pity. He was a fiercely independent man and put a high price on basic dignity, but in the end there was no choice but to admit that the cancer had won. He was rushed into hospital on the afternoon of 17 August 2008 and died the following evening.

I'm sure he knew that he was surrounded by people who loved him and it was, when it came, a peaceful end to what had been a remarkable life. The last words in this account of his life must be his own. He was always a brilliant writer but what follows was, I think, his finest piece of writing. Many people struck down by cancer have written about it but never, I think, quite like this. He finished it within hours of his diagnosis. It was witty, irreverent and wise. I hope this book and these, his final words, may stand as a tribute to a great journalist and a good man. We shall miss him more than my own words can convey.

John Humphrys

A Matter of Hours

You shouldn't be reading this about me!

Hell, I shouldn't be writing this about me!

You should be reading this about somebody else and I should be writing this about somebody else. Except I'm not. It is about me.

There's an awful lot of 'me's there, but I'm rather afraid this is a subject where 'I', 'me' and 'my' are going to dominate, because it's not happening to somebody else. It's going to affect lots more – my wife, my three kids, even my cats who seem remarkably aware of my change of mood in the last three hours – but at the end of the line it's me, 'numero uno', who's got to face this thing. This thing called 'death'. There, I've said it. It's only been three hours, and already I'm coming to terms with my own mortality.

Maybe I've been coming to terms with it for a bit longer than that – ever since my doctor, Trevor, who also doubles up as a friend, said I could probably do with an X-ray to sort out some pains I was getting in my chest and shoulder. I put it down to writing this book, crouched over a laptop on the kitchen table. Bad posture, got to be. Nothing to worry about. He sort of agreed – he might even be able to write it up in a medical journal – but, just to be on the safe side . . .

I made the appointment with the hospital. 'Next week?' asked the girl on reception. 'Bit difficult . . . how about the week after?'

She looked at her appointments. 'It's a Bank Holiday on the Monday, how about Tuesday the twenty-seventh?' We had a deal. But what if I'd said I couldn't make it on the twenty-seventh? What if I had a prearranged filling at the dentist's or just didn't fancy getting up early after a Bank Holiday night out. Then, I wouldn't be feeling like this now. I'd be in that blissful state of ignorance. I'd still be blaming bad posture, swallowing the odd anti-inflammatory and worrying about the credit crunch and the price of fuel. But no, I'd said I go on the twenty-seventh and I did.

It's funny how fate jumps in front of you, pulls a funny face and runs off cackling when you're facing up to inner fears. I was having an innocent Sunday evening pint with the papers at the pub after Manchester United's Champions League win against Chelsea a few days earlier. I was tempted to skip the match report – I'd wanted Chelsea to win after all – but I'd paid for the *Sunday Times* and I was going to read it.

There was a passage that leapt out at me, a poignant memory from Alex Ferguson about his dad.

> There are too many examples of people who retire and are in their box soon after. Because you are taking away the very thing that makes you alive, that keeps you alive. I remember my dad had his 65th birthday and the Fairfields shipyard gave him a dinner in Glasgow with 400 people there. It was a big night for my dad. I was in Aberdeen and came down for it on a Friday. The next week my mother phoned and said, 'Your dad's going in for an X-ray, he has pains in the chest.' I said, 'It'll be emotion.' Well, it was cancer. A week, one week.

Thanks, Sir Alex. Just what I wanted to hear. I've just retired, I've got pains in my chest and I'm going for an X-ray. That's all I need to read. But then a big furry creature called 'Rationalisation' appears and puts his arm around me. 'C'mon, Bob,' he purrs. 'How many people have an X-ray for pains in the chest and are soaking up the sun in St Tropez as we speak? Well, yeah, OK, not many, but that's down to the exchange rate of the pound against the euro rather than the fact that they've ended up in their box. Anyway, old Fergie was writing about the mid-eighties. Think how treatment has progressed since then!'

'You're right, Big R,' I reasoned and turned over to read the headline: 'The Exodus Begins'. The *Sunday Times* was talking about Avram Grant leaving Chelsea. For a moment I thought they might be on about me!

The X-rays were deceptively mundane. 'George Robert Humphrys?' a nurse calls out. It helps having an abbreviation as your work-name. It saves the embarrassment of having the old ladies in their cardigans turning to their husbands and saying, 'Ooh look . . . it's him off the telly. Does the sport or something!' A couple of quick clicks, 'Put your shirt back on' – a merciful release for the woman pressing the button – a slightly apprehensive jest about 'Got a good picture?' and it's time to go home. 'Your doctor should have the results in a week . . . but ring before you go. They might not have turned up by then.'

That wasn't so bad, then. Even if the local evening paper does chip in with a story about a woman raising money for Velindre, Wales's specialist cancer treatment centre. Her husband was telling the story – about her organising a ball to raise funds for the hospital. The sting in the tail? She herself was diagnosed with lung cancer and died five weeks later, before the ball could be held. Jeez, not good, I thought. Five weeks? That's barely the time it takes to work out one of Garth Crooks's interminable post-match questions. Where's my old pal 'Rationalisation' when you need him?

I didn't have to ring the doctor before I went to see him for the results. He came to me. It was about four hours ago. I'd just had a phone call from my wife about getting the road tax done for our daughter's car, followed by another more tetchy one as she rang again two minutes later for more details from our bank card. 'Couldn't you have asked that five minutes ago?' I muttered irritably. It was probably the last time in my life I'm going to be annoyed about minutiae.

Two minutes later the doorbell was sounding. I'd bought the ridiculous chiming set of ring tones to annoy Julie a few years ago, so it could have been 'Happy Birthday' or maybe 'Au clair de la lune'. I didn't notice. I was more concerned about the figure just about discernible through the stained glass. It was Trevor. This was not good.

I guessed there was something wrong. He knew there was something wrong. Somehow small talk about the weather seemed out of place.

'I don't know how to say this, Bob.' I was tempted to point out that if he didn't know how to do it, perhaps he shouldn't try, but I didn't. The time for being a smart arse had gone. 'You've got a mass on your lung . . . it's malignant.'

Aah, I was right, this was not good. Not good at all. What are you meant to say? How about, 'I watched an episode of *House* a couple of weeks ago, Trev. Guy on there was diagnosed with lung cancer and it turned out they were wrong. He sued them for millions. Better make sure you're right on this one, boy!' Somehow, that didn't strike the right tone either. I rather think that if he rings the doorbell now and says, 'Sorry, mate, bad batch of film . . . bit of a mistake, there's nothing wrong with the X-ray at all. Carry on as normal', I'd waltz him round the room and open a bottle of my 1983 St Emilion Grand Cru rather than get on the phone to Lawyers-for-you.

There was a bit of a chat about CT scans and discovering whether it was secondary or primary, but I thought this was no time to discuss schools. It did, though, seem rather unjust. I'd had one puff of a cigarette in my life when I was ten, and had spent all of the following day throwing up. Punishment enough, it seemed, but no! Lung cancer was meant to affect those who smoked cigarettes next to me in pubs all my adult life. Maybe there was a clue there. I'd always been in favour of the smoking ban in pubs. It's just a pity it was all a little late.

'I think I'd probably prefer to be alone, Trev.' What a dreadful line, I might have said on any other occasion, totally over the top, much too melodramatic, and then I realised it was me saying it. Did I want him to go? I suppose I had to tell my wife. She didn't answer her phone, probably pissed off with my earlier irritability. I tried my brother. The fastest, least personal answerphone message in the world told me to leave a message and get off. I did. I thought that possibly 'Hi John. Maybe – nope, probably – dying. Talk later. Cheers' was a bit terse, even for his busy world.

I noticed my mobile phone was on the blink. Shit, this was definitely not my day! At least – unlike my wife and brother – Vodafone answered eventually. The girl at the end of the line, who might or might not have been recording my call for training purposes, sounded remarkably chipper. 'Whoa, my lovely,' I was tempted to say in my most patronising way, 'I want none of this bonhomie. I'll have you know I've just received news that I could be about to shuffle off the old mortal coil. I could soon be an ex-person.' I didn't, of course. I just listened as she told me the nearest store to take the Nokia N95 to. I wondered if they could fix malignant masses on the lung too.

The world outside the front door seemed awfully normal. The car was just as I left it last night. A weird thought came into my mind about how life – like history – could now be divided into two: BC and AD . . . 'Before Confirmation' and 'After Diagnosis'. BC was everything up to an hour ago; AD is everything since. They're very different places. AD – and I've only been here five or so hours now – has me looking at the woman pushing the shopping trolley or the workman shovelling the cafeteria lunch in his mouth and thinking,

'So what's the biggest problem in your life, eh? A pint of milk being the price of a long weekend in Paris, the fact your darts team lost last night? Pah, luxury, a mere bagatelle . . . I can beat yah hollow.'

There will need to be readjustments. I bumped into an acquaintance as I went to fill a prescription in the local chemist – I suspect there'll be a lot of that in the future – and there was the usual, means-nothing greetings: 'Hi, Dickie . . . all right?' 'Yeah, Bob . . . you?' 'Fine.' 'Fine!' I'm telling him I'm *fine*! I'm not fine at all. I'm walking and I'm talking, but inside I'm feeling like one of those characters shuffling along in *Night of the Living Dead*. 'I'm not one of you any more, Dickie . . . the pod has hatched inside me!'

On the television the hammer still comes down on antiques that people didn't really want to sell in the first place, would-be home-buyers look at properties that would have been thirty per cent cheaper if they'd waited until now, and C-list celebrities salivate over what a TV chef can do with a chicken leg and a bunch of carrots. It's all so familiar yet so alien. And outside the rain still comes down. It reminds me of a conversation I had with a friend when I was about twelve. It was chucking it down and we were talking for some reason about funerals. 'I want it to be raining really hard when it's mine,' I said. 'That way everyone will be miserable with me!' There was an obvious flaw in the argument of the twelve-year-old me, but I know how he felt. I feel like that now.

So what does the future hold six hours AD? Do I go to the pub and smile and joke and pretend everything's all right? Do I google 'malignant masses on the lung' and scare myself shitless? Do I e-mail the BBC's Pensions Department and say, 'You know I ticked that box saying I didn't want to take an enhanced pension until I was sixty-five? Is it too late to change my mind?'

I've told my wife now, but John's answerphone is still on. My son Jamie is doing his GCSEs. Would knowing affect his chances in the exams? Should I tell my daughter Claire, the vet, who texted me this morning to ask the results of my tests? And what about Emma, who's just finished her university finals? She should be enjoying herself, not thinking about me.

There's much to ponder. Will I sleep tonight? That prescription might help . . . it was for Temazepam. And will there be much pain? I don't think I'm keen on pain. It has to be said, I'm scared . . .

Acknowledgements

Bob Humphrys did not live long enough to write the acknowledgements to this book, but there are a great many people whom he would have wished to thank. It is to our great sorrow that he was unable to do so.

The publishers would like to make grateful acknowledgement for permission to reproduce extracts from the following: *The X Factor* by Graham Henry with Bob Howitt (published by Queen Anne Press); *Number Nine Dream* by Rob Howley with Graham Clutton (published by Mainstream Publishing); *Operation Seal Bay* by Pat Molloy (published by Gomer Press); *One Cap Wonders* by Grahame Lloyd (published by Robson Books); and *Eye of the Storm* by Garin Jenkins with Gareth Roberts (published by Mainstream Publishing). The publishers would also like to make grateful acknowledgement to the *Western Mail* (for the article on pp. 2–3 and the photographs of Bob Humphrys on p. 4), to PA Photos (for the photograph of *Sir Galahad* on p. 5), to Allsport (for the photographs on p. 6) and to Getty Images (for the photographs on pp. 14–15) for permission to reproduce photographs; and to Alastair Milburn and Jamie Owen for their assistance. While every effort has been made to obtain permission from holders of copyright material reproduced herein, the publishers would like to apologise for any omissions and will be pleased to incorporate missing acknowledgements in any further editions.